PUTTING CIVIL SOCIETY
IN ITS PLACE

Also available in the Civil Society and Social Change series

The Foundational Economy and Citizenship
Comparative Perspectives on Civil Repair
Edited by **Filippo Barbera** and **Ian Rees Jones**

HB £75.00 ISBN 978 1 4473 5335 5
286 pages September 2020

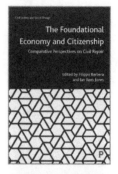

Civil Society and the Family
By **Esther Muddiman, Sally Power** and **Chris Taylor**

HB £75.00 ISBN 978 1 4473 5552 6
208 pages October 2020

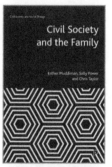

Civil Society Through the Life Course
Edited by **Sally Power**

HB £75.00 ISBN 978 1 4473 5483 3
200 pages October 2020

Published with the Wales Institute of Social & Economic Research, Data & Methods Civil Society Research Centre

For more information about the series visit
bristoluniversitypress.co.uk/civil-society-and-social-change

PUTTING CIVIL SOCIETY IN ITS PLACE

Governance, Metagovernance and Subjectivity

Bob Jessop

First published in Great Britain in 2022 by

Policy Press, an imprint of
University of Bristol
1-9 Old Park Hill
Bristol
BS2 8BB
UK
t: +44 (0)117 954 5940
e: bup-info@bristol.ac.uk

Details of international sales and distribution partners are available at
policy.bristoluniversitypress.co.uk

British Library Cataloguing in Publication Data
A catalogue record for this book is available from the British Library

ISBN 978-1-4473-5496-3 paperback
ISBN 978-1-4473-5495-6 hardcover
ISBN 978-1-4473-5498-7 ePub
ISBN 978-1-4473-5497-0 ePdf

Cover design: Clifford Hayes
Front cover image: Black and white geometric pattern © Freepik.com

Bristol University Press and Policy Press use environmentally responsible
print partners.

Printed and bound in Great Britain by CPI Group (UK) Ltd,
Croydon, CR0 4YY

FSC
www.fsc.org
MIX
Paper from
responsible sources
FSC® C013604

Dedicated to the memory of my brother,
Richard John Jessop (1947–2017)

Contents

List of tables and figures

Tables

Figures

Abbreviations

BHPS	British Household Panel Survey
CPE	Cultural political economy
CSO	Civil society organization
ESRC	Economic and Social Research Council
EU	European Union
EZ	Enterprise Zone
FBO	Faith-based organization
GSP	Global social policy
HE	Higher education
IMF	International Monetary Fund
IWA	International Workingmen's Association
LEP	Local Enterprise Partnership
LSP	London Science Park
MLG	Multilevel governance
MSMG	Multispatial metagovernance
NCRM	National Centre for Research Methods
NGO	Non-governmental organization
OECD	Organization of Economic Co-operation and Development
OMC	Open method of coordination
Q	*Quaderno* (*Notebook*)
QUALITi	Qualitative Research Methods in the Social Sciences: Innovation, Integration and Impact (2005–08), a research unit at Cardiff University focused on qualitative research methods, especially the social contexts in which research methods and methodologies are situated
R&D	Research and development
SRA	Strategic-relational approach
STF	Spatio-temporal fix
TPSN	Territory, place, scale, network
UK	United Kingdom
UN	United Nations
US	United States
WHO	World Health Organization
WISER	Wales Institute of Economic and Social Research
WISERD	Wales Institute of Social & Economic Research, Data & Methods

Note on the author

Bob Jessop is Distinguished Professor of Sociology at Lancaster University. He previously taught in the Department of Government at Essex University and has held visiting fellowships in the European University Institute, Florence, the Department of Sociology at the University of Wisconsin (Madison), the School of Geography at Manchester University, and the Post-Growth College at the Friedrich Schiller University, Jena (Germany).

His research interests are state theory, critical governance studies, critical political economy, cultural political economy and welfare state restructuring. He has published extensively in books, anthologies and journal articles. His recent work includes: *Towards a Cultural Political Economy* (co-authored with Ngai-Ling Sum, Edward Elgar, 2013); *The State: Past, Present, Future* (Polity, 2015); *Financial Cultures and Crisis Dynamics* (co-edited with Brigitte Young and Christoph Scherrer, Routledge, 2014); *Transnational Capital and Class Fractions: The Amsterdam School Perspective Reconsidered* (co-edited with Henk Overbeek, Routledge, 2018) and *The Pedagogy of Economic, Political and Social Crises: Dynamics, Construals, and Lessons* (co-edited with Karim Knio, Routledge, 2019). Other work is cited in the References.

Acknowledgements

Writing this book was triggered by my participation in 2016–19 as a part-time research fellow in the Economic and Social Research Council's Civil Society programme hosted by the Wales Institute of Social & Economic Research, Data & Methods (WISERD) (Grant Number: ES/L009099/1). I was based at Lancaster University and occasionally visited Cardiff, Llandridnod Wells, Aberystwyth, Bangor and Swansea to participate in WISERD-funded events to learn from colleagues and deliver lectures on my account of civil society. I chose to interpret civil society as a shifting horizon of action rather than a fixed reality with a definite substance and became convinced, following the example of Michel Foucault, that it should be studied as a pluralistic ensemble of governance or governmental arrangements with diverse agents. Thus, the book examines civil society from a governance theoretical viewpoint, which gives it a more abstract theoretical quality than many readers might expect. It does not take civil society as its primary theoretical object but introduces governance, governance failure, metagovernance and metagovernance failure before turning to the two phases of the WISERD Civil Society programme and my own examples. In this sense, it draws on my long-established pre-WISERD studies as well as my involvement with the WISERD programme.

In writing this book I have benefited from the support of Martin Jones, David Beel, Paul Chaney, Esther Muddiman, Ian Rees Jones and Victoria Macfarlane in the WISERD project, and from Ngai-Ling Sum and Andrew Sayer at Lancaster University. I alone am responsible for errors, omissions and theoretical inconsistencies. Laura Vickers-Rendall at Policy Press was helpful in bringing the book to completion and Millie Prekop assisted with publicity. Dawn Rushen was a superlative copyeditor.

I dedicate this book to my younger brother, Richard John Jessop, who was born on 17 September 1947 and died on 28 December 2017.

Licensing information

I have drawn on my previously published work in writing this book and have secured licences to reproduce my work in more or less modified form with the permission of the respective licensors through PLSclear. The articles and chapters concerned are:

- Bob Jessop (1997) 'The Governance of Complexity and the Complexity of Governance: Preliminary Remarks on Some Problems and Limits of Economic Guidance', in A. Amin and J. Hausner (eds) *Beyond Markets and Hierarchy: Interactive Governance and Social Complexity*, Cheltenham: Edward Elgar, 111–47. PLSclear licence ref: 36147. Drawn on in Chapter 2.
- Ngai-Ling Sum and Bob Jessop (2013) *Towards a Cultural Political Economy: Putting Culture in its Place in Political Economy*, Cheltenham: Edward Elgar, 247–50. PLSclear licence ref: 36267. Drawn on in Chapter 3.
- Bob Jessop (2009) 'Governance and Metagovernance: On Reflexivity, Requisite Variety, and Requisite Irony', in H. Bang (ed) *Governance as Social and Political Communication*, Manchester: Manchester University Press, 101–16. PLSclear licence ref: 36263. Drawn on in Chapter 3.
- Bob Jessop (2015) 'Global Social Policy and Its Governance: A Cultural Political Economy Approach', in A. Kaasch and Merton (eds) *Actors and Agency in Global Social Governance*, Oxford: Oxford University Press, 18–42, including Table 2.1. PLSclear licence ref: 36140. Drawn on in Chapter 8 to discuss global social policy.
- Bob Jessop (2002) 'Liberalism, neoliberalism, and urban governance: A state-theoretical perspective', *Antipode*, 34(3): 464–9 of 458–78. PLSclear licence ref: 36260. Drawn on in Chapter 8 to discuss 'good governance'.
- Bob Jessop (2000) 'The Dynamics of Partnership and Governance Failure', in G. Stoker (ed) *The New Politics of British Local Governance*, Basingstoke: Macmillan, 11–32. PLSclear licence ref: 36264. Drawn on in Chapter 9 to discuss regional governance strategies.
- Bob Jessop (2015) 'Corporatism and Beyond: Governance and Its Limits', in E. Hartmann and P.F. Kjaer (eds) *The Evolution of Intermediary Institutions in Europe: From Corporatism to Governance*, Basingstoke: Palgrave, 29–46. PLSclear licence 36265. Drawn on in Chapter 9 to discuss the periodization of corporatism.

- Bob Jessop (2015) 'The course, contradictions, and consequences of extending competition as a mode of (meta-)governance: Towards a sociology of competition and its limits', *Distinktion: Scandinavian Journal of Social Theory*, 16(2): 167–85. Tandfonline open licence. Drawn on in Chapter 10 to discuss competition as a mode of governance.

Preface

As a more-or-less distinctive set of political practices, governance has a long history. Nonetheless, theoretical interest in these practices under the rubric of 'governance' has mostly emerged in the last 40 to 50 years. This was initially prompted in the late 1960s and 1970s by growing elite concerns in liberal democracies about governmental overload, state failure, legitimacy crises and general ungovernability – concerns that triggered a search for political and social arrangements to address these problems. One response was to seek to lower expectations by informing the public of the limits to what any government could achieve faced with growing global turbulence and scarce resources. Another was neoliberal calls for 'more market, less state'. A third response, more significant for this book, was growing theoretical and practical interest in the potential of coordination through self-organizing networks, partnerships and other forms of reflexive collaboration and, relatedly, in an alleged 'shift from govern*ment* to govern*ance*' in the polity and similar shifts from hierarchical authority to networked or 'heterarchical' coordination in many other social fields. This amounted to a rediscovery of the potential contribution of civil society to problem-solving without representing a direct engagement in philosophical reflection.

Relatedly, there has been growing interest from the late 1970s onwards in whether and how 'civil society' in one guise or another might enhance state capacity in the face of growing complexity and/or whether or how they might provide new ways to overcome old problems that postwar state intervention and the more recent (re)turn to market forces seem to have left unsolved, if not aggravated. Civil society is sometimes regarded as a flanking and supporting mechanism of neoliberalism and authoritarian statism. Involving civil society actors, organizations and partnerships raises hopes or expectations that policy-making and implementation will thereby be improved and made more accountable, either to relevant stakeholders and/or to pre-given criteria of efficiency, effectiveness, transparency and moral standards. This interest in civil society as a supplement to government occurs on all scales from the local state through metropolitan and regional governments to national states, and can also involve various intergovernmental arrangements at the international, transnational, supranational and global levels. This is reflected in the rise of civil society organizations (CSOs) in the operations of the European Union (EU) and international governance mechanisms. Likewise, new forms of partnership, negotiation and networking have been introduced or extended by state managers as they seek to address the declining legitimacy and/or effectiveness of other approaches to policy-making and implementation. Such innovations also redraw the inherited public–private divide, engender new forms of interpenetration between the political system and other functional systems, and modify relations between these systems and the lifeworld as the latter impacts on the nature and exercise of state power (on the lifeworld-vs-system distinction, see Habermas, 1987). Since that critical juncture 40 to 50 years ago, interest in governance has exploded, either explicitly or indirectly through work on parallel concepts and trends.

In this sense, civil society is a well-worn theme in social and political theory, conceptual history and democratic theory. The present book takes a very distinctive approach to the topic. It does not provide one more analysis of the concept through a conventional history of ideas or a normative theoretical approach, but seeks to locate how CSOs, partnerships and associations (in various guises and linked to different discourses) are being mobilized in response to market failure and state failure. In other words, it locates civil society in the context of critical governance studies and seeks to show how it has become the point of intersection between two contrasting sets of political strategy that seek to revive and recontextualize the significance of civil society. One strategy is to promote individual and collective self-responsibilization in order to lighten the governance burdens of local and central states. The other is to facilitate collective self-emancipation through social innovation, community mobilization and creating the commons to limit or escape the constraints of market and state. In both cases, governance can be located at the intersection of networks and solidarity as alternatives to market exchange and hierarchical command.

Given growing disillusion with the neoliberal formula, 'more market, less state', civil society has become a central stake in political struggles, as seen in new forms of resistance, such as the Occupy movement, the appeal of Bernie Sanders and Jeremy Corbyn, the *gilets jaunes*, the rise of right-wing populism, the vote for Brexit in 2016 or the increasing incivility in political discourse. It is also evident in the churning of terms like 'Big Society' or the development of community initiatives such as food banks as austerity tightens. Self-responsibilization and solidarity are also evident in responses to the global COVID-19 pandemic in 2020. This makes this book relevant to current political debates.

Governance is clearly a notion whose time has come. It appears to move easily across philosophical and disciplinary boundaries, diverse fields of practical application, the manifold scales of social life and different political camps and tendencies. Yet even a cursory glance at the literature reveals that the meaning of governance varies by context and it is being deployed for quite contrary, if not plain contradictory, purposes. These range from philosophical and theoretical ends through shaping problem construals and policies (including the marketing of quick governance fixes as one-size-fits all solutions to quite heterogeneous problems) to efforts to implement new constitutional and ethical solutions to global problems (for example, the concept of 'good governance' as advanced by the World Bank).

Thanks to these terminological uncertainties and heterogeneous applications, it is doubtful whether governance *sans phrase* can really provide a persuasive theoretical entry-point for analysing contemporary social transformation or, again, a plausible practical entry-point for coping with complexity and turbulence. It is this paradox that I wish to pursue and resolve in this text. Its ultimate intention is to provide a clear account of the nature and limitations of governance and metagovernance in a complex world. It also introduces a typology of forms of governance related to their distinctive coordinating logics, principal domains of application and tendential forms of failure.

This set of objectives has two aspects. First, I want to put governance, governance failure and metagovernance at the centre of the analysis rather than treating them as having secondary significance at best. Second, I want to put governance, governance failure and metagovernance in their place within a more comprehensive analysis of social relations. These practices have distinctive features and effects that cannot be theorized or explained without a broader theory of social relations. Thus, rather than develop a state- or society-centred account of governance, which comprise two well-rehearsed perspectives in the literature, I develop a strategic-relational analysis of governance that identifies its general and specific features, its strengths and weaknesses, and associated responses to the inherent improbability and empirically recurrent experience of governance failure. In this regard, I follow Foucault's analysis of civil society as a set of governmental discourses and practices (see Chapter 7).

This book seeks to avoid one-sided interpretations of the shift from government to governance by combining four main theoretical approaches: complexity theory, institutional and evolutionary economics, including especially a 'plain Marxist' approach that treats Marxist analysis as posing important problems even if the answers given to date are not always satisfactory (or, indeed, relevant to all potential topics of investigation), and the strategic-relational approach (hereafter

SRA) (see especially Jessop, 2007c). These elements are presented in Chapters 1 to 4.

Different governance arrangements are better suited to the pursuit of some types of strategy than others because they mobilize different resources, appeal more to some identities, values and interests than others, have different operational logics and are prone to different kinds of failure. Indeed, following disillusion with the turn to 'more market, less state' in the 1980s, in the 1990s there was growing recognition of failures in the new (or newly revived) forms of governance intended to address these earlier failures. This was followed from the mid-1990s by growing theoretical and practical interest in different kinds of metagovernance. In its most basic and general sense (but also most eclectic sense), metagovernance denotes the governance of governance. Other work on governance and/or metagovernance has examined the self-organization of organizations, the constitution of organizational identities, the modalities of coordination of interorganizational relations, and issues of organizational intelligence and learning. Overall, metagovernance occurs on many sites and scales and with different orders of 'meta-ness'. Higher-order metagovernance, or collibration, has become a key activity of states and can be seen as a countertrend to the shift from government to governance. In other words, while the early interest in governance was associated with this alleged shift, there has been growing interest in a shift from governance to metagovernance.

In this context, the SRA adopted below advances four more or less distinctive claims. First, it identifies four ideal-typical modes of governance – market exchange, imperative coordination, reflexive networks and unconditional solidarity – and argues that each of these 'first-order' forms of governance is prone to its own distinctive kinds of failure. They can also exist in hybrid forms. The same growing complexity that generated the demand for new governance mechanisms also contributes to their tendential failure to achieve what is expected of them, resulting in repeated patterns of failed attempts to resolve problems through promoting first one, then another, form of governance. These governance cycles prompt attempts to modulate the forms and functions of governance. This is the field of different kinds of metagovernance. Thus, second, the SRA identifies four ideal-typical responses that correspond to these four main modes of governance. These 'second-order' responses aim to improve, respectively, the efficiency of markets, the effectiveness of command, the responsiveness of networks and the level of trust and solidarity in communities. Third, in addition to attempts to improve the operation and outcomes of the first-order modes of governance through second-order governing practices, there can be efforts to alter the weight of the four individual modes of governance so that the overall ensemble of governance arrangements at a higher or more comprehensive level of social organization is better adapted to coordinate complex social relations. This can be described as 'third-order' metagovernance.

And fourth, whereas second-order governing occurs in many arenas and policy fields and need not involve the state (which is primarily concerned in these terms with the effectiveness of command), third-order governing is more likely to involve the state as the addressee in the last instance of appeals to solve societal problems by taking responsibility for the overall balance among modes of governance. This is where the shift from governance to metagovernance directly involves the state or close substitutes for the state. In all cases, however, despite significant differences between their respective modes of complexity reduction (which inevitably marginalizes some features essential to effective governance), the continuing excess or surplus of complexity – especially deep complexity – is a major cause for failure in efforts at governance and metagovernance alike. Collibration reorders the relative weight of alternative modes of governance (Dunsire, 1996). It can also be seen as 'third-order' metagovernance based on observing how first-order modes perform and how second-order attempts to improve them succeed or fail. It involves reflexive governance of the articulation of social conditions and relations and their modes of governance. We should note here that there is no master meta-governor, no single summit from which metagovernance is performed: the sites, stakes and agents of metagovernance itself are highly contested and its modalities reflect a changing equilibrium of compromise.

In terms of a research agenda on (meta)governance, the preceding remarks invite the following questions. First, given the inherent complexity of the real world, what role does semiosis (that is, sense- and meaning-making) play in reducing complexity and, *a fortiori*, defining collective problems? This is a field where critical discourse analysis has much to offer not only in understanding the discursive framing or construction of social problems but also in the critique of ideology. Second, given the inherent complexity of the real world, what role does structuration play in limiting compossible social relations? This set of issues is one where an SRA to structurally inscribed strategic selectivities and, *a fortiori*, to patterns of domination, has much to offer. Third, given the importance of disciplinary, normalizing and regulatory practices in both regards, what specific modes of calculation and technologies of power or knowledge are involved in governance?

There are some interesting and productive links here to Foucauldian analyses of governmentality and questions of power or knowledge relations. And fourth, because of the lack of social closure in a hypercomplex, discursively contested, structurally underdetermined and technically malleable world, what scope is there for social agency to make a difference? This is where questions of conjunctural analysis, strategic calculation and social mobilization belong.

If we accept the incompleteness of one-sided attempts at coordination (whether through the market, the state, networks or solidarity) as inevitable, then we need to adopt a satisficing approach to these attempts. This, in turn, has three key dimensions: a self-reflexive orientation to what will prove satisfactory in the case of failure, a self-reflexive cultivation of a repertoire (requisite variety) of responses so that strategies and tactics can be combined to reduce the likelihood of failure and to alter their balance in the face of failure, and a self-reflexive 'irony' in the sense that participants must recognize the likelihood of failure but proceed as if success were possible.

Finally, in terms of practical recommendations on governance and metagovernance and their recurrent forms of failure, I advocate a principled and pragmatic reliance on romantic public irony combined with participatory governance. I juxtapose 'romantic public irony' to fatalism, stoicism, cynicism or opportunism. The fatalist concludes that, since everything fails, there is no point in trying to achieve anything, and therefore lapses into passive resignation. The stoic agrees but carries on regardless, out of a ritualistic sense of duty or obligation. The cynic shares the fatalists' 'pessimism of the intellect' but seeks, sometimes in a self-deluding manner, to deny evident failures or to redefine them as successes or else manipulates appearances so that success seems to have occurred. The opportunist recognizes the possibilities (indeed, probability of failure) but hopes to bail out in time as a winner, leaving others to carry the costs of failure. In contrast to the cynics and opportunists, ironists are sceptical and romantic. They act in 'good faith' and are prepared to admit to failure and bear its costs. One cannot choose to succeed completely and permanently in a complex world, but one can choose how to fail. This makes it imperative to choose wisely!

Given the main alternatives (markets, imperative coordination, self-organization and solidarity) and what we know about how and why they fail, the best chance of reducing the likelihood of failure is to draw on the collective intelligence of stakeholders and other relevant partners in a form of participatory democracy. This does not exclude resort to other forms of coordination, but it does require that the scope granted to the market mechanism, the exercise of formal authority, the contribution of networks or the resort to solidarity is subject as far as possible to decision through forms of participatory governance or commoning that aim to balance efficiency, effectiveness and democratic accountability. This provides the public dimension to romantic irony. Key substantive outcomes to be added here include sustainable development, the prioritization of social justice and respect for difference. In this sense, public romantic irony is the best mechanism for working out which modes of governance to resort to in particular situations and when collibration is required. It is not the only method to be adopted in each and every situation.

1

Introduction

This book explores the roles of markets, organizations, networks and solidarity as modes of governance, their respective strengths and weaknesses, and how they are combined and operate in hybrid ways in the real world. Civil society is not the main object of this book, which seeks instead to locate this field of social relations within a governance approach. Civil society can be said to exist at the intersection of networks and solidarity as opposed to markets or command, and its agents have the potential to guide markets and state action. In these terms, civil society may serve as a means of self-responsibilization as well as self-emancipation, and this can be seen in dialogues around the 'Big Society', social enterprise, social innovation, the formation of the commons, and so forth, as well as in practices of societal organization in response to disasters and crises. In this regard the governance approach rejects the tripartite classification of market, state and civil society inherited from the Enlightenment in favour of an analysis of hybrid relations of governance.

First comments on civil society

Let me confess that I find 'civil society' problematic on conceptual as well as empirical grounds. It is hard to separate 'civil society' fully from the economy (which is always socially embedded, although the forms of embeddedness vary) and from the state (defined by Gramsci, for example, as 'political society + civil society', 1971: 242; 1975, Q15, §10: 1765). Gramsci added that the state can be understood as '[t]he entire complex of practical and theoretical activities with which the ruling class not only justifies and maintains its dominance, but manages to win the consent of those over whom it rules' (Gramsci, 1971: 244; 1975, Q15, §10). Nicos Poulantzas (1978) developed this idea further when he defined the state as a social relation. This is an elliptical statement that draws on Marx's own statement that capital is not a thing but a social relation between people, established through the instrumentality of things (Marx, 1996 [1883]: 753). For Poulantzas, this meant that state power is a social relation between politically relevant forces mediated through the institutional structure of political society (Poulantzas, 1978: 128–9). Both Gramsci and Poulantzas adopted a

1

class-theoretical approach to state power. This is not required in a governance-theoretical strategic-relational approach (SRA), but can be useful for some purposes.

I do not support a concept of 'civil society' as denoting a specific institutional site with its own structured coherence. This is problematic, especially as there is no definition of civil society that corresponds to the modern territorial state. 'Civil society' comprises a heterogeneous set of institutional orders and pluralistic set of agents, many of which are operationally autonomous and resistant to control from outside – whether through market forces, top-down command or horizontal networking. It is also the site of identities and interests that are not grounded in any specific institutional order but crosscut them by virtue of their relationship to the experience and 'lifeworld' of whole persons. This is reflected in David Lockwood's questioning of sociologists' focus on class formation over citizenship and his recognition of the politics of intersectionality (cf Lockwood, 1999: 531, 537, 547). Indeed, people with multiple roles and complex personal identities and in addition, complex multifunctional organizations, often attempt to integrate their personal and organizational lives by retaining autonomy and resisting state intervention. This is where demands for empowerment and capacity-building become relevant. But identity politics and empowerment could become just another opportunity for capital to appropriate more flexible labour power, to commodify other institutional orders, to restructure consumption even as its tendencies towards economic polarization continue on a global scale, to seek legitimacy through the domestication of calls for corporate social responsibility, and so forth. This would limit attempts to ensure the inclusion of all citizens within each order.

This raises the question of whether 'civil society' is an autonomous domain of social life with its own logic, or comprises no more than a heterogeneous set of social relations that are not (yet) dominated by other institutional orders. The former approach can be illustrated through Habermas's analysis of the public sphere with its dialogical role in elaborating the 'public interest' (1989). In contrast, the latter approach sees 'civil society' as a horizon of action or 'environment' for other institutional orders (such as the economy or political system and their relevant actors) that form the main object of analysis. I incline more to the latter view, especially as the increasing functional differentiation of modern societies along with the tendential globalization of different functional systems (such as economics, law, science, education, health, politics or military security) makes it harder to identify a distinct site on which 'civil society' might be unproblematically located. Indeed, it is precisely this increasing decomposition or formlessness of 'civil society' that makes it such a significant (if often imaginary) stake in so many different struggles.

Not only are there what Habermas calls 'colonizing' attempts to penetrate civil society and subordinate it to the requirements of specific institutional orders (for example, market, law, science, education, healthcare, politics, foreign or homeland security). Civil society also serves as a heterogeneous site of struggles to resist such colonization in defence of identities and/or interests that lie outside and/or crosscut the relevant institutional orders (for example, in defence of class, gender, race, nationality, generation, stage in the life course, citizenship, human rights or the natural environment). In this sense 'civil society' is an essentially contested space (as well as an essentially contested concept) for representatives of very different types of interests, norms and values. It serves both as a horizon of action for strategies to secure the dominance of a given institutional order, and as a reservoir of antagonistic 'instincts' (rooted in other identities) and social resources for resisting such colonization (Habermas, 1989).

This was expressed well by Maurizio Lazzarato, in the following:

> In order for governmentality to preserve its global character, in order for it to not be separated in two branches (the art of economics and juridical government), liberalism invents and experiments [with] a series of techniques (of government) which are exerted on a new level of reference that Foucault calls civil society, society or the social. But here civil society is not the space for the making of autonomy from the state, but the correlative of certain techniques of government. Civil society is not a first and immediate reality, but something that belongs to the modern technology of governmentality. Society is not a reality in itself or something that does not exist, but a reality of transactions, just like sexuality or madness. At the crossing of these relations of power and those which continue to escape them emerge some realities of transaction that constitute in a way an interface between the governing and the governed. At this junction and in the management of this interface liberalism is constituted as an art of government and biopolitics is born. (Lazzarato, 2005: 2–3)

These practical concerns are also reflected in new theoretical and policy paradigms that highlight the need to govern in and across different systems or institutional orders. Relevant concepts include the 'triple helix' formed by government, business and universities, the desirability of 'joined-up thinking' in promoting international competitiveness and the improbability of effective intersystemic cooperation to promote sustainable development. In addition to explicit use of the word 'governance' to denote these issues, analogous terms such as steering, networks, stakeholding and partnerships are also liberally deployed nowadays.[1] Nor has civil society escaped this fascination with new forms of governance. Indeed, with its growing pluralization of individual and collective identities and its multiplication of social movements, civil society is seen as ripe for their development. This is linked to a continuing search for forms of inclusion in the political process that go beyond the relationship of individual citizens to their respective sovereign states and for forms of participation that would enable various stakeholders to influence the operation of other systems too. As such, civil society is a rich and confused site of multiple and contestable identities that can be mobilized for both pro- and anti-systemic purposes. Compounding this already ample complexity are recommendations that governance be used to guide interactions between systems and the lifeworld in response to issues such as ecological crisis, the dialectic of globalization–regionalization, social exclusion and the risk society.

Governance

This introductory chapter presents the theoretical background to interest in governance, shows the etymological roots of the concept, offers some reasons for the explosion of interest in governance in the 1960s and 1970s, and describes the main features of governance practices. Chapters 2 and 3 of Part I then frame the discussion of governance in terms of a dialectic between the governance of complexity and the complexity of governance. This highlights the relation between the increased interest in governance that is associated with more recognition of the growing complexity of world society and that the greater resort to governance, whatever its modalities, often ends in governance failure. This is intended to counter the 'governance optimism' that exaggerates the potential of new (or rediscovered) governance practices and to provide the basis for my recommendations about approaching governance in a spirit of romantic public irony. Chapter 4 introduces supplementary arguments about the spatio-temporal complexities of the objects and modalities of governance, and makes a case for approaching the meso- and macro-level governance of complex objects in terms of their multispatial (and multitemporal) dimensions as well as other substantive features. It argues that neglect of its spatio-temporal complexities is one dimension of governance failure.

Chapter 5 of Part II shows how WISERD (Wales Institute of Social & Economic Research, Data & Methods) is concerned with the politics and policy concerns of civil society, and has developed an interest in civic stratification and civic repair in its second five-year funding round. Chapter 6 extends this interest to the political economy of civil society by drawing on the insights of Marx and Gramsci. Chapter 7 introduces the work of Michel Foucault and Foucauldian scholars to illustrate the politics of governance and its role in civil society.

Part III then comprises two chapters that illustrate the preceding arguments from case studies drawn from different fields of governance and metagovernance, and focuses on their forms of failure. In Chapter 8, the examples chosen are global social policy (GSP) and the discourse of 'good governance' in cities. Chapter 9 discusses regional economic governance and the nature of corporatism. Chapter 10 examines attempts to use competition as a mode of governance. Chapter 11, the Conclusions, returns to the theme of romantic public irony and its implications for participatory governance based on an expanded civil society.

Why governance, why now?

The notion of 'governance' seems to encapsulate and condense a wide range of concerns in the contemporary world and therefore carries enormous theoretical, descriptive, practical and normative weight. There has been growing interest from the late 1970s onwards as to whether and how new (or revived) forms of governance (or steering), such as networks, public–private partnerships, multilevel governance (MLG), the cooperative state or the enabling state might enhance state capacity in the face of growing complexity and/or whether or how they might provide new ways to overcome old problems that postwar state intervention and the more recent (re)turn to market forces seem to have left unsolved, if not aggravated.[2] It has also been applied to a wide range of social issues and to every scale of social organization from the micro- through the meso- and macro- to the meta-social level. As such, governance has become an increasingly significant theme in the standard anglophone social science lexicon (and elsewhere), and is employed liberally in the social and management sciences, in social practices and in the rhetoric and narratives of social transformation. It has also become a 'buzzword' in various lay circles. Unsurprisingly, it has acquired multiple meanings and can be inserted into many different paradigms and problematics. For the same reasons, however, governance has become a rather fuzzy term that can be applied to almost everything. Indeed, the very popularity of the term increases the likelihood that those who use it will talk past each other, leading to ill-founded misunderstandings and pointless disagreements.

Perhaps one reason for this is that governance is not – indeed, cannot be – defined in the same abstract terms as statehood, the state or government as this is conceived in general state theory. This is because it can be applied in many different fields of social action rather than being concentrated in just one apparatus or institutional ensemble. This is indicated by common use of the definite article for *the* state but not for governance. While the state is often treated as if it were a (fictive) subject or single actor or, alternatively, reified as a thing (an instrument, machine or cybernetic device), governance lacks such a fixed, albeit often illusory, reference point. In another context, of course, as critical governance studies has argued, one might question the validity of general state theory. Sticking with general state theory, however, one implication of this contrast is that, to paraphrase Marx, just as there is neither production in general nor general production, there is no governance in general nor general governance. Rather, there is only particular governance and the totality of governance (cf Marx, 1973b [1857]: 99; Jessop, 1990a: 186). There are only definite objects of governance that are shaped in and through definite modes of governance. It is important to note that this excludes any general theory that would apply to all forms of governance, whether outside or inside the state. This explains why governance often figures in debates on the state in terms of qualities or properties of the state, such as the planning state, network state, liberal market state, cooperative state, therapeutic state, and so on.

It follows that one should focus instead on the many and varied struggles over the constitution of governance objects, competing strategies and techniques of governance in these and other regards, and the contingently necessary incompleteness or failure of efforts to govern them. It is the failure fully to govern (and so stabilize or at least, modulate) potential objects of governance that creates, in turn, space for competing governance strategies and ensures that the future remains pregnant with a surplus of possibilities around how social relations are defined as objects of governance (or not) and how their governance is approached (or not).

These complexities and the surplus of possibilities lead to conceptual fuzziness, especially where governance practices are decentred, dispersed or lack clear borders. This is reflected in the many typologies of governance developed for different purposes and in significant (often unspoken) disagreement about what is included, and excluded, from the concept. Indeed, Claus Offe (2009) questioned its value, describing it as polysemic, as having a multitude of possible meanings, as an irredeemably overstretched concept, as a ritualized or fetishized linguistic sign, as a bridge concept, and as an empty signifier. The main problem, it seems, is that 'governance' is both *equivocal*, because it has different but stable meanings in different contexts, and *ambiguous*, as its meanings vary even in similar contexts. These issues matter because there is no direct equivalent to governance in many European languages, let alone beyond Europe (witness the broad contrast between the governance, *gouvernance*, *gobernia* family of words in romance languages and that of steering, *Steuerung*, *styring* and so forth in North European languages). Similar problems occur outside Europe for the concept of state, which reveals the Eurocentric nature of much work addressing the state and state power. This is why governance is often proposed as an alternative, less Eurocentric, approach to studying government.

Even after some 30 to 40 years of widespread deployment, social scientific usages of governance are often 'pre-theoretical' and eclectic. Lay usages are just as diverse and contrary. Indeed, governance theory tends to remain at the pre-theoretical stage of critique and theorists of governance operate within several, often disparate and fragmented, problematics. It is generally much clearer what the notion of governance is against than what it is for. In theoretical terms, governance, then, comprises the 'other' modality (or set of modalities) for a wide range of dominant concepts or paradigms in the social sciences. This is reflected in a proliferation of typologies of governance mechanisms constructed for different purposes and a large measure of (often unspoken) disagreement about what is included, what is excluded, from the overall concept (vivid examples of different typologies can be found in Campbell et al, 1991; Kitschelt, 1991; Thompson et al, 1991; Grabher, 1993; Kooiman, 1993b).

Nonetheless, in general terms, two closely related, but nested, meanings can be identified in the literature over the last 40 to 50 years. First, governance can refer to any mode of coordination of interdependent activities. Among these modes, four ideal-typical forms are relevant here: the anarchy of exchange; organizational hierarchy; self-organizing and self-reflexive 'heterarchy';[3] and solidarity rooted in unconditional commitments. Some governance theorists have correlated these types of governance to different sets of social relations, respectively: exchange with markets; hierarchy with the world of states and interstate relations; self-reflexive heterarchy with networks and civil society; and solidarity with real or imagined communities. They also link them to different kinds of social logic. Thus, market exchange involves *ex post* coordination based on the formally rational pursuit of self-interest by individual agents; hierarchical command corresponds to various forms of *ex ante* imperative coordination concerned with the pursuit of substantive goals established from above and imposed on organizational members; self-organizing networks are suited for systems (non-political as well as political) that are resistant to top-down internal management and/or direct external control and that coevolve with other (complex) sets of social relations with which their various decisions, operations and aims are reciprocally interdependent; and solidarity is especially well-suited as the primary mode of governance for sustainable social cooperation (for example, in the social economy or for community empowerment, cultural emancipation, and so on). In each case, successful coordination depends on the performance of complementary activities and operations by other actors, whose pursuit of their activities and operations depends in turn on such activities and operations being performed elsewhere in the relevant social ensemble.

The second, more restricted, meaning is heterarchy (or self-organizing networks), and this is often the main reference in the revival of the governance paradigm, whether in theoretical or policy guise. Interest in this specific mode of governance developed because it is alleged to integrate complexity more explicitly, reflexively, and, it is hoped, effectively than reliance on markets or command and, to the extent that it is ever considered, solidarity. Indeed, far from just responding to demands from social forces dissatisfied with both state and market failure, state managers themselves have actively promoted these new forms of governance as adjuncts to and/or substitutes for more traditional forms of top-down government. They have done so in the expectation and/or hope that policy-making and implementation will thereby be improved in terms of efficiency, effectiveness and transparency and also made more accountable to relevant stakeholders and/or moral standards, thereby leading to 'good governance'. This is reflected in growing concern with the role of various forms of political coordination that not only span the conventional public–private divide but also involve 'tangled hierarchies', parallel power networks or other forms of complex interdependence across different tiers of government and/or different functional domains. More generally, new forms of partnership, negotiation and networking have been introduced or extended by state managers as they seek to cope with the declining legitimacy and/or effectiveness of other approaches to policy-making and implementation. Such innovations also redraw the public–private divide, engender new forms of interpenetration between the political system and other functional systems and modify relations between these systems and the lifeworld as the latter impacts on the nature and exercise of state power. Where solidarity is involved, we also find arguments that the broader networks, especially coordinated through the state, can provide a means of community empowerment, prevent the isolation of local initiatives and generalize feelings of solidarity to a wider (imagined) community.

Etymology, genealogy and discourse

It is important to distinguish words from concepts. This applies especially to governance. It has a long and chequered past, dating back to medieval Latin and earlier. Its recent revival suggestively highlights a major paradigm shift in political (and economic) analysis as it provides a narrative and/or analytical framework in the contemporary world. The anglophone term 'governance' can be traced to the classical Latin and ancient Greek words for the 'steering' of boats. It originally referred mainly to the action or manner of governing, guiding or steering conduct, and as such, it overlapped with 'government'. The first recorded uses of 'governance' occur in the 14th century and refer mainly to the action or manner of governing, guiding or steering conduct. It is only in the last 40 to 50 years that there has been a sustained revival in explicit theoretical and practical concern with governance as opposed to government. In short, as far as the anglophone world is concerned, the recently renewed interest in regulation and governance can be dated to the mid-1970s. For a long time, usage was mainly limited to constitutional and legal issues concerning 'affairs of state' and/or to the direction of specific institutions or professions with multiple stakeholders.

The key factor in its revival has probably been the need to distinguish between 'governance' and 'government' in response to crucial changes in the external demarcation and internal organization of the state apparatus and the nature of state powers (plural). Thus, governance came to refer to the modes and manner of governing, government to the institutions and agents charged with governing, and governing to the act of governing itself. The analogous German concept of

Steuerung (steering, guiding) proved popular in the 1970s and 1980s for much the same reasons.

There are also significant historical precursors to the idea of metagovernance as well as some close contemporary equivalents. Its antecedents include Greek and Roman notions of a balanced constitution; the medieval and Renaissance 'mirror of princes' literature on the art of government (such as Machiavelli's *The Prince*, 1988); various notions of 'police' (*policey* or *Polizei* concerned with the structures and practices that would help to promote a sound political economy, good governance and state security; see Heidenheimer, 1986); and political principles of statecraft and diplomacy such as the mixed constitution at home and the wisdom and necessity of maintaining an international balance of power.

These traditional interests in governance and metagovernance have survived in different forms. But governance has also been discussed without explicit use of this term, and this provides a rich repertoire for illuminating the analysis of governance, whether explicitly in these terms or not. For example, theories of governance have obvious precursors in institutional economics, work on statecraft and diplomacy, research on corporatist networks and policy communities and interest in 'police'[4] or welfare. And although the idea of 'governance' has now gained widespread currency in mainstream social sciences, it has by no means displaced other research on economic, political or social coordination. In addition, newer theoretical paradigms have turned their attention from governance (or its equivalents) to metagovernance for their own reasons, at different times, and in their own ways. An influential contemporary analogy is Foucault's approach to governmentality as 'the conduct of conduct' (1991; 2003: 138), especially as developed by the Anglo-Foucauldian school of governmentality studies (see, for example, Miller and Rose, 2008). It is also evident in the increasing interest in resilience (see, for example, Joseph, 2016, 2018).

It is nonetheless worth noting one major source of ambiguity in the mobility of 'governance' between theoretical inquiries and practical politics. This is the fact that governance offers both a theoretical and a policy paradigm. Wallis and Dollery (1999) distinguish between them as follows:

> ... policy paradigms derive from theoretical paradigms but possess much less sophisticated and rigorous evaluations of the intellectual underpinnings of their conceptual frameworks. In essence, policy advisers differentiate

policy paradigms from theoretical paradigms by screening out the ambiguities and blurring the fine distinctions characteristic of theoretical paradigms. In a Lakatosian sense, policy paradigms can be likened to the positive heuristics surrounding theoretical paradigms. Accordingly, shifts between policy paradigms will be discontinuous, follow theoretical paradigm shifts, but occur more frequently than theoretical paradigms since they do not require fundamental changes in a negative heuristic. (Wallis and Dollery, 1999: 5)

Drawing on this distinction helps us to understand that the explosion of interest in governance has policy as well as theoretical roots, and that the transfer of ideas and arguments across these two types of paradigm may be both limited and subject to serious misunderstandings. Conversely, failure to make this distinction is likely to contribute to two complementary fallacies. The first is that governance, when viewed largely from the ideas that inform the policy paradigm, is seen as an essentially incoherent concept. This is especially problematic in the case of 'good governance' as a discursively mediated policy paradigm. This is reinforced when it is shown that the discourse of 'good governance' often serves to legitimate neoliberalism, serving as a flanking and supporting mechanism for an essentially inegalitarian and unjust economic and political project (see Chapter 8). The second fallacy is that, when measured against the demands for analytical rigour of governance as a scientific concept and practice, it is claimed that governance practices are bound to produce no more than 'muddling through' at best and failure at worst. This poses at least three problems in exploring theoretical and policy paradigms. What is the best way to link theoretical and policy paradigms without committing errors? The first error is to reduce one to the other. The second is to subject policy paradigms to a purely theoretical critique or seek to derive immediate policy lessons from the theoretical paradigm. The third is to adopt the normative assumption that the practical necessity of governance justifies any and all attempts at governance,[5] or to make the fatalistic claim that the practical impossibility of fully effective governance practices nullifies all such attempts.

Theoretical background to governance

These general etymological and conceptual accounts do not explain why a relatively dormant concept with limited scope and restricted usage came to be revitalized at a particular time and has been applied by so many individuals, agencies and organizations to so many different topics. An important general answer (with varied instantiations) to the 'why this concept, why now' question is a convergent reaction to perceived inadequacies in earlier theoretical paradigms. It is particularly tempting in the political and social sciences to suggest that the 'other' of governance is government (considered as state or organizational hierarchy).[6] Thus theories of governance are primarily concerned with a wide range of 'social' modes of social coordination rather than with narrowly political (sovereign, juridico-political, bureaucratic or at least hierarchically organized) modes of social organization. In this context, social coordination refers to the ways in which disparate but interdependent social agencies are coordinated to achieve specific social objectives. And in these terms, one could define the general field of governance studies as concerned with the resolution of (para-)political problems (problems of collective goal attainment or the realization of collective purposes) through specific configurations of governmental (hierarchical) and extra-governmental (non-hierarchical) institutions, organizations and practices.

In theoretical terms, this can be linked to certain paradigmatic crises in the social sciences in the 1970s and 1980s – crises partly due, in turn, to dissatisfaction with their capacity to describe and explain the 'real world'. An interest in 'governance' as a major theme is rooted in the rejection of several simplistic dichotomies that inform the social sciences. These include market vs hierarchy in economics; market vs plan in policy studies; private vs public in politics; and anarchy vs sovereignty in international relations. Indeed, Fritz Scharpf (1993) was prompted to write:

> Considering the current state of theory, it seems that it is not so much increasing disorder on all sides that needs to be explained as the really existing extent, despite everything, of intra- as well as interorganizational, intra- as well as intersectoral, and intra- as well as international, agreement and expectations regarding mutual security. Clearly, beyond the limits of the pure market, hierarchical state, and domination-free discourses, there are more – and more effective – coordination mechanisms than science has hitherto grasped empirically and conceptualized theoretically. (Scharpf, 1993: 57; translated by BJ [author])

In general terms, it could be suggested that the various approaches to governance share a rejection of the conceptual trinity of market–

state–civil society that has tended to dominate mainstream analyses of modern societies. Thus reflexive self-organization has been greeted as a new social-scientific paradigm, as a new mode of problem-solving that can overcome the limitations of anarchic market exchange and top-down planning in an increasingly complex and global world, and as a solution to the perennial ethical, political and civic problems of securing institutional integration and peaceful social coexistence. In part, this recent interest involves little more than an attempt to put old theoretical wine in new bottles and/or reflects one more turn in the never-ending policy cycle whereby disenchantment with one mode of coordination leads to excessive faith in another – until that, too, disappoints.

Political scientists, for example, have expressed growing dissatisfaction with a rigid public–private distinction in state-centred analyses of politics and its associated top-down account of the exercise of state power. Whereas statehood (or, less abstractly, authoritative government) presupposes a state apparatus, territory and population, the notion of governance lacks this core juridico-political or otherwise relatively fixed institutional reference point. If statehood is a concept that applies in the first instance to the polity, then governance relates more to politics and policy. It concerns public politics, public policies or public affairs (Larsson, 2013: 107) rather than the state-cum-polity that provides the framework in which these unfold. However, it is even broader in scope because governance practices are not limited to the polity and indeed, are often advocated as a means to avoid the iron fist (even when concealed in a velvet glove) of state power. This has been reflected in growing concern with various forms of political coordination that not only span the conventional public–private divide, but also involve 'tangled hierarchies', parallel power networks or other forms of complex interdependence across tiers of government and/or different functional domains.

The Köln School has been an influential contributor to governance studies under the rubric of *Steuerung* (steering).[7] It has thereby developed a distinctive approach to the problems of governing functionally differentiated, organizationally dense and complex societies. Its leading figures recognized that these problems involved both the steering capacity of governing subjects and the governability of the objects to be governed (Mayntz, 2003: 29; cf also Mayntz, 1993). While these problems can lead to 'steering pessimism' (for example, in the work of Niklas Luhmann), the Köln School was more optimistic, influenced, perhaps, by specific examples of successful administrative reform and the overall record of neocorporatism in

13

Germany in promoting economic development and sustaining a high-waged, high-tech, globally competitive 'Modell Deutschland' (German Model). Two key figures in developing these ideas were Renate Mayntz and Fritz Scharpf who codirected the Max Planck Institute for the Study of Societies at Köln for many years. A distinctive feature of this school is its actor-centred institutionalism, namely, its interest in how the interaction between micro- and meso-level actors and institutional factors shapes the possibilities of effective governance. Indeed, Mayntz (2004) later emphasized that the actor-centred political steering (*Steuerung*) approach to policy-making was quite distinct from the governance (*Regulierung*) approach, which is more institutionalist and deals with regulatory structures combining public and private, hierarchical and network forms of action coordination. In this spirit, the Köln School explored how to (re)design the interaction between institutions and actors to improve the chances of overcoming policy problems. This is yet another way in which the topic of metagovernance (or, in this context, metasteering) has emerged.

Theoretical background to metagovernance

The notion of metagovernance obviously builds on that of governance. As noted, in its most basic and general sense, it denotes the governance of governance. Whereas some scholars and practitioners explicitly refer to metagovernance, many other terms have been used to denote or connote this phenomenon. This linguistic variety is linked in part to the relatively 'pre-theoretical' nature of work on governance and metagovernance, to the diversity of theoretical traditions with which more rigorous work is associated, to the different political traditions and tendencies that have shown interest in governance, to the great heterogeneity of the subjects and objects of governance and, *a fortiori*, of metagovernance, and to the challenges involved in translating theoretical reflections on governance and metagovernance into policy paradigms or indeed, commercial consultancy in the public, private and third sectors.

This is illustrated neatly in Louis Meuleman's work on metagovernance (2008: 73). He shows some significant routes to interest in metagovernance in two theoretical traditions (rational choice vs sociological) and with respect to the three most commonly identified modes of governance (market, hierarchy and network). Of particular interest in his analysis is an implicit distinction between first-, second- and third-order governance, to which we return below, as well as the key role this distinction accords to reflexivity, deliberation and normative commitments in second- and third-order governance, which are also the two main sites of what he identifies as metagovernance.

One of the two authors most often cited as the originator of the term 'metagovernance' is the Dutch scholar, Jan Kooiman, who belongs to a broader Dutch tradition of sociocybernetic inquiry (see, for example, Kickert et al, 1997; Edelenbos and Klijn, 2007; Meuleman, 2008; see also Deutsch, 1963). Interested in the problems that states faced in governing complex societies, he drew on sociocybernetics to explore state–society interactions not only in terms of automatic cybernetic mechanisms but also in terms of conscious guiding actions (Kooiman, 1993a, 2003). Rather than assume that the state stands over and against society, he viewed governments as cooperating with key societal actors to guide societal development.

Accordingly, he stressed the need for requisite variety among modes of government–society interactions that range from hierarchical governance (top-down intervention) through cogovernance (joint action) to self-governance (societal self-organization without government interference). Whereas Kooiman recognized that each mode has its own specific properties, he argued that they also interact to produce hybrid, or mixed, patterns of governance (Kooiman, 2003: 7). He further noted the importance for effective governance of cultivating the capacity to reflect on, and rebalance, the mix among these modes in response to changes in the challenges and/or opportunities that exist at the interface of market, state and civil society. Governing in modern society requires an interactive perspective concerned to balance social interests and facilitate the interaction of actors and systems through self-organization, co-arrangements or more interventionist forms of organization. Thus, for Kooiman, the key problem is how best to 'strike a balance' among different kinds of actors and steering mechanisms at the micro, meso and macro levels of society.[8]

Kooiman distinguishes first-, second- and third-order governing. First-order governing is problem-solving; second-order governing occurs when attempts are made to modify the institutional conditions of first-order governing when, according to Kooiman, these conditions are out-dated, dysfunctional or detrimental in governance terms; and third-order governing (or, for Kooiman, metagovernance) involves attempts to change the broad principles that concern the way governing takes place: it is the governance of governance or governors through modification of the (normative) framework in which first- and second-order governing activities evolve (Kooiman, 2000, 2002).

Whereas the literature on governance and metagovernance has shown much interest in issues of institutional design appropriate to different objects of governance, work on governmentality has explored attempts to change the subjects of governance and their values. The neoliberal project, for example, clearly requires attempts to create entrepreneurial subjects and demanding consumers aware of their choices and rights as well as actions to expand the scope of the market mechanism. Anglo-Foucauldian scholars have explored the role of power and knowledge in shaping the attributes, capacities and identities of social agents and, in the context of self-reflexive governance, in enabling them to become self-governing and self-transforming (cf Miller and Rose, 2008). This raises questions about the compatibility of modes of governance not only institutionally but also in terms of individual and collective capacities to pursue creatively and autonomously the strategies and tactics required to sustain contrasting modes of governance. This indicates that collibration demands more than the search for a technical, problem-solving fix. It also involves specific objects, techniques and subjects of governance and efforts to manage the wider 'unstable equilibrium of compromise'. Applied to metagovernance, this means comparing the effects of failure or inadequacies in markets, government, self-organization and solidarity, and regularly reassessing how far current actions are producing desired outcomes. This, in turn, requires monitoring and modulating mechanisms, and a willingness to reevaluate objectives.

Political contexts

Given such theoretical pre-histories and current theoretical alternatives, it is worth asking whether other factors might lie behind the recent interest in governance. Here one should certainly consider the strong practical dimension to such paradigm shifts. Current fascination with the nature and dynamics of governance is closely linked to the failure of many taken-for-granted coordination mechanisms in the postwar world. Here we could mention the competitive threat to Anglo-American capitalism posed by other models of capitalism (such as Continental European or East Asian variants); the crisis of US hegemony in a post-Cold War order and the attendant search for post-hegemonic and/or 'post-national state' solutions to global problems; the crisis of the postwar Keynesian welfare national state and its typical modes of economic and political coordination, including tripartite macro corporatism; and the eruption of identity politics and new social movements that threaten established forms of social and political domination. In these circumstances we find concern with both corporate governance and national competitiveness; managing new (or newly defined) economic, military, demographic, environmental and other threats to global security; with 'good' rather than 'bad' governance in 'Third World' polities, whose authoritarianism and corruption can no longer be simply defended as preferable to totalitarian communist rule;[9] with compensating for the failure of hierarchical decision-making and 'top-down' planning in a turbulent environment marked by complex reciprocal interdependence; and with resolving the disciplinary crisis of an allegedly dependency-inducing 'state of welfare' by instituting new forms of 'regulated self-discipline' in an 'enterprise society'. On a more meso-level scale there was also growing interest in clinical governance in medicine, the governance of schools and universities, the self-regulation of the scientific community and the governance of sport.

It is certainly worth noting that the increased interest in governance coincided with the crisis of Atlantic Fordism and the Keynesian welfare national state, and it was strengthened, in the mid-1990s, as recognition grew of the limited success of an over-enthusiastic and fetishistic turn to the market. This was also a period when civil society was celebrated and efforts made to integrate community organizations and old and, especially, new, social movements into policy-making and implementation. These responses also opened up the space for some governance scholars to assert or predict that the sovereign national state was losing authority and influence, and to intone the 'government to governance' mantra. The plausibility of this claim was reinforced because governance arrangements were identified within and across many different social fields and functional systems, at and across different scales of social organization, and transversally to the conventional juridico-political boundaries between the state and society. In short, the turn to governance theoretically and in practice seemed to be a general trend that extended beyond the state or political system. The state and the modalities of state power nonetheless remained central to some analyses that regarded governance as an integral part of state projects and strategies. Overall, then, these empirical and theoretical trends opened up the space for society- and state-centred approaches to governance as well as for accounts that sidestepped or crosscut this familiar, indeed, often reified, distinction.

Another aspect of the changing economic and political order in this period was the reshaping of the world economy by a complex dialectic of globalization–regionalization under the dominance of capitalist relations that combined growing integration of the world order together with the survival of a plurality of national states. This process is alleged to make it more difficult for (national) states to control their own domestic economies let alone the global dynamic of capital accumulation. At the same time, capital accumulation was said to depend on an increasing range of extra-economic factors generated on various spatio-temporal scales through other institutional orders (see, for example, Chesnais, 1987; Castells, 1989; Porter, 1990; Reich, 1991; Nelson, 1993; Boyer, 1996). Major changes were also occurring in the (global) political system with equally paradoxical effects. Thus, on the one hand, there has been a tendential denationalization of the state system through the movement of state power upwards, downwards and sideways as attempts are made by state managers to regain operational autonomy (if not formal sovereignty as such) and thereby enhance the state's own strategic capacities. On the other hand, there has been a tendential destatization of politics (a shift from the primacy of top-down government towards more decentred governance mechanisms) as political capacities are seen to depend on the effective coordination of interdependent forces within and beyond the state (for a review of these and related trends, see Jessop, 2015). It is in this context that governance (or 'partnership') strategies were strongly advocated as alternatives to market anarchy and organizational hierarchy in promoting economic development.

Interest in metagovernance was related to the growing perception of the problems generated in the 1990s by a combination of state and market failure and/or by a decline in social cohesion in the advanced capitalist societies. This was reflected in notions such as governmental overload, legitimacy crisis, steering crisis and ungovernability. It prompted theoretical and practical interest in the potential of coordination through self-organizing heterarchic networks and partnerships and other forms of reflexive collaboration. Most of the early studies of governance were concerned with specific practices or regimes oriented to specific objects of governance, linked either to the planning, programming and regulation of specific policy fields or to issues of economic performance. Concern with problems of governance and the potential contributions of metagovernance followed during the mid-1990s, and the nature and dynamics of metagovernance have since won growing attention.

The real world of governance

Many practices now subsumed under 'governance' have been examined under other rubrics. Thus corporatism, public–private partnerships, industrial districts, trade associations, statecraft, diplomacy, interest in 'policing', policy communities, international regimes and the like all involve aspects of what is now termed 'governance'. In this sense, we find pre-cursors of current interest in governance in various disciplines. One could interpret this in four ways. First, regardless of the changing importance or otherwise of heterarchy (neither anarchy nor hierarchy) and solidarity, the significance of governance in lay discourses has changed, and this is reflected in social science scholarship. Second, a stable but recently subterranean stream of heterarchic practices has resurfaced and begun to attract renewed attention. Third, after becoming less significant compared with other modes of coordination, heterarchy has once again become important. And fourth, an upward trend has continued, is becoming dominant, and is likely to continue to do so. There is a kernel of truth in each interpretation.

The first possibility is suggested by the expansion of governance discourses. These range from 'global governance' through 'multilevel governance' (MLG) and the shift from 'government to governance' to the issues of 'the stakeholding society' and 'corporate governance'. Given the close, mutually constitutive relationship between the social sciences and lay discourses, this suggestion would be worth exploring further.

The second possibility is the persistence of underlying realities beneath the vagaries of intellectual fashion. So-called 'governance' mechanisms (as contrasted to markets or hierarchy) have long been widely used in coordinating complex organizations and systems. There have always been issues and problems for which heterarchic governance is, so to speak, the 'natural' mode of coordination.[10] Certain forms of interdependence are inappropriate for (or at least resistant to) market and/or imperative coordination. For example, public–private partnership is theoretically well-suited in cases of organized complexity characterized by a loose coupling of agents, complex forms of reciprocal interdependence and complex spatio-temporal horizons. In addition, different state traditions have given scope for market forces and/or self-regulation to operate in their economies and civil societies. There are also normative preferences for self-organization in certain contexts. This socially necessary minimum of heterarchic practices makes it even more curious that they have only recently attracted focused scientific interest. This is almost certainly related to the blind spots associated with specific disciplinary paradigms or prevailing forms of 'common sense'. Thus, during the postwar period of growth based on a virtuous circle of mass production and mass consumption in North America and Western Europe, when the 'mixed economy' was a dominant paradigm, institutions and practices intermediate between market and state were often neglected. They had not actually disappeared; they were simply marginalized theoretically and politically. Subsequent disenchantment with the state in the 1970s, and with markets in the 1990s, has renewed interest in something that never really disappeared.

A third factor contributing to the rise of governance is the cycle of modes of coordination. All modes are prone to dilemmas, contradictions, paradoxes and failures, but the problems differ with the mode in question. Markets, states, networks and solidarity fail in different ways. One practical response to this situation is to combine modes of policy-making and vary their weight over time – thereby shifting the forms in which tendencies to 'failure' manifest themselves and creating room for manoeuvre (Offe, 1975a, b). This suggests that the current expansion of networks at the expense of markets and hierarchies and of governance at the expense of government may involve little more than a specific stage in a regular succession of dominant modes of policy-making. In this sense, what we are witnessing today is really discontinuity in continuity: oscillation within a repeated policy cycle. In other words, the rediscovery of governance could mark a fresh revolution in this process – a simple cyclical response to past state failures (especially those linked to attempts to manage the emerging crisis of Atlantic Fordism from the mid-1970s) and more recently, market failure (and its associated crisis in corporate governance).

An alternative explanation would be that, for various reasons, there has been a shift in the institutional centre of gravity (or 'institutional attractor') around which policy cycles operate due to some qualitative shift in the basic problems that regularizing or governmentalizing policies must address. Here we would be dealing with continuity in discontinuity: the revival of familiar governance mechanisms for qualitatively new purposes. If there is a major transition from Fordism to post-Fordism (linked additionally to new technologies, internationalization and regionalization), then such a long-term shift may be at work. Similar possibilities are indicated by the crisis of the national state – with a proliferation of cross-border and multitier problems that can no longer be coordinated within national state hierarchy or through neorealist anarchy of market (see Jessop, 1995). Here, too, we could anticipate that the expansion of networks and/ or governance is a sign of a qualitative shift rather than a simple pendular swing within a policy cycle. Rather than prejudge this issue, however, one should recognize that there could be various path-dependent possibilities.

The fourth possibility is that a fundamental secular shift in social relations has occurred. Important new economic and social conditions and attendant problems have emerged that cannot be managed or resolved readily, if at all, through market-mediated anarchy or top-down state planning. This secular shift reflects the dramatic intensification of societal complexity that flows from growing functional differentiation of institutional orders in an increasingly global society – which leads, in turn, to greater systemic interdependencies across various social, spatial and temporal horizons of action. As Scharpf (1994: 37) notes:

> ... the advantages of hierarchical coordination are lost in a world that is characterized by increasingly dense, extended, and rapidly changing patterns of reciprocal interdependence, and by increasingly frequent, but ephemeral, interactions across all types of pre-established boundaries, intra- and interorganizational, intra- and intersectoral, intra- and international.

A similar argument could be made about the declining advantages of market coordination. In this sense, the recent expansion of networks and solidarities at the expense of markets and hierarchies and of governance at the expense of government is not just a pendular swing in some regular succession of dominant modes of policy-making. It reflects a shift in the fundamental structures of the real world and a corresponding shift in the centre of gravity around which policy cycles move.

Introducing some conceptual clarity

Faced with the wide range of factors that have prompted interest in governance and metagovernance and the wide range of usages and parallel vocabularies, it is useful to distinguish words from concepts. This holds especially where the terminology is not only unclear but also essentially contested. The latter is particularly common in periods of rapid social change and/or when new fields of academic inquiry are emerging. Both sets of circumstances apply in the present case. This illustrates the close, mutually constitutive, links among academic discourse, political practice and changing realities.[11] This reflects the fact that the question of governance is more often and more directly related to problem-solving and crisis management in a wide range of fields than the regulation approach in heterodox economics. While this can have salutary effects in diverse fields, it also risks falling into a 'floating eclecticism'[12] by working both within and against old paradigms in a wide range of terrains. The risk of eclecticism is reinforced in some cases by the interest of governance theorists in issues of institutional design, which has led some governance theorists to focus more on specific collective decision-making or goal-attainment issues in relation to specific (socially and discursively constituted) problems. In this sense, governance theorists have sometimes inclined towards instrumentalist analyses that are less concerned to speak truth to power than to become its advisers. This is a temptation in the WISERD Civil Society programme.

More disinterested governance scholars are also interested in the diversity of policy regimes that emerge in response to crises, emergencies and other social problems and the political dynamic behind regime shifts. This often leads to an innovation process oriented to solving the purported governance problems and doing so in a more or less turbulent environment; new forms of governance will emerge on condition that collective action problems are resolved through one (or more) of the attempted solutions and become part of new patterns of conduct. Thus, one might examine how failure in established forms of governance and/or an emerging 'crisis' of governance is perceived by political actors (broadly conceived) and is then translated into demands for restructured and/or new governance regimes. This helps to explain the growing breadth of interest in the relative weight of government and governance.

Defining governance

Having emphasized the polyvalent, polycontextual and essentially contested nature of 'governance', I will now engage in the seemingly self-defeating exercise of offering a definition of governance. But at least this will provide a basis for later discussion in this book and illustrate ironically the importance of self-reflexive irony in addressing complex problems. This approach involves two analytical steps, the first identifying the broad field of coordination problems within which governance can be located, the second providing a narrow definition that identifies the *differentia specifica* of governance within this broad field. In broad terms, governance is one of several possible modes of coordination of complex and reciprocally interdependent activities or operations. What makes these modes relevant for our purposes is that their success depends on the performance of complementary activities and operations by other actors – whose pursuit of their activities and operations depends in turn on the performance of complementary activities and operations elsewhere within the relevant social ensemble (see Table 1.1).[13] In general, the greater the material, social and spatio-temporal complexity of the problems to be addressed, the greater the number and range of different interests whose coordination is necessary to resolve them satisfactorily, and the less direct the reciprocities of these interests, the greater will be the difficulties of efficient, effective and consensual coordination regardless of the method of coordination that is adopted (for further discussion of complexity, see the chapters in Part I). It is still useful to distinguish four main forms of coordination of complex reciprocal interdependence: *ex post* coordination through exchange (for example, the anarchy of the market); *ex ante* coordination through imperative coordination (for example, the hierarchy of the firm, organization or state); reflexive self-organization (for example, the heterarchy of ongoing negotiated consent to resolve complex problems in a corporatist order or horizontal networking to coordinate a complex division of labour); and coordination through drawing as needed on unconditional commitments based on more or less extensive solidaristic

Table 1.1: Modalities of governance

	Exchange	Command	Dialogue	Solidarity
Rationality	Formal and procedural	Substantive and goal-oriented	Reflexive and procedural	Unreflexive and value-oriented
Criterion of success	Efficient allocation of resources	Effective goal attainment	Negotiated consent	Requited commitment
Ideal typical example	Market	State	Network	Love
Stylized mode of calculation	*Homo economicus*	*Homo hierarchicus*	*Homo politicus*	*Homo fidelis*
Spatio-temporal horizons	World market, reversible time	Organizational space, planning	Rescaling, path shaping	Any time, any where
Primary criterion of failure	Economic inefficiency	Ineffectiveness	'Noise', 'talking shop'	Betrayal, mistrust
Secondary criterion of failure	Market inadequacies	Bureaucratism, red tape	Secrecy, distorted communication	Codependency, asymmetry
Significance	Anarchy	Hierarchy	Heterarchy of civil society	

Source: Jessop (2017)

relations in an imagined community. It is the third type of coordination that I refer to as 'governance' when the term is otherwise unqualified.

Reflexive self-organization can be distinguished from the other three types of coordination in terms of the basic rationale for its operations and its institutional logic (see Table 1.2). Thus, market exchange is characterized by a formal, procedural rationality that is oriented to the efficient allocation of scarce resources to competing ends. In contrast, imperative coordination has a substantive, goal-oriented rationality that is directed to the effective realization of specific collective goals established from above. In turn, governance, as defined here, has a substantive, procedural rationality that is concerned with solving specific coordination problems based on a commitment to a continuing dialogue to establish the grounds for negotiated consent, resource sharing and concerted action. As such, it is a form of self-organization that, in contrast to the anarchy of exchange, depends not on purely formal, *ex post* and impersonal procedures, but on substantive, continuing and reflexive procedures.

Solidarity, conversely, relies on an unreflexive and value-oriented rationality. It has roots in the voluntary giving of public goods, akin to classical liturgical associations (Kelen, 2001: 7–40). Since then it has taken many forms in ancient societies, analysed by Marcel Mauss (1990) in his book on gift giving, and it appears across history in diverse forms of commoning based on solidarity, mutuality and conviviality (de Angelis, 2017). More recently it is seen to depend on attitudes of mutual acceptance, cooperation and mutual support in times of need (Banting and Kymlicka, 2017: 3). Following Banta and Kymlicka (2017: 4), we can distinguish three dimensions of solidarity:

- *Civic solidarity:* this involves mutual tolerance; a commitment to living together in peace, free from intercommunal violence; acceptance of people of diverse ethnicities, languages and religions as legitimate members of 'our' community; and openness to newcomers from diverse parts of the world.
- *Democratic solidarity:* this involves support for basic human rights and equalities; support for the rule of law and for democratic norms and processes, including equal participation of citizens from all backgrounds; tolerance for the political expression of diverse political and cultural views consistent with basic rights and equalities; and acceptance of compromises among legitimate contending interests.
- *Redistributive solidarity:* this involves support for redistribution towards the poor and vulnerable groups; support for the full social

inclusion of people of all backgrounds to core social programmes; and support for programmes that recognize and accommodate the distinctive needs and identities of different ethnocultural groups.

Governance procedures are concerned to identify mutually beneficial joint projects from a wide range of possible projects, to redefine them as the relevant actors attempt to pursue them in an often-turbulent environment and monitor how far these projects are being achieved, and to organize the material, social and temporal conditions deemed necessary and/or sufficient to achieve them. Moreover, in contrast to the hierarchy of command, reflexive self-organization does not involve actors' acceptance of pre-given substantive goals defined from above on behalf of a specific organization (for example, a firm) or an imagined collectivity (for example, a community or nation) and the centralized mobilization of the resources to achieve these goals. Instead it involves continued negotiation of the relevant goals among the different actors involved and the cooperative mobilization of different resources controlled by different actors to achieve interdependent goals. For these reasons and to distinguish it from the anarchy of the market and the hierarchy of command, it is also common to refer to these forms of reflexive self-organization as heterarchic in character.

Reflexive self-organization

There are various forms of reflexive self-organization. One way to classify them is in terms of the level of social relations on which they operate. We can distinguish collaboration based on informal interpersonal networks, the self-organization of interorganizational relations, and the indirect steering of the coevolution and structural coupling of intersystemic relations. The individuals who are active in interpersonal networks may represent only themselves and/or articulate the codes of specific functional systems. However, although they may also belong to specific agencies, groups or organizations, they are not mandated to commit the latter to a given line of action. In contrast, interorganizational relations are based on negotiation and positive coordination in task-oriented 'strategic alliances' derived from a (perceived or constructed) coincidence of organizational interests and dispersed control of the interdependent resources needed to produce a joint outcome that is deemed to be mutually beneficial. The key individuals involved in interorganizational relations are also empowered to represent their organizations and to negotiate strategies on their behalf for positive interorganizational coordination. Another layer of complexity is introduced by the more programmatic or mission-oriented, decentred, context-mediated nature of intersystemic steering. Whereas noise reduction involves the mediated nature of intersystemic steering, here noise reduction and negative coordination are important means of governance. Noise reduction comprises practices that are intended to facilitate communication and mutual understanding between actors and organizations oriented to different operational logics and rationalities; negative integration involves taking account of the possible adverse repercussions of one's own actions on third parties or other systems and exercising self-restraint as appropriate.[14]

Although governance in the sense of reflexive self-organization occurs on all three levels, the term itself is often limited to interorganizational coordination mechanisms and practices. However, where the relevant agencies, stakeholders or organizations are based in different institutional orders or functional systems, problems relating to intersystemic steering will also affect the 'self-organization of interorganizational relations' even if they are not explicitly posed as such in this context. Indeed, more generally, all three forms of reflexive self-organization may be linked in tangled hierarchies. For example, interpersonal trust often helps to maintain markets and hierarchies (cf Granovetter, 1985). It can facilitate interorganizational negotiation and/or help build less personalized, more 'generalized trust' as organizations and other collective actors (including interorganizational

Table 1.2: Two-dimensional hybridity

	Primacy of profitability	Primacy of command	Primacy of dialogue	Primacy of solidarity
Secondary role of exchange	n/a	Mafias, new public management	Benchmarking, good governance	Trade unions, syndicalism
Secondary role of command	Firms, mixed economy	n/a	Public–private partnerships, deliberative democracy	*Bund*, commune, associational democracy
Secondary role of dialogue	*Guanxi*, network economy	Parties, soft law, cooperative state	n/a	Community, communitarianism
Secondary role of solidarity	Social enterprises, cooperatives, social economy	Commune, subsidiarity	Social movements, civil society	n/a

Source: Jessop (2017)

partnerships) are seen to sacrifice short-term interests and reject opportunism (cf Luhmann, 1979: 120–2; Marin, 1990).

In turn, interorganizational dialogue across systems eases intersystemic communication by reducing the 'noise' that can arise from major differences between systems in their respective institutional logics, operational codes and modes of calculation. If organizations representing different systems can formulate and communicate these contrasting desiderata and legitimate them in terms of their respective functional requirements, this may promote mutual understanding and the search for mutually beneficial trade-offs. It thereby permits 'systemic trust' (in the integrity of other systems' codes and operations) by promoting mutual understanding and stabilizing reciprocal expectations around a wider 'societal project' as the basis for future self-binding and self-limiting actions. In turn, the resulting noise reduction can promote interpersonal trust by enhancing mutual understanding and by stabilizing expectations. In negotiated economies, for example, a few formal organizations and forums are entrusted to formulate and represent the identities and interests of different subsystems at the same time as they contribute to the definition and promotion of a wider 'societal project'.

The rise of governance practices

The rise of governance is partly due to secular shifts in political economy that have made heterarchy and solidarity more significant than markets or hierarchies for economic, political and social coordination. I now consider the reasons for this by undertaking two tasks: first, identifying the logic of governance as a distinctive coordination mechanism in contradistinction to markets and imperative coordination; and second, considering more fully what societal (or macro-social) changes might have made heterarchy more appropriate as an economic coordination mechanism.

First, the most general case for the shift from government hierarchy and pure market exchange to heterarchic governance can be made in terms of the evolutionary advantage (the relative capacities to innovate and learn in a changing environment) that it offers in certain circumstances. Self-organization is especially useful in cases of loose coupling or operational autonomy, relations where a plurality of interdependent but autonomous organizations, each controlling important resources, need to coordinate their actions in the face of complex reciprocal interdependence, complex spatio-temporal horizons and shared interests or projects to produce a joint outcome that is deemed mutually beneficial. Mayntz (1993) has discussed networks as a form of heterarchic governance in these terms. She suggests that their typical logic is that of *negotiation* directed to the realization of a joint product, such as 'a specific technical innovation, a city plan, a strategy of collective action, or a problem solution in public policy' (Mayntz, 1993: 11). In this way, common short-term objectives can be identified, and their self-interested realization used to promote generalized compliance with interorganizational expectations and rules (Marin, 1990: 15; Scharpf, 1994). Crucial to the success of such arrangements is the building of interorganizational capacities that synergetically reinforce those of individual organizational members. These arguments can be illustrated from the emergence and dynamics of the so-called 'negotiated economy' that was realized in Scandinavia (cf Nielsen and Pedersen, 1988, 1993; Andersen et al, 1996).

I would add that such negotiation typically occurs in the context of more or less complex forms of interpersonal and interorganizational *networking* that bring and keep together those involved in negotiation; that the key to successful negotiation is *noise reduction*, that is, reducing mutual incomprehension in the communication between different institutional orders in and through attempts to enhance understanding and sensitivity to their distinctive rationalities, identities and interests; and that, once agreements are reached, they form the basis for *negative* and *positive coordination* of activities. In short, if reliance on heterarchy has increased, it is because increasing interdependencies are no longer so easily managed through markets and hierarchies.

Second, turning to the macro-social changes that might explain the growth of heterarchy, I focus on the interdependencies in and across the economy and polity. The world economy is being reshaped by a complex dialectic of globalization–regionalization. This has allegedly made it more difficult for (national) states to control economic activities within their borders let alone global capitalist dynamics. Once the relative coincidence of coherent economic spaces and national territories typical of postwar Atlantic Fordism (in the US, Northwestern Europe, Canada, Australia and New Zealand) was undermined by internationalization of the economy (especially among the advanced capitalist economies), faith in the national state's capacities to govern the economy was undermined. A corresponding increase in the 'unstructured complexity' of the economy on a world scale has triggered attempts on various spatial scales (from local to global) to reimpose some structure and order through resort to heterarchic coordination.

These changes also make public–private partnerships and other forms of heterarchy more relevant than conventional legislative, bureaucratic and administrative techniques. This is seen in a turn from the 'Keynesian welfare national state' to a more complex, negotiated system oriented to international competitiveness, innovation, flexibility and an 'enterprise culture'. The primary coordination instruments in the Keynesian welfare system were the market and the state. They were articulated in a 'mixed economy' in which big business, big labour and the big state often engaged in tripartite concertation at the national or regional level. In the emerging Schumpeterian workfare regime (Jessop, 1993, 2002b), the market, the national state and the mixed economy have lost significance to interfirm networks, public–private partnerships and a multilateral and heterarchic 'negotiated economy'. Moreover, in contrast to the primarily national focus of the mixed economy, these new forms of negotiated economy also involve 'key' economic players from local and regional as well as national and increasingly, international, economic spaces. This is linked to the partial 'hollowing out' of national states through the expansion of supranational government, local governance regimes and transnationalized local policy networks in an attempt to enhance the 'decentred context-mediated steering' of capitalist economies. And this latter shift poses further coordination problems concerning the management of the interscalar as well as intersystemic dependencies.

Likewise, the traditional models of the large, vertically integrated firm of the 1960s, and of the small autonomous, single-phase firm of the 1970s and part of the 1980s are replaced by a new type of large networked firm, with strongly centralized strategic functions extending in several directions, and by new types of small enterprise, integrated into multicompany local networks. Across these networks, a system of constantly evolving power relationships governs both the dynamics of innovation and the capacity of partners to capture returns. The network firm is attracted towards diversified mass production and a single firm's competitiveness is its control of complementary assets in the hands of its potential partners (Capello, 1996: 490).

Governance failure

The early interest in governance and the later interest in metagovernance indicate that markets, states, governance and solidarity all fail as modes of coordinating relations of complex reciprocal interdependence. This is not surprising because failure is a central feature of all social relations, for 'there is no such thing as complete or total control of an object or set of objects – governance is necessarily incomplete and as a necessary consequence must always fail' (Malpas and Wickham, 1995: 40). Indeed, given the growing structural complexity and opacity of the social world, failure becomes the most likely outcome of most attempts to govern it with reference to multiple objectives over extended spatial and temporal horizons – whether through markets, states, partnerships or another mechanism.

This is often recognized. However, while failure in other modes of coordination is regarded as inevitable, in the preferred mode of coordination it is typically seen as exceptional and corrigible. For example, for liberals, although the state is prone to failure, a turn to the market will solve the problem. If the market fails, however, it can be improved. Conversely, for statists, the response to market failure is government. If government fails, however, it should be improved. This polarization is reflected both in the succession of governments and in policy cycles within governments in which different modes of policy-making succeed each other as the difficulties of each become more evident. These issues are further explored in Part I.

Overall, then, this book explores:

- The implications of complexity theory for the inevitability of failure. This is a new approach in terms of critical policy studies and critical governance studies (Chapter 2).
- A taxonomy of modes of governance and their hybrid forms. This typology is more comprehensive than others, grounded theoretically and historically as well as in a survey of empirical analyses (Chapters 2, 3 and 4).
- An analysis of governance and governance failure in terms of the limits, contradictions and dilemmas of different modes of governance (Chapter 4).
- A theory of metagovernance, metagovernance failure and responses to failure (Chapters 2, 3 and 4).
- Locating civil society in terms of the theory of governance (and governance failure) as a potential point of intersection of networks and solidarity as modes of governance and resources for other modes of governance (Chapters 1, 2, 3 and 4).
- Locating civil society as a point of intersection between competing strategic responses to market and state failure: top-down self-responsibilization and bottom-up self-emancipation. This represents a major challenge to current policy, practice and thinking in the field of government and governance practice (this holds for the following bullet points too) (Chapters 1, 2 and 7).

- An analysis of the struggles to integrate self-responsibilization and self-emancipation into broader strategies for governance and metagovernance (Chapter 7).
- A series of case studies to illustrate some of the points at issue above. These case studies will include, but are not confined to, research conducted within the WISERD Civil Society programme (Chapters 5, 8, 9 and 10).

PART I

Complexity, contingency and governance

2

The governance of complexity and the complexity of governance

The natural and social worlds (and their interconnections) are far too complex to be *understood* in all their complexity or effectively *governed* in all their complexity in real time. This pair of statements is too simple: complexity is complex. This is reflected in the tendency for complexity to become a chaotic concept – especially in the social sciences, where mathematical formalization is difficult and metaphorical expression is common. It follows that we must first reduce the complexity of complexity in order to connect it to problems of governance and metagovernance. Indeed, faced with complexity, simplification is essential for any operating system or agent to be able to 'go on' in the world. Ontological complexity enforces selection on natural and social systems alike. One way to study such systems is in terms of how they select selections. In the social world, complexity is reduced in two main ways. The first is simplification through semiosis (sense- or meaning-making), which is associated with specific systems of meaning and forms of representation and tied to personal and collective identities. The second is simplification through various modes of structuration, which set limits to action repertoires and composable sets of social relations in time–space, and through attempts to articulate (collibrate) different forms of structuration. Governance is relevant in both respects: its success depends on the adequacy of social imaginaries to the complexities of the real world and on the adequacy of the modes of governance to the objects that are to be governed.

Given these remarks, this chapter addresses the recent discovery of 'governance' as the complex art of steering multiple agencies, institutions and systems that are both operationally autonomous from one another and structurally coupled through various forms of reciprocal interdependence. This discovery could reflect the dramatic intensification of societal complexity that flows from growing functional differentiation of institutional orders within an increasingly global society with all that this implies for the widening and deepening of systemic interdependencies across various social, spatial and temporal horizons of action. Indeed, governance appears to have moved up the theoretical and practical agendas because high levels of (increasingly globalized) functional differentiation undermine the basis for hierarchical, top-down coordination under the aegis of a single centre at the peak of a given societal formation let alone at the peak of a global social system with its continuing territorial division into national states still jealous of their declining formal sovereignty (cf Willke, 1987, 1990; Luhmann, 1992).

Complexity

While recognizing that a governance practice bandwagon has been rolling for some decades, I am reluctant to leap onto it – certainly in an uncritical fashion – as if it were taking us down a virtuous path that could solve all our theoretical and practical problems. Instead, I argue that governing complexity is far from simple and indeed, that governance failure is common. In developing this argument, I introduce the concept of 'contingent necessity' to problematize that of social complexity before considering problems of governance. This first set of remarks has two main purposes. They are intended to show how complexity risks becoming a 'chaotic conception' (Marx, 1973b [1857]; cf Sayer, 1992) that serves neither as a coherent research object nor as a coherent explanatory principle. And they are meant to correct an unfortunate celebratory tendency in some contributions to debates on governance (for example, uncritical accounts of the potential of stakeholding, associational democracy, learning regions, promoting the social economy and social innovation or mobilizing 'Big Society' to boost resilience). While many contributors allege that unstructured complexity somehow dooms market forces and/or bureaucratic planning to failure in realizing collective goals or goods, they also imply (even if they do not directly claim) that, with sufficient goodwill and skilful institutional design, other forms of governance could succeed in almost any circumstances. They could reduce and structure complexity to such an extent that the real world becomes collectively manageable and agencies charged with its governance can be rendered collectively accountable. There are powerful arguments, however, against strong versions of this presumption. I develop these based on some general reflections on 'contingently necessary complexity'. But these remarks will also inform a more modest account of conditions that might contribute to more localized, provisional and partial successes for attempts at governance.

I then attempt to reduce the risk of chaotic conceptions of complexity and its governance by distinguishing forms of complexity in interpersonal, interorganizational and intersystemic relations, and by linking the resulting problems of these different forms of complexity to issues of 'requisite variety', adaptability and learning in possible governance mechanisms. This second set of ideas is drawn from recent work on social complexity, self-organization and 'autopoietic' (self-referential, self-reproducing) systems. This work is important for its concern with complexity in social as opposed to natural systems or engineered mechanical artefacts. But it also risks neglecting the specific forms of complexity in different institutional orders and the contrasting problems these pose for governance. Accordingly, by combining these general ideas on complexity with principles drawn from institutional and evolutionary economics, an SRA to social analysis and the Marxist critique of capital as a social relation, I hope to cast new light on problems of governance in political economy and cognate social spheres.

Contingent necessity

My approach to issues of complexity has been shaped by earlier work on the distinctive features of 'contingent necessity'. This term, with its seeming *contradictio in adjecto*, refers to the nature of 'real-concrete' phenomena. It assumes that everything that happens in the real world must happen; in other words, that it is in some sense 'necessary'. Rejecting this assumption would render much scientific enquiry pointless. It is the precise meaning of necessity, however, that is at stake in 'contingent necessity', for it need not, does not and cannot mean that whatever happens in the real world is due to a *single* causal mechanism. Instead, the concrete actualization of events results from the *interaction* of diverse causal tendencies and countertendencies. Now, while it may be tempting to argue that this interaction itself can serve as the single causal mechanism that necessarily generates the necessary happening, this is invalid because such interactions cannot be attributed to the operation of any single causal mechanism, because they, too, result from interaction among diverse causal tendencies and countertendencies. This opens the route to an infinite explanatory regress into the path-dependent past. To avoid this, events are best studied 'genealogically' in terms of their provenance as *necessary* products of *contingent* interactions among different sets of causal mechanisms. Contingent necessity also implies an unbounded surplus of (unmanageable, often mutually exclusive) future possibilities, thereby ensuring that the world has an 'open' structure (cf Luhmann, 1979: 6, 13). Governance mechanisms reduce this surplus of future possibilities and its resulting social complexity.

What do contingent necessity and complexity imply for analyses of the real world? *Ontologically*, complexity refers to the events or phenomena in the real world. As Marx noted, the 'real-concrete' is 'the complex synthesis of multiple determinations' (Marx, 1973b [1857]: 101). This excludes any simple algorithm to generate explanations of complex phenomena. Contingent necessity in the real world calls, in turn, for complexity reduction. *Epistemologically*, if 'contingent necessities' really exist, to adequately explain them requires one to combine concepts, assumptions and principles of analysis from different theoretical domains and to link them to a given, theoretically defined, explanandum. Since the real world is infinitely complex, however, it is also analytically inexhaustible. Thus, an explanation is only more or less satisfactory relative to a given explanandum that has been isolated (and thus 'constructed') by an observer from that infinite complexity. *Methodologically*, this requires a 'method of articulation' that respects contingent necessity and complexity. One way to understand this is to see it as based on the dual movement from abstract to concrete along one plane of analysis and from simple to complex as more analytical planes are introduced in order to produce increasingly adequate explanations (Jessop, 1982: 213–19).

All three implications apply to 'observation' of the real world as well as to that which is observed, for observation itself occurs in the real world and is therefore also open to (self-)observation. By applying these principles to their own observational practices, observers can reflect on the contingent necessity (situatedness) of their own concepts and categories. This sort of self-reflexiveness may also help secure the relative success of governance mechanisms in localized contexts and for limited periods. In both cases, of course, such (self-)observation and (self-)reflection generates the paradox that complexity reduction mechanisms and practices add to the complexity of the real world (cf Poggi, 1979; Luhmann, 1983).[1]

We can now state the general links between contingent necessity, complexity and governance. Contingent necessity, as it concerns real world phenomena and events, indicates their *de facto* causal determination (necessity) and *ex ante* indeterminability (contingency). As a feature of the real world, contingent necessity implies that world's ontological complexity. Indeed, if the development of the real world involves an infinite succession of contingently interdependent as well as contingently necessary 'contingent necessities', then it must also be infinitely complex. This poses a series of questions about how one can best grasp the 'complexity of complexity' in the real world and simplify it in dealing with that world. Later the text returns to semiosis (sense- and meaning-making) and structuration as two potentially complementary (but also potentially disjunctive) modes of complexity reduction. For now, however, governance can be interpreted as one way to self-reflexively transform unstructured (because infinite) into structured (because simplified) complexity (cf Marin, 1990: 21; Delorme, 2010: 102–5) based on appropriate social imaginaries and coordination procedures. We should also note that this does not ensure the ability to control the (nth order) effects of such simplification and structuration.

For Hayek, the complexity of the social world rules out effective planning and implies that the only epistemologically sound mode of economic governance is the market mechanism (Hayek, 1947, 1972). But, as recent recognition of the plurality of governance mechanisms implies, one's choice in this regard is not restricted to a rigid dichotomy based on market vs hierarchy. Hayek's arguments on contingent necessity and social complexity and his conclusion as to the inevitability of planning failure do not exclude alternative forms of governance additional to pure market forces. This is not just a matter of abstract logic but is also confirmed by the wide range of at least partially successful governance mechanisms in various institutional contexts.

Semiosis and structuration as a means of complexity reduction

Given the complexity of the natural and social worlds, we need to consider how social agents reduce this complexity as a condition of being able to go on within the world. This is especially significant for relations of complex reciprocal interdependence. One way to approach this task is through the tools of cultural political economy (CPE) (Jessop, 2004, 2009; Jessop and Sum, 2001; Sum and Jessop, 2013). This studies semiosis and structuration as essential mechanisms of complexity reduction in the field of political economy, but this approach can also be generalized to all social relations. These mechanisms are potentially complementary but can be contrary or disconnected.

For social agents to be able to 'go on' in the world, they must reduce complexity by selectively attributing meaning to some of its features rather than others and impose limits to compossible sets of social relations through structuration. Thus actors (and observers) must focus selectively on some aspects of the world as the basis for becoming active participants therein and/or for describing and interpreting it as disinterested observers. These 'aspects' are not objectively pre-given in the real world and nor are they subjectively pre-scripted by hard-wired cognitive capacities. Instead they depend for their selective recognition and misrecognition largely on the currently prevailing meaning systems of relevant actors and observers as these have been modified over time. In turn, meaning-making helps to shape the overall constitution of the natural and social world insofar as it guides a critical mass of self-confirming, path-shaping actions that more or less correctly diagnose the scope for the world to be different and therefore contribute to realizing what was previously there only in potentia.

A recent illustration of the importance of complexity reduction (and its limitations) is the well-known confession by Alan Greenspan, Chair of the US Federal Reserve (1987–2006). Asked by Representative Henry Waxman whether he thought that his ideology had pushed him into making decisions that he had since come to regret in light of the continuing financial crisis, he replied:

> … remember what an ideology is: a conceptual framework for people to deal with reality. Everyone has one. You have to – to exist, you need an ideology. The question is whether it is accurate or not.… I've found a flaw. I don't know how significant or permanent it is. But I've been very distressed by that fact.… A flaw in the model that I perceived as the critical functioning structure that defines how the world works, so to speak. (Greenspan, 2008)

This ideology was the efficient market hypothesis, a key element in neoclassical economics, and the basis of his conviction that markets could and indeed, should, be left to manage themselves. If necessary, the state would step in later to clear up any problems. Of course, there are many other economic 'ideologies' or, as I prefer to call them, 'imaginaries', which simplify economic relations in different ways. And there are countless other ways of reducing complexity through sense-making that attribute meaning to other aspects of the natural and social world, construing them in one or another way in a this-worldly and/or other-worldly fashion. The latter would include, for example, spiritual and religious imaginaries.

But, while all social *construals* are equal (insofar as all social agents must engage in meaning-making in order to be able to 'go on' in the world), some interpretations are more equal than others in their impact on the social *construction* of the social world (Sayer, 2000: 40, 53, 61). The role of intellectuals is clearly important here, but we should not fall prey to the intellectuals' temptation to think that theirs are the only imaginaries that become hegemonic or dominant. The role of semiosis in this respect cannot be understood or explained without identifying and exploring the extra-semiotic conditions that both enable meaning-making and make it more or less effective, not only in terms of comprehension but also in terms of practical action. This highlights the role of variation, selection and retention in the development and consolidation of some construals rather than others and in their embodiment and embedding in practices that transform the natural and social world. As one moves from variation through selection to retention, extra-semiotic factors linked to specific communication channels and broader social configurations play an increasing role in determining which discourses or imaginaries are translated into durable social constructions and become part of actors' bodily and mental condition (which Pierre Bourdieu, 1984, calls 'hexis'), shape their personal and social identities, promote certain social dispositions and routines (Bourdieu's 'habitus'), get enacted in organizational routines or become institutionalized in various ways. Inquiring into such processes is especially important where meaning systems have become so sedimented (taken-for-granted or naturalized) that their socially contingent nature goes unremarked. Another intriguing question concerns the relation between micro-social diversity and stable macro-social configurations, and this is where structuration enters the investigation.

Structuration establishes possible connections and sequences of social interaction (including interaction with natural worlds) that facilitate routine actions and set limits to path-shaping strategic actions. While *structuration* refers to a complex, contingent, tendential process that is mediated through action but produces results that no actors can be said to have completely willed, *structure* refers to the contingently necessary outcome of diverse structuration efforts (for an influential sociological account of structuration, see Giddens, 1984 [1976]; for a more complicated interpretation, with a more nuanced analysis of structure–agency dialectics, see Jessop, 2007c). With its mix of constrained opportunities, recursiveness, redundancy and flexibility, structuration facilitates social reproduction somewhere between an impossible stasis and the edge of chaos. Reproduction is not automatic but is mediated through situated social action that occurs in more or less structured contexts. It involves complex assemblages of asymmetrical opportunities for social action, privileging some actors over others, some identities over others, some ideal and material interests over others, some spatio-temporal horizons of action over others, some coalition possibilities over others, some strategies over others, and so on (Jessop, 2007c). In this sense, structural constraints always operate selectively: they are not absolute and unconditional but always temporally, spatially, agency- and strategy-specific. Conversely, to the extent that agents are reflexive, capable of reformulating within limits their own identities and interests, and able to engage in strategic calculation about their current situation, they may be able to alter these selectivities.

Where these two forms of complexity reduction complement each other, they transform meaningless and unstructured complexity into meaningful and structured complexity. In terms of societal configurations, this involves hegemonic imaginaries and institutional and spatio-temporal fixes (STFs) that together produce zones of relative stability based on active or, more likely, passive consent and structured coherence. The social and natural world becomes relatively meaningful and orderly for actors (and observers) insofar as not all *possible* social interactions are *compossible* in a given time-space envelope. This excludes many other meanings and many other possible social worlds. This does not prevent competing imaginaries of different fields of social action or indeed, rival principles of societal organization more generally, for, in a social world characterized by exploitation, oppression and exclusion, there are many possible standpoints for construing the world and many sources of social disruption. How relatively stable social orders emerge in particular time-space envelopes in the face of such complexity is one of the enduring challenges in the social sciences.

Lived experience, social imaginaries and ideologies

Semiosis is an umbrella concept for all forms of the production of meaning that is oriented to communication among social agents, individual or collective. An imaginary is a semiotic ensemble (without tightly defined boundaries) that frames individual subjects' lived experience of an inordinately complex world and/or guides collective calculation about that world. There are many such imaginaries and they are involved in complex and tangled relations at different sites and scales of action (see Althusser, 1971; Taylor, 2001). As noted above, without them, individuals cannot 'go on' in the world and collective actors (such as organizations) could not relate to their environments, make decisions or pursue more or less coherent and successful strategies in a complex, often deeply complex, environment.

While some social imaginaries are organized around (oriented to, help to construct) specific systems of action (for example, economy, law, science, education, politics, health, religion, art), others are more concerned with different spheres of life, the 'lifeworld' (broadly interpreted)[2] or 'civil society'. The latter kind of imaginaries may nonetheless acquire system-relevance through their articulation into the operation of system logics (for example, the use of gender to segment the labour force, the mobilization of 'racial' identities to justify educational or political exclusion). System-relevant and lifeworld imaginaries provide the basis for identities and interests, whether individual, group, movement or organizational. Agents normally have multiple identities, privileging some over others in different contexts. This has prompted the recent interest in 'intersectionality' – in other words, the study of the effects of different mixes of system-relevant and 'lifeworld' identities.

Given this multiplicity of identities, their differential intersection and the problems that this poses for social mobilization, effective social agency often depends on strategic essentialism (Spivak, 1987). This involves the discursive and practical privileging of one identity over others for the purposes of collective action in particular conjunctures, even though this temporarily ignores or suppresses real differences within a movement. Examples include the appeal to nationalism in inter-imperialist wars, successive waves of feminism or the mobilization of regional identities to create the social as well as economic bases of regional competitiveness.

Everyone engages in social construal because meaning-making is the basis of lived experience. But not everyone makes an equal contribution to the social construction of social relations. Each system and the different spheres of the 'lifeworld' have their own semiotic divisions of labour that overlay, differentially draw on and feed into lived experience. Some individuals and/or collective intellectuals (such as political parties and old and new social movements) are particularly active in bridging these different systems and spheres of life, attempting to create hegemonic meaning systems or to develop sub- or counter-hegemonic imaginaries. And, of course, increasingly, semiosis is heavily 'mediatized', that is, influenced by mass media and social media.[3] Given the diversity of systems and the plurality of identities in the 'lifeworld', it would be mistaken to assume that one type of social actor will be the leading force in semiosis in general or hegemony-making in particular. Likewise, given competing societalization principles, there can be no guarantee that one principle of structuration will dominate the others.

As Maarten Hajer (2009: 13) notes: 'Rethinking strategies of governance needs to fully incorporate an understanding of what a mediatized politics implies. At the same time, however, there is a need for those working in media studies to rethink their understanding of contemporary politics.'

Hajer (2009) continues with the following remark on network governance:

> It is a form of governing which seeks to develop an interaction with publics drawing on discursive interaction within a well-defined setting. Here the authority of governance is not a derivative of the institutional rules and conventions, but is actively created in the joint experience of being political between policy-makers and publics. Thirdly, we see a field of political techniques, staging an extended form of reasoned elaboration between stakeholders, outside the classical-modernist order and often removed from the view of "the general public". (Hajer, 2009: 180)

Returning to the main argument, when analysing meaning systems, the three main analytical steps required to avoid simplistic critiques of semiosis as always-already ideological are: (1) recognize the role of semiosis as a meaning pool in complexity reduction, that is, regard signs and symbols as elements from which ideation and communication draw; (2) identify social imaginaries, that is, specific clusters of meaning (or semiotic) systems, and describe their form and content, recognizing that they are never fully closed and are frequently rearticulated; and (3) analyse their contingent articulation and contribution to processes of structuration that secure specific patterns of exploitation, oppression and domination that serve the particular interests of specific individual agents or social forces.

Governance as the art of complexity

We can now develop these arguments by making an explicit connection between the increased salience of the policy and theoretical paradigms of governance and the increased salience of complexity in policy-making and theoretical debates respectively. There is some merit in suggestions that the current interest in governance is just another turn in a never-ending policy cycle and/or involves little more than an attempt to put old theoretical wine in new bottles. But it is more plausible to argue that there has been a secular increase in governance practices because society itself is becoming more complex and that this makes it harder to rely on the anarchy of the market or the hierarchy of the state as means of coordination (Jessop, 1998). On the one hand, the growing interest of practitioners in governance (and, *a fortiori*, good governance) directly reflects growing recognition of the complexity of the policy environment in which they must now make and implement policies. And on the other hand, the growing interest of theorists in governance can be related to their growing recognition that modern societies are becoming more functionally differentiated and hypercomplex and/or post-modern societies are becoming fragmented and chaotic.

John Urry (2002) suggested that sociological hypotheses about the real world are generated through metaphor and that, as the real world changes, sociologists should adopt new metaphors. Ignoring the seeming contradiction in this account and the risk that metaphors are used to tell 'good stories' rather than provide 'solid arguments', we can agree that recent interest in complexity reflects a *Zeitdiagnostik* (temporal surmise) – right or wrong – that the social world has become more complex. The spread of governance practices into so many spheres and the growth of governance studies in so many disciplines can be seen to represent a general response to a dramatic intensification of societal complexity. This, in turn, has led social agents to search for new ways to reduce complexity and address its problems. Among the many reasons recently advanced for a dramatic intensification of societal complexity are the following:

- Increased functional differentiation in contemporary societies combined with increased interdependence among the resulting functional systems.
- Increased fuzziness and contestability of some institutional boundaries, for example, concerning what counts as 'economic' in an era of increased competitiveness in a knowledge-based economy.
- The multiplication and rescaling of spatial horizons and the increasingly complex dialectic of deterritorialization and reterritorialization as the taken-for-grantedness of the national sovereign state continues to erode.
- The growing complexity and interconnectedness of institutionalized temporalities and temporal horizons at different sites and scales of action, ranging from split-second timing (for example, computer-driven trading) to growing awareness of the acceleration of the glacial time of social and environmental change.
- The multiplication of identities and the reimagination of the political communities to which the political system is oriented together with new state projects to redefine the nature and purposes

of the state and new hegemonic projects to redefine the imagined general interest of these new political communities.

- This is related to the increased importance of knowledge and organized learning, and, as a result of the above, to the self-potentiating nature of complexity. This denotes that complex systems generally operate in ways that engender opportunities for additional complexity.[4]

But recognition of growing social complexity, even assuming that this could be measured accurately and compared with earlier periods and/ or across different kinds of societies in today's asynchronous, unevenly developing world society, does not, per se, justify the appropriation of models of complexity from mathematics and the natural sciences without regard to the differences between the natural and social worlds. In particular, it ignores the meaningfulness of the social world and the scope for agents to respond reflexively to complexity (for the counterview that perception, boundary-drawing and meaning-making occur in all systems, see Barbieri, 2008).

This suggests that we should distinguish complexity in general from specific modes of complexity. All complex systems share some features – or at least, for the sake of reducing the complexity of complexity, it makes sense to identify these features. These include non-linearity, scale dependence, recursiveness, sensitivity to initial conditions and feedback. Even at this level of analysis, however, complexity can be studied in many ways, including algorithmic, deterministic and aggregative analyses (Rescher, 1998). While some complex systems can be modelled more-or-less adequately for given purposes, others are characterized by 'deep complexity', that is, are hard to reduce in a satisficing way and therefore pose problems about how to reduce this complexity (Delorme, 2010). Ontological complexity excludes any simple algorithm to generate explanations of complex phenomena or to provide the basis for planning. This requires mechanisms of complexity reduction or simplification at the cognitive, organizational and practical levels (Rescher, 1998).

The market is often presented as an appropriate mechanism to address problems of complexity because it draws on the dispersed knowledge of many actors and allows for self-correction in response to changes in price signals. Yet it remains a purely formal and procedural mechanism that operates *ex post* and requires demanding conditions if it is to work efficiently, even in its own limited terms. This is reflected in the fact that even market-friendly economists have long recognized that it is often rational to adopt non-market modes of coordination.

But top-down planning is also problematic in the face of growing complexity, for, in addition to the usual problems of creating and maintaining appropriate organizational capacities, the algorithms required for effective *ex ante* coordination in a complex and turbulent environment impose heavy cognitive demands.

Top-down command makes excessive demands on prior centralized knowledge or accurate anticipation of the likely interaction among operationally autonomous systems with different institutional dynamics, modes of calculation and logics of appropriateness. This tends to result in the failure to achieve collective goals because of the unintended consequences of top-down planning or simple bureaucratic rule following. In addition, both market and imperative coordination are prey to the problems of bounded rationality, opportunism and asset specificity[5] (Coulson, 1997).

Governance is often said to overcome these problems in providing a 'third way' between the anarchy of the market and top-down command. Self-organization is especially useful in cases of loose coupling or operational autonomy, complex reciprocal interdependence, complex spatio-temporal horizons and shared interests or projects (cf Mayntz, 1993; Scharpf, 1994).

It is the combination of operational autonomy and mutual interdependence of organizations and systems that encourages reliance on governance. While their interdependence makes them ill-suited to simple, blind coevolution based on the 'invisible hand' of mutual, *ex post* adaptation, their respective operational autonomies exclude primary reliance on a single hierarchy as a mode of coordination among relevant agencies, institutions and systems. On the one hand, the incrementalism of the post hoc operation of market forces is suboptimal from a governance viewpoint because market forces often fail to address the positive and negative externalities involved in situations of complex and continuing interdependence. This leads to short-run, localized, ad hoc responses to market opportunities that ignore the paradox of autonomy and interdependence characteristic of modern societies. This paradox is especially acute when what is at stake is the governance of relations among functionally differentiated subsystems that are stretched out over space and time (cf Willke, 1987, 1990; Jessop, 1990b; Offe, 1996).

Before examining functionally differentiated subsystems, I identify three levels of 'embedded' social organization relevant to governance. These are: (1) the social embeddedness of interpersonal relations (cf Granovetter, 1985); (2) the institutional embeddedness of interorganizational relations (cf Keohane, 1984; Grabher, 1993);

and (3) the 'societal' embeddedness of functionally differentiated institutional orders (especially those that can be interpreted as autopoietic subsystems)[6] in a complex, decentred societal formation (cf Polanyi, 1957; Glagow and Willke, 1987; Luhmann, 1992). Each type of embeddedness is linked to a corresponding type of heterarchy and its associated problems of negative and positive coordination. The latter, in turn, may be resolved, at least in a provisional and partial manner, in and through different patterns of governance.

Solidarity involves a minimally unconditional commitment or loyalty to members of a real or imagined community. As Angus Mason puts it, 'members must give each other's interests some non-instrumental weight in their practical reasoning [and that] ... there must be no systematic exploitation or (on some versions) no systematic injustice' (2000: 27). Or, as Hauke Brunkhorst states it more succinctly, 'it expresses the reciprocal duty of everyone to everyone' (2005: 60). It provides 'the bridge between the different modes of social and systemic integration of society' (Brunkhorst, 2005: 5). And, as Judith Dellheim argues, '[a] solidaristic economy is associated with the appropriation, defence and building up of the public – with common goods in citizens' hands, with socially and economically sustainable economic activity, production and reproduction of the commons' (2014: 2; translated by BJ [author]).

Each form of governance has its own distinctive problems, its inherent weaknesses and its characteristic forms of failure.

Levels of heterarchic governance

The simplest form of heterarchy arises from the selective formalization of interpersonal networking. Individual actors build on their past familiarity with others in various interpersonal networks to form a more exclusive, more targeted partnership; partners share an imagined community of interests and orientation to the future and use selective memories to reinforce trust (Elchedus, 1990: 197–8; see also Macneil, 1974; Luhmann, 1979: 16–19). In the first instance, partners represent only themselves, but they may also be regarded as speaking informally on behalf of institutional orders from which they are recruited. If their actions are confined to interpersonal networks, however, partners cannot commit the organizations or institutions from which they may be recruited and/or which they represent symbolically.

More complex is heterarchic governance through *interorganizational negotiation* systems. The 'self-organization of interorganizational relations' is a familiar form of governance in many different contexts. It emerges where materially interdependent but formally autonomous organizations, each of which controls important resources, must coordinate their actions to secure a joint outcome that is deemed mutually beneficial. To this end they negotiate to identify common objectives and engage in positive coordination to achieve these aims. The continued pursuit of common long-term objectives typically depends on the realization of shorter-term objectives and general compliance with established or emerging interorganizational expectations and rules. Crucial to the success of such partnerships is *resource synergy*, that is, the 'added value' that comes from partners combining resources rather than acting alone (Hastings, 1996). This should be linked in turn to the building of interorganizational capacities that surpass the powers of any individual member organization.

Each of these levels of heterarchic governance has its own problems within the general pattern of governance failure associated with self-organizing networks. Interpersonal networks are associated with an acute problem of trust as more actors get involved and/or the material stakes increase. This is due to the many-sided 'double contingencies' of social interaction (grounded in the fact that ego's behaviour depends on expectations about alter's conduct and vice versa). Such problems are reinforced on an interorganizational level by difficulties in securing the internal cohesion and adaptability of individual organizations, and in making their respective operational unities and independence compatible with their de facto material, social and spatio-temporal interdependence on other organizations. Finally, intersystemic heterarchy poses the problem of the material and social interdependence of operationally autonomous (or closed) functional systems, each with its own autopoietic codes, programmes, institutional logics and interests in self-reproduction. Thus, partnerships that cross institutional boundaries face further problems due to difficulties in mutually coordinating (let alone unilaterally controlling) institutional orders that operate according to their own distinctive logics.

Guidance as heterarchic governance

The most complex form of governance emerges in attempts to facilitate the mutual understanding and coevolution of different functional systems whose structural coupling and strategic coordination affect the attainment of societal objectives. A generic mechanism serving these strategically self-reflexive purposes in both interorganizational and intersystemic contexts can be identified in *decentralized, cooperative context-steering* that is oriented to producing controlled structural change (Glagow and Willke, 1987). This is often described simply

49

as 'guidance' and will be so labelled below. An initial account should be useful. This form of governance involves the coordination of differentiated institutional orders or functional systems (such as the economic, political, legal, scientific or religious systems), each of which has its own complex operational logic such that it is impossible to exercise effective overall control of its development from outside that system. The political and legal systems, for example, cannot control the overall development of the economy through coercion, taxation, legislation, judicial decisions, and so forth. This does not exclude specific external interventions to produce a particular result; it does exclude control over that result's repercussions on the wider and longer-term development of the whole system. This indicates that there may be better prospects of 'steering' systems' overall development by taking serious account of their own internal codes and logics and modifying the structural and strategic contexts in which these continue to operate, and by coordinating these contexts across different systems in light of their substantive, social and spatio-temporal interdependencies. Such steering is mediated not only through symbolic media of communication such as money, law or knowledge, but also through direct communication oriented to intersystemic 'noise reduction', negotiation, negative coordination and cooperation in shared projects (these terms are defined above). Intersystemic coordination is typically decentred and pluralistic and depends on specific forms of governance (Glagow and Willke, 1987).

From a strategic-relational viewpoint, such guidance involves both (1) modifying the structurally inscribed strategic selectivities of different levels of socially embedded, socially regularized action; and (2) modifying the self-understanding of identities, strategic capacities and interests of individual and collective actors in different strategic contexts and hence their implications for preferred strategies and tactics. Whereas modifying the former serves to alter pay-offs in different strategic contexts, modifying the latter provides both common orientations and a basis for the self-guidance of relevant actors and subsystems within the limits of their respective operational autonomies. A key aspect to this process is the transformation of cognitive expectations within and across systems by generating new information about reciprocal interdependencies among actors, organizations, institutions and systems. This information can then become the basis for self-transformation and self-regulation on the part of relevant actors in light of their own codes or selection criteria (Willke, 1987: 27–28). In this way guidance can create 'concerted', highly predictable environments and stabilize expectations (cf Marin, 1990: 15–16).

In functionally differentiated societies, 'context-steering' procedures work on an intersystemic level by encouraging operationally closed systems to take account – even as they try to maintain their operational autonomy – of their resource dependence on their environment, functional interdependence with other such systems and high levels of contextual interpenetration. This sort of learning and mutual understanding can occur in various ways: for example, through developing convergent internal models of how other systems perceive their environments and operate within it; through self-reflexive calculation and concern about how a system's own operations will ultimately react back on its own future development through their mediated impact on other systems; and through debates among representatives of various systems in a 'negotiated economy' type of social dialogue to promote self-reflection and strategically coordinated coevolution. Such strategic linkages can arise through single agents (whether people or organizations) with multiple roles, interpersonal networks, dialogue between organizations or the interfaces that exist between subsystems (whether boundary roles, boundary structures, bi- or multivalent resources such as taxation or explicit linking procedures) (cf Luhmann, 1982a: 71–85; Teubner, 1989: 78, 104, 119; Jessop, 1990b; Théret, 1992: passim).

Such coordination is most likely to occur where conditions are sufficiently stable and the options sufficiently restricted that reflexive monitoring and dynamic social learning can occur, and individual systems can refine their own internal 'forecasting' models about the dynamic of other systems. This does not mean that subsystems must abandon their own distinctive codes or undergo de-differentiation; merely that the individual programmes that they use to specify the operational implications of these codes must be modified at the margins to facilitate continued negative and/or positive coordination of their respective operations. Such reflexive monitoring, dynamic learning and incremental change can be seen in evolutionary terms as sources of variation; relatively stable, non-turbulent environments will facilitate the selection of responses that stabilize governance mechanisms to the extent that joint goals are being achieved and/ or non-achievement is attributed to temporary difficulties in those mechanisms or their environment. Conversely, turbulence means that any lessons from previous successes or failures may not be applicable in rapidly changing circumstances. This argument also applies, of course, to the use of imperative coordination. Those who see markets as discovery mechanisms also presuppose some measure of stability in the environment.

In all cases, however, what is crucial is the structural mediation of these procedures – the self-reflexive use of self-organization (self-structured system complexity) linking limited sets of actors to reduce unstructured complexity (hence uncertainty) thereby provides a basis for coordinated action. In this sense the retention (institutionalization, stabilization, regularization) of given governance mechanisms is closely linked to their structurally inscribed strategic selectivities and the strategic capacities of their agents to self-reflexively monitor how specific actions affect interdependent individual and collective goals.

Guidance need not exclude a state role, but the latter would incline more towards metagovernance than government. Thus, in their account of sectoral governance in the US economy, Lindberg et al (1991: 31) note that:

> ... the state ... is capable of influencing governance in many complex ways, most of which are not available to organizations in civil society ... other actors cannot behave like the state because they cannot serve as gatekeepers, allocate resources and information, influence and structure property rights, or affect governance and governance transformations in other ways as does the state.

I am not arguing here that such forms of strategic context steering rest on simple, unconstrained, democratic consensus on the 'common good' of various reciprocally interdependent subsystems. On the contrary, social forces from different systems often compete to stabilize orientations and expectations through multilateral agreement around their own preferred 'joint project', with each project simplifying social relations, marginalizing some forces, regions, time horizons, and so on, in their own system interests.

A hegemonic project achieves this by resolving the abstract problem of conflicts between particular interests and the general interest. If successful, it stabilizes networks of social relations linking different social domains in real time and space as well as in 'functional' time and space – networks that serve the reproduction interests of their own particular system as well as those of the (imagined) wider community or totality. The emergence of any hegemonic project is uncertain, however, and even if present, it never rests on total unanimity or blind obedience. Instead it provides a conception of the common good and a framework within which different forces can cooperate and/or coexist with a relative degree of harmony. Nonetheless, viable hegemonic projects (and, one might add even more forcefully, accumulation strategies) must have some organic connection to the dominant mode of growth. They cannot simply be 'arbitrary, rationalistic, and willed' but must have some prospects of forming and consolidating a specific historical bloc, that is, some structural correspondence between the mode of economic growth and its modes of regulation and governance (Gramsci, 1971: 376–77; 1975: Q7, §19; for more detail, see Jessop, 1996). A key role in this regard is played by political parties (or similar forces) that link governance strategies with a broader, national hegemonic project and/or supply political privileges, resources and policies that help to sustain a continuing commitment to interorganizational negotiation and coordination.

In addition to interpersonal networking and interorganizational negotiation and positive coordination, two further mechanisms are crucial. The first is *noise reduction*, that is, reducing 'noise' in intersystemic communication by enhancing mutual sensitivity to the autonomous logics or rationales of complex autonomous systems and thereby promoting mutual understanding through dialogue rather than the forceful colonization (or penetration) of other systems by the rationale and logic of one, dominant system. The second mechanism is *negative coordination*, that is, encouraging agents/agencies to take account of the possible adverse repercussions of their own actions on third parties or other systems and to exercise self-restraint as appropriate. Likewise, if negative coordination is not to become a disguised form of imperative coordination, it should also be based on genuine pluralism rather than the sheer dominance of one system, its operational codes and social dynamic. Together these mechanisms may help to realize an intersystemic consensus around visions or missions that provide, within a more general framework of 'decentralized context steering', a basis for more specific interorganizational partnerships oriented to the *positive coordination*[7] of relevant activities around specific objectives.[8] These arguments can be illustrated from work on national systems of innovation (see, for example, Lundvall, 1992; Nelson, 1993). This is the situation that existed in the period of Atlantic Fordism with its commitment to full employment and social welfare as the context for specific interorganizational projects as well as intersystemic cooperation. It is something that the neoliberal hegemonic project also sought to achieve.

Intersystemic concertation is subject to real, if paradoxical, limitations. On the one hand, entire subsystems (such as the economy, law, politics and education) can never be real acting subjects with capacities for conscious action. Thus, to avoid blind coevolution based entirely on *post hoc* structural coupling, intersystemic concertation must be mediated through subjects who can engage in *ex ante* self-regulatory strategic coordination, monitor the effects of that coordination on goal attainment and modify their strategies as appropriate. On the other hand, such bodies can never fully represent the operational logic (let alone fully comprehend the current conjuncture and future direction) of whole subsystems. Indeed, they could even promote their own private interests in maintaining interorganizational exchanges (or simply their own survival as organizations) at the expense of effective intersystemic concertation. In short, whereas the complexities of strategic interdependence among systems do require specific forms of interorganizational concertation, the latter needs regularizing to limit the risks of self-serving 'privatization' and to guide strategic interaction so that it remains in line with the 'public interest'. This depends, in turn, on a hegemonic consensus or project that provides the various forces involved with common programmatic objectives despite differing codes, identities, and so forth.

Metagovernance involves not only institutional design but also the transformation of subjects and cultures. Whereas there has been much interest in issues of institutional design appropriate to different objects of governance, less attention has been paid by governance theorists to reforming the subjects of governance and their values. Yet the neoliberal project, for example, clearly requires attempts to create entrepreneurial subjects and demanding consumers aware of their choices and rights as well as needing actions to shift the respective scope and powers of the market mechanism and state intervention. This is an area where Foucauldian students of governmentality offer more than students of governance. They have been especially interested in the role of power and knowledge in shaping the attributes, capacities and identities of social agents and, in the context of self-reflexive governance, in enabling them to become self-governing and self-transforming (see Chapters 8 and 9). This raises important questions about the compatibility of different modes of governance insofar as this involves not only questions of institutional compatibility but also the distribution of the individual and collective capacities needed to pursue creatively and autonomously the appropriate strategies and tactics to sustain contrasting modes of governance.

Modalities and objects of governance

Much of the literature on governance assumes that the objects of governance pre-exist their coordination in and through specific governance mechanisms. However, as the preceding remarks indicate, at the very least, attempts at governance affect the conduct of agents and their conditions of action. In many cases governance mechanisms are also actively involved in constituting governing agents, identities, interests and strategies. Hence some governance theorists argue that 'objects of governance are only known through attempts to govern them' (Hunt and Wickham, 1994: 78).[9] In other words, the very processes of governance co-constitute the objects that come to be governed in and through these same processes. Thus, while its objects may indeed pre-exist governance attempts as potential 'raw material', they only become real objects of governance to the extent they are subject to specific, more or less effective, governance mechanisms. Pertinent examples include industrial 'clusters', flexible industrial districts, cross-border regions and 'negotiated economies'. Such phenomena cannot be adequately understood without reference to their co-constitution through forms of governance that conform neither to pure market nor pure hierarchy. In this sense, then, governance reduces the unstructured complexity of the 'raw material' (or elements) of governance and adds to structured complexity (by transforming these elements into 'moments' of the governed object). But the emergence of conflicting attempts at governance and/or of uncoordinated governance mechanisms produces, in turn, new forms of unstructured complexity. The latter could well become constituted as a 'problem' for attempts at higher-order governance (or metagovernance), and so on ... in an endless spiral of governance/metagovernance strategies. There is no point at which any final metagovernance instance can be established to coordinate myriad subordinate forms of governance – this would reintroduce the principle of hierarchy that social complexity rules out.

Metagovernance does not amount to the installation of a monolithic mode of governance. Rather, it involves the metamanagement of complexity and plurality. Thus markets, hierarchies, heterarchies and solidarities still exist, but they operate in a context of 'negotiated decision-making'. Thus, on the one hand, market competition will be balanced by cooperation, the invisible hand will be combined with a visible handshake. On the other hand, the state is no longer the sovereign authority. It becomes but one participant among others in the pluralistic guidance system and contributes its own distinctive resources to the negotiation process. As the range of networks, partnerships and other models of economic and political governance expand, official apparatuses remain at best *primus inter pares*, for although public money and law would still be important in underpinning their operation, other resources (such as private money, knowledge or expertise) would also be critical to their success. The state's involvement would become less hierarchical, less centralized and less dirigiste in character. The exchange of information and moral suasion become key sources of legitimation, and the state's influence depends as much on its role as a prime source and mediator of collective intelligence as on its command over economic resources or legitimate coercion (cf Willke, 1992).

An SRA implies that governance is inherently spatio-temporal. This goes beyond the trite conclusion that, since time and space inevitably serve as external conditions and contexts of action, actions may need to be collocated and/or dislocated at particular points in time-space as well as coordinated over time and space to realize interdependent projects. One must recognize that time and space *qua* social relations are also key objects and stakes in the organization of governance. In short, governance constitutes its objects in spatio-temporal as well as other respects. The temporal and spatial are not separable here. The choice of time horizon will, in part, dictate the appropriate spatial scale at which governance is organized. In turn, the choice of spatial scale will partly determine the time horizon over which the object of governance will be constructed and governance objects pursued.

By way of illustration, the discursive constitution of the boundaries and nature of the (local) economy affects the temporal dimension of strategy-making as well as its spatial scale. This is quite explicit in many economic strategy documents, with powerful players seeking to shape both the spatial and temporal horizons to which economic and political decisions are oriented so that the economic and political benefits are 'optimized' (on the Thames Gateway in the UK, see Chapter 9). The match between spatial scale and time horizon may be a crucial factor shaping the success or failure of local economic development strategies associated with urban regimes. Stable modes of local economic growth typically involve building a structured complementarity (or coherence) between the local economy and one or more of its encompassing regional, national and supranational accumulation regimes. This structured complementarity can only be secured in time and space. Since capitalism is always marked by uneven development and tendencies towards polarization, the success of some economic spaces (and the success of the spaces whose growth dynamic is complemented by their own) will inevitably be associated with the marginalization of other economic spaces. This is seen in the changing hierarchy of economic spaces as capitalist growth dynamics are affected by the relative exhaustion of some accumulation strategies and modes of growth and/or the dynamic potential of innovations in materials, processes, products, organization or markets. Nonetheless, when space and time horizons are articulated more or less successfully, economic development will occur within relatively stable 'time-space envelopes' (cf Massey, 1994: 225; Sum, 1997).

All of this has major implications for the dynamic of governance mechanisms and their capacities to address challenges. In strategic-relational terms, social practices, organizations, institutions and systems typically have specific structurally inscribed temporal and spatial forms and are oriented to distinctive spatial and temporal horizons of action. Thus, specific forms of economic and political system privilege some strategies over others, access by some forces over others, some interests over others, some spatial scales of action over others, some temporal horizons over others, some coalition possibilities over others. Strategies can be oriented in turn to the transformation of these structurally inscribed (or socially embedded) spatio-temporal selectivities. This also suggests that successful governance may depend on the self-reflexive monitoring and transformation of how these (and other) selectivities impinge on embedded social practices and socially stabilized expectations.

Thus, governance mechanisms must provide a framework in which relevant actors can reach agreement over (albeit possibly differential) spatial and temporal horizons of action vis-à-vis their environment. They must also stabilize the cognitive and normative expectations of these actors by shaping and promoting a common 'worldview' as well as developing adequate solutions to sequencing problems, that is, predictably ordering various actions, policies or processes over time, especially where they have different temporal logics.[10] This does not exclude (and indeed, may well require) a certain ambivalence and real flexibility in governance mechanisms so that an adequate repertoire (requisite variety) of governance routines exists to ensure continued vitality in the face of a turbulent environment through the ability to alter strategies and select those that are successful (cf Willke, 1992; Grabher, 1994).

This need is based on recognition that complexity excludes simple governance solutions. Instead, effective governance requires a combination of mechanisms and strategies oriented to the complexities of the object to be governed. Combining strategies and tactics reduces the likelihood of failure, enabling their rebalancing in the face of governance failure and turbulence in the governance environment (Meuleman, 2008). It promotes the ability to alter strategies and select those that are successful. This may seem inefficient at first sight because it introduces slack or waste into organizations and movements, but it also provides major sources of flexibility in the face of failure. If every mode of economic and political coordination is failure-laden, relative success in coordination over time depends on the capacity to switch modes of coordination as the limits of any one mode become evident. This provides, in turn, the basis of displacing or postponing failures and crises.

On an intersystemic level, requisite variety can be secured through the separation of different institutional orders so that it becomes possible to displace the dominant and/or hegemonic role across systems in response to different problems, challenges or crises. It has often been noted that institutional separation of the economic and political orders in capitalist societies permits more flexibility in crisis management than their fusion does in state socialism (cf Kaminski, 1991).[11] This separation offers more possibilities both for a more effective self-regulation and for crisis displacement. The latter could amount to nothing more than a purely negative displacement through buck-passing, but it could involve using the resources generated by one complex system to solve problems confronting another (for example, transforming legal institutions or educational systems in response to institutional changes in the market economy). The latter response may well be explicitly pursued in the case of decentralized context-steering. Noise reduction, negative coordination and joint problem-solving based on horizontal as well as vertical subsidiarity[12] principles are well-suited to flexible control of intersystemic resources.

Strategic selectivities frame more specific governance strategies insofar as they privilege some strategies and hinder others. Hence, from a more self-reflexive (or metagovernance) perspective, there are also strategic choices about redrawing borders, altering spatio-temporal horizons and reordering temporalities. These choices may be linked to changes in time-space distantiation (the stretching out of governance capacities and horizons of action over space and the binding of 'future presents' into the present through path-shaping activities),[13] and/or to changes in time-space compression (the conquest of space by time and/or the domestication of time through enhanced capacities to discriminate events and so react appropriately within a given time period). Metastrategies intended to entrench or modify strategic selectivities are analogous to a Gramscian 'war of position' (Gramsci, 1971: 108–11, 120, 229–35, 237–8, 243; 1975, Q15, §17; Q10I, §89; Q1, §133–4; Q7, §16; Q13, §7). They allow those in privileged positions to capitalize acquired advantages, plan ahead and win a certain independence in the face of a turbulent environment (cf de Certeau, 1985: 36–7; cf Grabher, 1994, on redundancy).

Metaphorically, in a war of position, space is used to govern time. Michel de Certeau (1985) contrasts this strategy (which he equates with strategy in general) with the concept of 'tactics'.[14] This is pursued from outside entrenched positions, resorts to time to disrupt established structures of domination, and is especially effective in crises. As Régis Debray (1971: 90, 107) notes, 'political time moves faster in periods of crisis…. In every decisive crisis there is an inevitable hiatus between the need to make a decision and the available information on which to base it rationally'. Crises are also key moments of temporal compression, decisive moments when much is undecided and when decisive actions can therefore have unusually wide-ranging effects on future developments (cf Debray, 1971). Crises make it harder to govern, and this enables forces of resistance to intensify the disorder, turbulence and noise that are always already present in complexity. In de Certeau's words,

> … whereas strategies pin their hopes on the resistance that the *establishment of a place* offers to the erosion of time; tactics on a clever *utilization of time*, of the opportunities it presents and also of the play that it introduces into the foundations of power … the two ways of acting can be distinguished according to whether they bet on place or on time. (de Certeau, 1985: 38–9; original emphasis)

Collibration

Following Andrew Dunsire (1996), we can refer to third-order governing, when it is orchestrated by the state, as *collibration*. This has sound etymological roots as a term to describe the continual rebalancing of *several* modes of governance, whereas equilibration would serve well enough for just two modes of governance. It also serves to distinguish what is at stake here from other kinds of metagovernance.

Collibration is more than a purely technical or technocratic process that provides a technical, problem-solving fix: it always involves specific objects, techniques and subjects of governance and it is tied to the management of a wider 'unstable equilibrium of compromise'. As with other aspects of state power, it involves efforts to secure and/or rework a wider unstable equilibrium of compromise organized around specific objects, techniques and subjects of government and/or governance. Indeed, it is typically conducted in light of the 'global' (or most general) function of the state. In other words, it maintains social cohesion in a socially divided social formation. Governance and metagovernance cannot be reduced to questions of how to solve issues of a specific techno-economic, narrowly juridico-political, tightly focused social administrative or otherwise neatly framed problem. This is not only because of the material interconnections among different problem fields in a complex world, but also because every governance (and, *a fortiori*, metagovernance) practice has implications for the balance of forces.

Governments play a major and increasing role in many aspects of collibration. This is especially true during periods of crisis that threaten system integration and/or social cohesion. They get involved in redesigning markets, in constitutional change and the juridical reregulation of organizational forms and objectives, in organizing the conditions for networked self-organization, in promoting social capital and the self-regulation of the professions and other forms of expertise, and, most importantly, in the collibration of different modes of governance and first-order metagovernance. This role means that networking, negotiation, noise reduction and negative as well as positive coordination often occur 'in the shadow of hierarchy' (Scharpf, 1994: 40; see also Hodgson, 1988: 220–8).

The literature on metagovernance often considers the state in relatively conventional terms as a sovereign authority or alternatively, as the point of intersection of a parallelogram of political forces. Here I adopt an SRA. This makes three important points about the state and state power. First, as an *ensemble* of power centres and capacities that offer unequal chances to different forces within and outside the state, the state apparatus itself does not exercise power. Second, its powers are activated by changing sets of politicians and officials in specific sites, acting in specific conjunctures, using specific modes of governance and specific horizons of action. Thus, to talk of the state or its managers exercising power (or, *a fortiori*, engaging in metagovernance or collibration) is a convenient fiction that masks more complex political relations that extend well beyond the state system and its capacities. And third, as a social relation (more precisely, as an institutionally mediated condensation of a shifting balance of forces located within the state, the wider political system and the wider sets of social relations within which the state is embedded), it involves far more than the state in its narrow, juridico-political sense. This is reflected in the expanded, or integral, definition of the state, proposed by Gramsci, which points beyond the state apparatus and political society to the dependence of state power on civil society (1971: 262–3: 1975, Q6, §88; and below).

The need for such a state role is especially acute in light of the wide dispersion of governance mechanisms and the corresponding need to build appropriate macro-organizational capacities to address far-reaching interorganizational changes without undermining the basic coherence and integrity of the (national) state of coordination that is deemed valuable but prone to collapse. This role can be seen in:

- Subsidizing the production of public goods; organizing side-payments for those making sacrifices to facilitate effective coordination.
- Contributing to the meshing of short-, medium- and long-term time horizons and temporal rhythms across various sites, scales and actors, in part to prevent opportunistic exit and entry into governance arrangements.
- Trying to modify the self-understanding of identities, strategic capacities and interests of individual and collective actors in diverse strategic contexts and so alter their import for preferred strategies and tactics.
- Organizing redundancies and duplication to sustain resilience via requisite variety in response to unexpected problems.
- Taking material and/or symbolic flanking and supporting measures to stabilize forms.
- Organizing redundancies and duplication to sustain resilience through requisite variety in response to unexpected problems.[15]
- Assuming political responsibility as addressee in last resort in the event of governance failure in domains beyond the state (based in part on Jessop, 2002b: 219; see also Bell and Hindmoor, 2009).

This collibratory role tends to fall to the state because of its heightened paradoxical position as an institutional subsystem that is simultaneously merely part of a wider, more complex society (and thus unable to control the latter from above) (cf Offe, 1987; Jessop, 1990b, 2002b). Such collibratory practices suggest that governance (in its various forms) occurs 'in the shadow of hierarchy' (Scharpf, 1994: 40). In other words, there is a continuing role for the state in the organization of self-organization as well as other modes of governance (see also Meuleman, 2008; Bevir, 2010). Indeed, for Bell and Hindmoor (2009), metagovernance is the government of governance.

Generalizing Dunsire's arguments, reflexive self-organization based on stakeholding or public–private partnerships can be seen as a form of 'passive revolution'; as an attempt to absorb the energies and expertise of leading figures in subaltern groups and indeed, of whole 'stakeholder groups'; to defuse a loss of political legitimacy; to recuperate problems of government overload; to turn potential sources of resistance or obstruction into self-responsibilized agents of their own subordination; and to enhance the efficiencies of economic, political and social domination through forms of micro management that penetrate into the pores of an increasingly complex social formation that is intransparent to any single point of observation, command and control, and that cannot be left to the invisible but benign hand of market forces.

Collibration is where the 'shadow of hierarchy' is most evident. This phrase was introduced (initially by Scharpf, 1993) to denote the indirect influence that states may exercise over other actors or forces in political and civil society through the real or imagined threat of executive or legislative action that draws on the state's unique capacities and powers, including coercion (see also Héritier and Rhodes, 2011). While the Gramscian redefinition above highlights the state's role in collibration, other scholars have suggested that there are functional equivalents to the state's 'shadow' role in this regard. These include: (1) the more or less spontaneous, bottom-up development by networks of rules, values, norms and principles that they then acknowledge and follow (Kooiman and Jentoft, 2009; Torfing et al, 2012); (2) increased deliberation and participation by civil society groups through stakeholder democracy, putting external pressure on the state managers and/or other elites involved in governance (Bevir, 2010); and (3) actions taken by international governmental and non-governmental agencies to compensate the inability of failed or weak states to engage in metagovernance (Börzel and Risse, 2010) – although this example seems to involve a rescaling of the shadow of hierarchy insofar as these actions are typically backed, as Börzel and Risse themselves note (2010), by powerful states.

A neo-Gramscian approach

Jonathan Davies (2011) provides a neo-Gramscian approach to governance that complements Gramsci's redefinition of the integral state but is more tightly focused on neoliberal globalizing capitalism. Specifically, he interprets the movement from hierarchy (via, he suggests, markets) to governance as an aspect of the continuing struggle for hegemony under neoliberalism (2011: 128; cf Provan and Kenis, 2008). In this context he emphasizes, against claims that network governance is symmetrical (at least in the sense that it is not hierarchical), that it is strongly asymmetrical and that these asymmetries are rooted in, and also mediate, the wider, contradictory totality of capitalist social formations with their vast concentrations of power and wealth, intensifying competition and chronic instabilities. On this basis he outlines a novel typology of forms of network governance *within neoliberalism* that ranges from inclusive governance through subhegemonic to counter-hegemonic forms, and examines the conditions for emancipation through networks. He asks why powerful networks of actors with similar material and cultural endowments have more influence than other types of networks, and why nodal actors in different networks are more closely related than other actors (Davies, 2011: 131). He also remarks that network coordination tends to degenerate into hierarchical coordination because networks fail to cultivate governing subjects (he calls them 'connectionist citizen-activists') able to solve policy and management problems in depoliticized, trust-based networks. He concludes that network governance failure moves state power along the Gramscian consensus–coercion continuum from hegemonic leadership towards domination (Davies, 2011: 132). In the terms presented above, this could also be described as a reassertion of the shadow of hierarchy, but one tied to a particular class project. This approach need not be confined to neoliberalism but can be extended to the role of governance whenever its objects involve 'wicked problems' rooted in part in social relations of exploitation and/or domination.

Concluding remarks

This chapter has ranged over many issues, from abstract aspects of contingent necessity and complexity through the importance of complexity reduction via semiosis and meaning-making to more specific comments on the modalities and objects of governance. It has distinguished a set of first-order variants concerned with the reflexive redesign of individual modes of governance (such as markets, hierarchies, networks and solidarities) and a set of second-order metagovernance practices concerned with the collibration, or rebalancing, of different forms of governance and their metagovernance. Metagovernance comprises a complex array of more or less reflexive social practices concerned with the governance of social relations characterized by complex, reciprocal interdependence. Interest in the topic has grown in step with recognition, even among its strongest advocates, of the limits of heterarchy (self-organization) as a solution to the failure of other forms of governance (such as the anarchy of the market or the hierarchy of command) (cf Peters, 2009).

It is always hard for critical scholars to engage with governance and metagovernance because of the normative bias secreted in the definition of governance problems and solutions. Although there is a theoretical literature on governance and metagovernance (especially in the fields of critical political economy and governmentality studies), most research on governance is concerned with organizational and/ or policy issues in the private, third and public sectors and connected to irenic modes of problem-solving. This is especially clear in current concerns with 'democratic network governance' and 'good governance'. This has discouraged, as Renate Mayntz (2001) has noted, inquiries into the grounding of 'societal problems' in economic and political domination and, as I have argued in my own contributions to the critique of political economy, serious neglect of the extent to which the sources of governance failure are deeper rooted than issues of cognitive capacities, the discursive framing of problems, institutional design, the tools of governance or the willingness to engage in cogovernance. These are fundamental questions that must be integrated into an emerging research agenda on the governance of complexity and the complexity of governance. This requires more work on the theoretical assumptions rather than policy implications of interest in governance and metagovernance. This agenda will be explored and illustrated in subsequent chapters.

3

Governance failure, metagovernance and its failure

The growing fascination (bordering on obsession) with governance mechanisms as a solution to market and/or state failure should not lead us to overlook the risks involved in attempts to substitute governance through networks and solidarity for markets and/or hierarchies and the resulting likelihood of governance failure. 'Thinking about institutional design nowadays requires sociological input' (Hajer and Wagenaar, 2003: 2) – this means that the challenge is to develop relations between the spheres of civil society, the economy and the state that are less hierarchical and less paternalist, that are sensitive to the needs and aspirations of diverse groups (and especially those who tend to get marginalized) and that have a capacity to learn from diverse knowledge resources (Amin and Thrift, 1995; Storper, 1997; Moulaert, 2000; Healey et al, 2003).

Given contingent necessity, social complexity, structural contradictions,[1] strategic dilemmas[2] and multiple or at least ambivalent, goals, failure is a contingently necessary outcome of attempts at governance (on the sociology of failure, see Malpas and Wickham, 1995). What is necessarily contingent about governance attempts are their modalities, sites, forms, temporalities, spatialities, effects and capacities for recuperating or responding to failure. On the last point, indeed, Offe (1975b) notes that, since each and every mode of state policy-making is prone to failure, one must either accept that a stable state apparatus is impossible or that it is possible only to the extent that it has the capacity to flexibly shift modes of policy-making as the failures and contradictions of the dominant mode (or the prevailing policy-making mix) become more evident and threaten the state's rationality and legitimacy. Offe concludes that the state's long-run survival depends on specific organizational qualities of the state, including what I have elsewhere termed the articulation of government and governance. This is a powerful argument and can be generalized to other forms of (self-reflexive) coordination besides the national state.

Heterarchic governance through networks and solidarities is not always more efficient than markets or states in resolving problems of economic and/or political coordination. Much depends on the strategic capacities to sustain exchange, negotiation, hierarchy or solidarity as well as the specific nature of the coordination problems. Thus, while increasing functional differentiation makes hierarchical coordination increasingly problematic, it does not follow that the structural and strategic conditions for effective governance are sufficiently developed to outperform continued reliance on hierarchy or neoliberal preferences for marketized solutions. We must examine the self-reflexive, self-diagnosing and self-modifying capacities of governing agents and their institutional capacities to redesign themselves in response to failures. Indeed, second-best solutions may be more effective and stable when best solutions are too costly.

Strategic dilemmas in governance

Heterarchic governance mechanisms are prey to strategic dilemmas that may contribute towards failure. We will briefly comment on four of these below.

Cooperation vs competition: it is a commonplace that capitalist economies operate through an unstable and mutually implicated balance of cooperation and competition (cf Piore and Sabel, 1985; Hirst and Zeitlin, 1991). This poses a series of dilemmas for heterarchic governance. One horn of the resulting dilemmas concerns how to maintain interpersonal trust, secure generalized compliance with negotiated understandings, reduce noise through open communication and engage in negative coordination in the face of the many and varied opportunities such practices create for short-term self-interested competitive behaviour that could soon destroy the governance relationship. The other horn of the dilemmas is that an excessive commitment to cooperation and consensus could block the emergence of creative tensions, conflicts or efforts at crisis resolution that could promote learning and/or learning capacities and thereby enhance adaptability (cf Messner, 1994: 589–93). This second dilemmatic horn is especially acute when the environment is turbulent, speedy action is required, incrementalism is inappropriate and consensus would take time to build (and, perhaps, be irrelevant when it does emerge). Such dilemmas have been extensively discussed in economic analysis of flexible industrial districts, learning regions, innovative milieux, and so on. They also affect the political system in the form of the trade-off between partnership and partisanship (with multiple partnerships being linked with differential advantages for political parties, tiers of government or departmental interests). They also relate to differential economic interests. This poses dilemmas both regarding any given partnership and, even more acutely, regarding the opportunities that may exist for juggling multiple partnerships to secure partisan advantage.

Openness vs closure: heterarchies operate in complex, often turbulent, environments. They face problems in remaining open to the environment at the same time as securing the closure needed for effective coordination among a few partners. One horn of this dilemma is that closure may lock in members whose exit would be beneficial (for example, inefficient firms, underemployed workers, sunset sectors) or block recruitment of new social partners (for example, new firms, marginalized workers, sunrise sectors). The other horn is that openness may discourage partners from entering into long-term commitments and sharing long-term time horizons. This may encourage short-term opportunism in the (potentially self-fulfilling) case that partnerships dissolve or involve high turnover. This dilemma can be seen in networking, negotiation, noise reduction and negative coordination. It is reflected in the choice of maximizing the range of possible actions by expanding relevant bases of membership or favouring the 'small is beautiful' principle for the purpose of focused and timely action. It is also reflected in the choice of variable geometries of action versus fixed spatial boundaries for membership of a governance arrangement. An interesting variant of this latter version of the dilemma is whether to permit transnational partnerships or to insist on membership in national sovereignty.

Governability vs flexibility: heterarchic governance mechanisms are neither market-mediated nor hierarchically organized and can be described in terms of the 'self-organization of interorganizational relations'. One argument for the 'visible handshake' of heterarchy over the 'invisible hand' of the market and the 'visible hand' (if not 'iron fist', perhaps in a 'velvet glove') of the state is that it can provide longer-term strategic guidance (lacking in markets) while retaining flexibility (lacking in bureaucratic organizations with their rule-governed procedures). But this is also the site of a dilemma: that between governability (the capacity for guidance) and flexibility (the capacity to adapt to changed circumstances). This assumes several forms. Reducing complexity through operational rules as a precondition for governing a complex world needs to be balanced against the recognition of complexity to mobilize the 'requisite variety' of actors and resources. Avoiding duplication to limit resource costs needs to be balanced against maintaining an adequate repertoire of actions and strategic capacities. A third variant is posed in the choice between exploiting past organizational and interorganizational learning to standardize around 'best practice' and maintaining adaptability in the face of a turbulent environment by avoiding 'lock-in' to outmoded routines. This last problem is particularly associated with efforts to impose 'best practice' from above rather than encourage diversity and allow for horizontal communication and learning among partnerships.

Accountability vs efficiency: some public–private partnerships are expected to serve the public interest as well as to deliver private benefits. But this blurs the public–private distinction and poses a familiar dilemma in terms of accountability versus efficiency. On the one hand, there are problems about attributing responsibility for decisions and non-decisions (acts of commission or omission) in interdependent networks. These problems are especially acute when partnerships are interorganizational rather than interpersonal. On the other hand, attempts to establish clear lines of accountability can interfere with the efficient, cooperative pursuit of joint goals. A related dilemma is that public–private arrangements run the risk of allowing the exploitative capture of public resources for private purposes and/or extending the state's reach into the market economy and civil society to serve the interests of the state or governing party. A third version of this dilemma concerns the relative primacy of economic performance and social inclusion – how far the maximand in public–private partnerships is marketized economic performance as opposed to addressing problems of social cohesion.

These dilemmas can be managed collectively in several ways. Among these are the development of different institutions, apparatuses or agencies specializing primarily in one or other horn of a dilemma and changing the balance between them through differential allocation of resources, continuing competition for legitimacy in changing circumstances, and so on. Likewise, different horns can be handled at different scales. Thus, in neoliberal economies competition is often pursued more vigorously at the national level (privatization, liberalization, deregulation, and so forth) while cooperation is pursued more vigorously at the local or regional level (through public–private partnerships) (cf Gough and Eizenschitz, 1996). Different governance arrangements may also be instituted to deal with different temporal horizons. Thus, one partnership may have an open structure and long-term horizon while another may be relatively closed and pursue specific tasks or development activities with short-term time horizons.

This discussion of several (by no means exhaustive) dilemmas of governance has illustrated them from the complex articulation of the economic and political in capitalist democracies. This is only partly a presentational strategem. It also reflects an important point that is often overlooked in general discussions of governance: that governance mechanisms cannot end the structural contradictions and strategic dilemmas of capitalism. Howsoever it is governed, capitalism involves the self-valorization of capital based on employing labour power as well as transforming nature. What is more, as extra-economic functional domains tend to become more relevant to the dynamic of capital accumulation (reflected in ideas such as structural competitiveness), these, too, tend to be subsumed (or subordinated) to the logic of accumulation and this spreads its contradictions, dilemmas and forms of competition into other domains. In this sense, the rise of governance may serve to extend and intensify capitalist competition rather than substitute non-capitalist principles for those of the market.[3] It poses a major limitation to claims that heterarchic governance can tame the anarchy of the market and render planning apparatuses more accountable. Capitalism has always depended on a contradictory balance between the value form and non-value forms of organization of the capital relation. Although this was previously understood primarily in terms of market vs hierarchy (rooted in the institutional separation and resulting operational autonomy of economics and politics), the rise of governance has not introduced a neutral third term into this conflict but added another site where it is contested. New forms of governance provide a new meeting ground (as did tripartism before) for the logics of accumulation and political mobilization. They also introduce new logics related to other functional subsystems (such as education, science and health), and intensify the problems of interorganizational negotiation, noise reduction and negative coordination. The consequences of this are still being worked out as governance mechanisms undergo their own evolution.

Responses to failure

There is growing recognition of different levels or orders of governance. Metagovernance involves the organization of the conditions for governance in its broadest sense. Thus, corresponding to the four basic modes of governance (or coordination) distinguished above, we can distinguish four basic modes of metagovernance and one umbrella mode (see Table 3.1).

First, there is 'meta-exchange'. This involves the reflexive redesign of individual markets (for example, for land, labour, money, commodities, knowledge – or appropriate parts or subdivisions thereof) and/or the reflexive reordering of relations among two or more markets by modifying their operation, nesting, overall articulation, embedding in non-market relations or institutions, and so on. Market agents often resort to market redesign in response to failure and/or hire the services of those who claim some expertise in this field. Among the latter are management gurus, management consultants, human relations experts, corporate lawyers and accountants. More generally, there has long been interest in issues of the institutional redesign of the market mechanism, the nesting of markets, their embedding in non-market mechanisms and the conditions for the maximum formal rationality of market forces. There are also 'markets in markets'. This can lead to 'regime shopping', competitive 'races to the bottom', or, in certain conditions, 'races to the top'. Moreover, because markets function in the shadow of hierarchy and/or heterarchy, non-market agents may try to modify markets, their institutional supports and their agents to improve their efficiency and/or compensate for market failures and inadequacies.

Second, there is 'meta-organization', the reflexive redesign of organizations, the creation of intermediating organizations, the reordering of interorganizational relations and the management of organizational ecologies (that is, the organization of the conditions of organizational evolution in conditions where many organizations coexist, compete, cooperate and coevolve), the reflexive redesign of organizational authority structures (see, for example, Beer, 1990), the creation of intermediating organizations, the reordering of hierarchical

Table 3.1: First-order responses to governance failure

Meta-exchange	Meta-command	Meta-dialogue	Meta-solidarity
Redesign individual markets	Organizational redesign	Reorder networks	Develop new identities and loyalties
De- and reregulation	Reorder organizational ecologies	Reorganize conditions of self-organization	From old to new social movements
Reorder market hierarchies	Constitutional change	New forms of dialogue	New civil society, 'Big Society'

Source: Jessop (2017)

interorganizational relations, the management of organizational ecologies), and the promotion of new policy rhetorics to justify new approaches (cf Fischer, 2009; see also Hood, 1998). Reflexive managers in the private, public and third sectors may undertake such meta-organizational functions themselves (for example, through 'macro management' and organizational innovation) and/or turn to alleged experts such as constitutional lawyers, public choice economists, theorists of public administration, think tanks, advocates of reflexive planning, specialists in policy evaluation, and so forth. This is reflected in the continuing redesign, rescaling and adaptation of the state apparatus, sometimes more ruptural, sometimes more continuous, and the manner in which it is embedded within the wider political system.

Third, there is what one might call 'meta heterarchy'. This involves the reflexive organization of the conditions of reflexive self-organization by redefining the framework in which this occurs,[4] and can range from providing opportunities for 'spontaneous sociability' (Fukuyama, 1995; see also Putnam, 2000) through various measures to improved forms of interpersonal networking and interorganizational negotiation to institutional innovations to promote more effective intersystemic communication and/or innovations to promote 'institutional thickness' (Amin and Thrift, 1995). Next, in response to governance failure in its narrow sense, that is to say, the failure of self-organizing networks, interorganizational partnerships based on negotiation or the heterarchic steering at a distance of intersystemic relations, we can talk of 'meta-heterarchy' (on network management, see Jones et al, 1997; Sørensen and Torfing, 2009). Van Bortel and Mullins (2009) distinguish three forms of metagovernance in this context: network design to shape the organizational form of networks, framing to define their goals, material conditions and narrative rationale, and participation by metagovernor(s) in network operations to influence network activities and outcomes. To this list, Sørensen et al (2009) add network management concerned to smooth network operations and make them more efficient and effective.[5]

Lastly, at least for present purposes, there is meta-solidarity. This involves forms of therapeutic action, whether spontaneous or mediated through therapeutic intervention, to repair or refocus feelings of trust, loyalty and unconditional commitment. As presented in the Preface to this book, this involves attempts to develop new identities and loyalties, to move from old to new social movements, and to build a new civil society, influenced perhaps by 'Big Society' discourse. At stake in this field is to cultivate and connect new senses of solidarity to establish new bases of mobilization.

These responses are best described as involving second-order governance or, shifting perspective, first-order metagovernance. But there is no need to stop here, for there is another level of responses, one that, if it were not too confusing, could be called 'meta-metagovernance'. Better options are third-order governance (à la Kooiman) or second-order metagovernance, and best of all, in part because of their etymological roots as well as conceptual precision, are Dunsire's suggestions of co-libration and 'collibration'. Although these have not yet become standard terms in the field, collibration has become more frequent and is especially apt for third-order governance (or metagovernance in its most precise sense). In a lecture at the Max Planck Institute for the Study of Societies, Dunsire described collibration as a 'useful mode of state intervention' that enabled the state to secure some influence when faced with the growth of functional systems (such as law, economy, education, politics and health) marked by operational closure and self-referentiality that made it hard for the state (or any other outside force) to regulate such systems. The result, other things being equal, was growing regulatory failure (Dunsire, 1993).

Later, and more elegantly, Dunsire referred to co-libration, namely, the action of contributing with others to equilibration, and to 'collibration', a process that involves the state in 'the manipulation of balancing social tensions, the controlled shifting of a social equilibrium, the fine tuning of an oscillation of near-equal forces' (1993: 11). When this is successful, an unstable equilibrium of compromise (to use a Gramscian rather than Dunsirean phrase) is established within which the state can continue to exercise some influence (see Dunsire, 1993, 1996; see also Gramsci, 1971).

Dunsire identified four main responses to this situation: (1) government subsidies that depended on compliance; (2) public–private partnerships and other forms of corporatist intermediation; (3) reflexive forms of law that require attention to the circumstances and consequences of their implementation; and (4) the use of various measures to indirectly influence the balance of forces. Each mechanism is said to transform in its own way the self-referentiality of functional systems from a problem into an asset that can be used to steer modern societies. But each also creates its own problems and must therefore be used reflexively and incrementally, monitoring effects and engaging in further rounds of intervention (Dunsire, 1993).

Collibration can be defined for present purposes as the judicious rearticulating and rebalancing of modes of governance to manage the complexity, plurality and tangled hierarchies found in prevailing modes of coordination with a view to achieving optimal outcomes as viewed by those engaged in metagovernance. It is the organization of the conditions for governance and involves the judicious mixing of market, hierarchy, networks and solidarity to achieve the best possible outcomes from the viewpoint of those engaged in metagovernance. In this sense, it also means the organization of the conditions of governance in terms of their structurally inscribed strategic selectivity. This would involve the asymmetrical privileging of different modes of coordination and their differential access to the institutional support and the material resources needed to pursue reflexively agreed objectives. The key issues for those involved in metagovernance are: '(1) how to cope with other actors' self-referentiality; and (2) how to cope with their own self-referentiality' (Dunsire, 1996: 320). Unfortunately, since every practice is prone to failure, metagovernance and collibration are also likely to fail. This implies that there is no Archimedean point from which governance or collibration can be guaranteed to succeed.

Collibration is no more the preserve of one actor or set of actors than it is confined to one site or scale of action. Instead it should be seen, like the various first-order forms of coordination of complex reciprocal interdependence and the various second-order forms of meta coordination, as fractal in character, which means taking self-similar forms in many different social fields (on fractal relations, see, classically, Mandelbrot, 1982).

Governments and metagovernance

Governments play a key role in metagovernance or collibration. They provide the ground rules for governance and the regulatory order in and through which governance partners can pursue their aims. They ensure the compatibility or coherence of different governance mechanisms and regimes. They act as the primary organizer of the dialogue among policy communities. They deploy a relative monopoly of organizational intelligence and information in order to shape cognitive expectations. They serve as a 'court of appeal' for disputes arising within and over governance. They seek to rebalance power differentials by strengthening weaker forces or systems in the interests of system integration and/or social cohesion. They try to modify the self-understanding of identities, strategic capacities and interests of individual and collective actors in different strategic contexts and hence alter their implications for preferred strategies and tactics. And they also assume political responsibility in the event of governance failure. This is especially true in periods of serious crisis *in* (and, even more, *of*) institutional orders that are critical to societal reproduction. But, more generally, metagovernance depends on almost permanent institutional and organizational innovation to maintain the very possibility (however remote) of sustained economic growth.

Metagovernance involves both institutional design and cultural governance. Whereas there has been much interest in issues of institutional design appropriate to different objects of governance, less attention has been paid by governance theorists themselves to the reform of the subjects of governance. Yet the neoliberal project, for example, clearly requires attempts to create entrepreneurial subjects and demanding consumers aware of their choices and rights as well as actions to shift the respective scope and powers of the market mechanism and state intervention. This is an area where Foucauldian students of governmentality have more to offer than students of governance. They have been especially interested in the role of power and knowledge in shaping the attributes, capacities and identities of social agents and, in the context of self-reflexive governance, in enabling them to become self-governing and self-transforming. This raises important questions about the compatibility of different modes of governance insofar as this involves not only questions of institutional compatibility but also the distribution of the individual and collective capacities needed to pursue creatively and autonomously the appropriate strategies and tactics to sustain contrasting modes of governance.

Recognizing the contributions of institutional design and subjective governmentality to metagovernance is no guarantee of success. These are certainly not purely technical matters that can be resolved by those who are experts in organizational design, public administration and public opinion management. All the technical activities of the state are conducted under the primacy of the political, that is, the state's concern with managing the tension between economic and political advantages and its ultimate responsibility for social cohesion. This fact plagues the liberal prescription of an arm's-length relationship between the market and the nightwatchman state, since states (or at least, state managers) are rarely strong enough to resist pressures to intervene when political advantage is at stake and/or it needs to respond to social unrest.

More generally, we can safely assume that, if every mode of governance fails, then so will metagovernance! This is especially likely where the objects of governance and metagovernance are complicated and interconnected. This conjecture is more plausible where the relevant objects of governance and metagovernance are complicated, interconnected and, perhaps, internally and/or mutually contradictory, and where any impression of effective governance and metagovernance to date has depended on displacing certain governance problems elsewhere and/or on deferring them into a more or less remote future. This could well be one source of the 'steering optimism' as opposed to pessimism that one finds in the governance and metagovernance literatures – especially when such temporary spatio-temporal fixes are reinforced by the capacity to engage in *fuite en avant* to produce new fixes. In contrast, 'steering pessimism' tends to look at the underlying long-term structural obstacles to effective governance and metagovernance. Indeed, these obstacles, by virtue of the simplification of the conditions of action, often lead to the 'revenge' of problems that have been ignored, marginalized, displaced or deferred. This sort of simplification is evident in attempts to define problems as societal in scope and as requiring consensual governance solutions rather than as conflictual effects of exploitation, oppression or discrimination that can be solved only by addressing fundamental patterns of domination (cf Mayntz, 2001, 2003). This is reinforced by the normative assumptions that inform policy paradigms focused on governance, governance failure and metagovernance, where the emphasis is on different forms of cooperation that obviate the need for antagonism and violence. In this sense, prolonged resort to organized coercion tends to be excluded from governance policy paradigms other than as a clear sign of governance failure.

Challenges of governance and metagovernance

This analysis leads to three conclusions, intellectual, practical and philosophical, respectively. Once the incompleteness of attempts at coordination (whether through the market, the state or heterarchy) is accepted as inevitable, it is necessary to adopt a satisficing approach that has at least three key dimensions:

- Deliberate cultivation of a flexible repertoire (requisite variety) of responses. This involves recognition that complexity excludes simple governance solutions and that effective governance often requires a combination of mechanisms oriented to different scales, different temporal horizons, and so on, that are appropriate to the object to be governed. In this way strategies and tactics can be combined and rebalanced to reduce the likelihood of failure and to modify their balance as appropriate in the face of governance failure and turbulence in the policy environment and changing policy risks.

- A reflexive orientation about what would be an acceptable policy outcome in the case of incomplete success, to compare the effects of failure/inadequacies in the market, government and governance, and regular reassessment of the extent to which current actions are producing desired outcomes.
- Self-reflexive 'irony' such that the participants in governance recognize the likelihood of failure but proceed as if success were possible. The supreme irony in this context is that the need for irony holds not only for individual attempts at governance using individual governance mechanisms but also for the practice of metagovernance using appropriate metagovernance mechanisms.

I now comment on each of these in turn.

Requisite variety

The need for 'requisite variety' (with its informational, structural and functional redundancies) is based on the recognition of complexity. As initially introduced into cybernetics, the 'law of requisite variety' states that, in order to ensure that a given system has a specific value at a given time despite turbulence in its environment, the controller or regulator must be able to produce as many different counteractions as there are significant ways in which variations in the environment may impact on the system (Ashby, 1956). This principle has major implications for governance but, as specified, it is essentially static. In a dynamic and changing world the forces of natural and/or social entropy would soon break down any predefined control mechanism established using this concept. Because of the infinite variety of perturbations that could affect a system in a complex world, one should try to maximize its internal variety (or diversity) so that the system is well prepared for any contingencies. Thus, the law of requisite variety is better reformulated as follows: to minimize the risks of metagovernance as well as governance failure in a turbulent environment, and to maintain a broad and flexible spectrum of possible responses so that the governance mix can be modified as the limits of any one mode become evident. This involves the monitoring of mechanisms to check for problems, resort to collibrating mechanisms to modulate the coordination mix, and the reflexive, negotiated reevaluation of objectives.

Maintaining requisite variety may well seem inefficient from an economizing viewpoint because it introduces slack or waste, but it also provides major sources of flexibility in the face of failure (Grabher,

1994). If every mode of economic and political coordination is failure-prone, if not failure-laden, relative success in coordination over time depends on the capacity to switch modes of coordination as the limits of any one mode become evident. This provides one way to displace or defer failures and crises in response to internal and/or external turbulence. Since there are no simple governance solutions, appropriate complex solutions must combine different scales and different temporal horizons and orient them to 'fit' the nature of the object to be governed. Moreover, because different periods and conjunctures as well as different objects of governance require different kinds of policy mix, the balance in the repertoire will need to be varied as circumstances change.

In addition, since different conjunctures and periods require different kinds of policy mix, the balance within the repertoire will need to be varied. One should also recognize that, even if specific institutions and organizations are abolished, it might be necessary to safeguard the underlying modes of coordination that they embody. Overall this should promote the ability to alter strategies and select those that are relatively successful. Thus, a flexible, adaptable political regime should seek to maintain a repertoire of modes of policy-making and implementation.

Requisite reflexivity

This involves the ability and commitment to uncover and make explicit to oneself the nature of one's intentions, projects and actions and their conditions of possibility, and, in this context, to learn about them, critique them and act on any lessons that have been learned. Complexity requires, as we have seen, that a reflexive observer recognizes that she cannot fully understand what she is observing and must therefore make contingency plans for unexpected events. In relation to governance, this involves inquiring in the first instance into the material, social and discursive construction of possible objects of governance and reflecting on why this, rather than another object of governance, has become dominant, hegemonic or naturalized. It also requires thinking critically about the strategically selective implications of adopting one or another definition of a specific object of governance and its properties, *a fortiori*, of the choice of modes of governance, participants in the governance process, and so forth (on these particular issues, see Larmour, 1997). Thus, reflexivity involves the ability and commitment to uncover and make explicit one's intentions, projects and actions, their conditions of possibility, and what would be an acceptable outcome in the case of incomplete success. It involves cultivating the ability to learn about them, critique them and act on any lessons.

Applied to metagovernance, this means comparing the consequences of failure/inadequacies in different forms of governance and regularly reassessing whether current practices are generating expected results. It requires thinking critically about the strategically selective implications of adopting one or another definition of a specific object of governance and its properties, *a fortiori*, of the choice of modes of governance, participants in the governance process, and so forth (on these particular issues, see Larmour, 1997). It requires monitoring mechanisms, modulating mechanisms and a willingness to reevaluate objectives. And it requires learning about how to learn reflexively. There is a general danger of infinite regress here, of course, but this can be limited provided that reflexivity is combined with the second and third principles.

A second set of constraints concerns the insertion of reflexive self-organization into the broader political system. This particularly concerns the relative primacy of different modes of coordination and their differential access to the institutional support and the material resources necessary to pursue reflexively agreed objectives. Among crucial issues here are the flanking and supporting measures that are taken by the state; the provision of material and symbolic support; and the extent of any duplication or counteraction by other coordination mechanisms.

We can distinguish three aspects of this second set of constraints. First, as both governance and government mechanisms exist on different scales (indeed, one of their functions is to bridge scales), success at one scale may well depend on practices and events on other scales. Second, coordination mechanisms may also have different temporal horizons. One function of governance (as with quangos and corporatist arrangements beforehand) is to enable decisions with long-term implications to be divorced from short-term political (notably electoral) calculations. But there may still be disjunctions between the temporalities of different governance and government mechanisms that go beyond issues of sequencing to affect the very viability of heterarchy in the shadow of hierarchy. And third, although governance mechanisms may acquire specific techno-economic, political and/or ideological functions, state managers typically monitor the effects of governance failure and attempts at metagovernance on their own capacity to secure social cohesion in divided societies. They reserve the right to open, close, juggle and rearticulate governance not only in terms of particular functions but also from the viewpoint of partisan and global political advantage. This can often lead state managers to pursue self-interested action to protect their particular interests rather than to preserve the state's overall capacity to pursue an (always selective and biased) consensual interpretation of the public interest and to promote social cohesion. This provides the basis for displacing or postponing failures and crises. It also suggests that the ideologically motivated destruction of alternative modes of coordination could prove counterproductive: they may well need to be reinvented in one or another form. This is one lesson from the growing disillusion with neoliberalism.

Requisite irony

Finally, there is a philosophical dimension to metagovernance. This concerns the appropriate stance towards the intellectual and practical requirements of effective governance and metagovernance given 'the centrality of failure and the inevitability of incompleteness' (Malpas and Wickham, 1995: 39). This suggests that, in approaching policy-making and implementation, one should also respect what can be defined as 'the law of requisite irony'.

> Far from underestimating the power of words, what I suggest is that the morality of solidarity requires a more holistic understanding of humanitarian communication – one that takes its point of departure in the historical shift from the solidarity of pity to the solidarity of irony. (Chouliaraki, 2013: 22)

In a world of increasing complexity, 'irony – with its emphasis on context, perspective, and instability – is simply what defines "the present conditions of knowledge" … for everyone' (Hutcheon, 1994: 33).

To defend this strange idea, I distinguish irony from fatalism, stoicism, opportunism and cynicism. Fatalism leads to inaction, stoicism rests on passive resignation in the pursuit of familiar routines, opportunism is expressed in avoiding or exploiting the consequences of failure for self-interested motives, and cynicism leads to the stage management of appearances to claim success in the face of failure.

The cynic is overly influenced by a 'pessimism of the intellect' and assumes that new policies will work no better than old policies. This leads cynics into a state of 'being in denial' so that they deny failure or else redefine it as success; it also encourages a manipulative approach, with appearances being stage-managed so that success seems to have occurred. This is the realm of symbolic politics, accelerated policy churning (to give the impression of doing something about intractable problems) and the 'spin doctor', the realm of 'words that work but policies that fail' (Edelman, 1977).

In contrast to fatalism, stoicism, opportunism and cynicism, the ironist is a sceptic. This is particularly evident in the highly mediatized world of contemporary politics. If one is likely to fail, one can at least choose one's preferred form of failure. This is irony in the Rortyan sense, but it has a public, not private, form. Rortyan irony primarily concerns a contrast between public confidence about the permanency and validity of one's vocabulary of motives and actions and private doubt about their finality and apodicticity (Rorty, 1989: 73–4). Thus, for Richard Rorty,

> An ironist is a person who realizes that all nonpublic convictions and values, and even vocabularies are contingent, contestable, transitory, and exposed to alternatives that arise continually. The ironist's position, therefore, embraces privacy and plurality and denies any one specific view as a priori or automatic priority. We must, he says, be "*content to treat the demands of self-creation and of human solidarity as equally valid, yet forever incommensurable*". (1989: xv; original emphasis)

Now, as expressed by Rorty, purely private irony could lead to cynicism or fatalism, a distrust of the motives behind others' expressed motives and actions and self-serving manipulation of their beliefs, on the one hand, or passive resignation, laissez-penser, and laissez-faire vis-à-vis others' beliefs and actions, on the other. Yet Rorty does go on to spell out one implication of his philosophy, namely, a 'commitment to political freedom and free discussion' (1989: 84). Thus, one could conclude that the ironist is more inclined to an 'optimism of the will' than a 'pessimism of the intelligence'. In this sense the ironist is more romantic than cynical. Yet, while Rorty's irony may minimize both cynicism and fatalism, it also tends to privilege the educated intellectual at the expense of the non-reflexive citizen, and can encourage forms of elitism and even intellectual terrorism (cf Haber, 1994: 66–9).

The only possibility open for political ironists, then, is to stand apart from their political practices and at the same time incorporate this awareness of their ironic position into the practice itself. Thus, the public ironist is more romantic than cynical, committed to continuing public dialogue rather than a privatized world of laissez-penser, and also opposes passive resignation and opportunistic behaviour. The law of requisite irony entails that those involved in governance choose among forms of failure and make a reasoned decision in favour of one or another form of failure. In this respect it is important to note that, in contrast to cynics, ironists act in 'good faith' and seek to involve others in the process of policy-making, not for manipulative purposes, but in order to bring about conditions for negotiated consent and self-reflexive learning. In line with the law of requisite variety, moreover, they must be prepared to change the modes of governance as appropriate.

But for good philosophical reasons to do with empowerment and accountability, they should ideally place self-organization at the heart of governance in preference to the anarchy of the market or the top-down command of more or less unaccountable rulers. In this sense self-reflexive and participatory forms of governance are performative – they are both an art form and a life form. This indicates a preference for participatory over authoritarian forms of governance, bottom–up over top-down approaches, taking account of the identities, interests and values of those involved and/or affected by governance, and seeking maximum feasible participation (cf Moulaert and Nussbaumer, 2005). Like all forms of governance, they constitute their objects of governance, but they also become a self-reflexive means of coping with the failures, contradictions, dilemmas and paradoxes that are an inevitable feature of life.

Translated into the public domain of self-reflexive, deliberative governance and metagovernance, this could be expressed in terms of the need to combine 'optimism of the will' with 'pessimism of the intelligence'. The ironist accepts incompleteness and failure as essential features of social life but acts as if completeness and success were possible. She must simplify a complex, contradictory and changing reality in order to be able to act, knowing full well that any such simplification is also a distortion of reality and, what is worse, that such distortions can sometimes generate failure even as they are also a precondition of relatively successful interventions to manage complex interdependence.

Muecke has defined romantic irony as 'the ironical presentation of the ironic position of the fully-conscious artist' (1970: 20). Transposed from the artistic field to the art of governance, this suggests that self-reflexive governing agents should seek creative solutions while acknowledging the limits to any such solution. They must engage in calculation but also make judgements; they must be committed to the resulting governance projects but recognize the risk of failure; and they will need to combine passion and reason to mobilize support behind the project. Recognizing the inevitable incompleteness of attempts at governance (whether through the market, the state, network or solidarity), romantic ironists adopt a satisficing approach. They accept incompleteness and failure as essential features of social life but continue to act as if completeness and success were possible. Whether the ironic stance in this latter regard is purely private (individual) or public (shared) or again, is covert (unstated but implicit) or open (that is, expressed in a self-consciously ironical manner) is surely a contingent issue at this level of reflection and analysis. In any case, the political ironist must simplify a complex, contradictory and changing reality in order to be able to act, knowing full well that any such simplification is also a distortion of reality and, what is worse, that such distortions can sometimes generate failure even as they are also the necessary precondition of relatively successful interventions to manage complex interdependence. The only possibility open for political ironists, then, is indeed, to stand apart from their political practices and at the same time incorporate this awareness of their ironic position into the practice itself.

Moreover, if political ironists are to take account of the subjects as well as the objects of governance in their ironic attempts at governance, they must also choose the modes in and through which they do so. Requisite irony entails that those involved in governance choose among forms of failure and make a reasoned decision in favour of one or another form of failure. In this respect, it is important to note that, in contrast to cynics, ironists act in 'good faith' and seek to involve others in the process of policy-making, not for manipulative purposes, but in order to bring about conditions for negotiated consent and self-reflexive learning. In line with the law of requisite variety, moreover, they must be prepared to change the modes of governance as appropriate. But for good philosophical reasons to do with empowerment and accountability, they should ideally place self-organization at the heart of governance in preference to the anarchy of the market or the top-down command of more or less unaccountable rulers. In this sense, self-reflexive and participatory forms of governance are performative – they are both an art form and a life form. Like all forms of governance, they are constitutive of their objects of governance, but they also become a self-reflexive means of coping with the failures, contradictions, dilemmas and paradoxes that are an inevitable feature of life. In this sense participatory governance is a crucial means of defining the objectives as well as objects of governance as well as of facilitating the co-realization of these objectives by reinforcing motivation and mobilizing capacities for self-reflection, self-regulation and self-correction.

Concluding remarks

This review of the complexities of governance and the nature of governance failure has emphasized that, while self-reflexive organization is an alternative mode of coordination to the market and the state, it is not immune to failure. Indeed, I have emphasized here and elsewhere that all forms of coordination of complex reciprocal interdependence are prone to failure. Two reactions to the tendency of all forms of coordination to fail are cynical opportunism and fatalistic resignation. But a third form is also possible: public romantic irony. This involves a commitment to participatory forms of governance in which relevant social forces engage in continuing dialogue and mutual reflection to monitor the progress of their attempts at governance and to develop an appropriate repertoire of modes of coordination so that they can respond to signs of failure. This, in turn, requires a commitment to metagovernance practices that are concerned to create the conditions in which the scope for participatory governance is optimized in different policy domains and on different scales, and in which the contribution of market forces and top-down command (especially through the state) are subordinated to the logic of participatory governance. This does not exclude resort to the anarchy of exchange or the hierarchy of formal organization as a means of simplifying specific coordination problems, but it does require that the scope of the market mechanism and the exercise of formal authority should be subject as far as possible to forms of participatory governance that aim to balance efficiency, effectiveness and democratic accountability in and through self-reflexive deliberation in conditions that minimize social exclusion. In this context, while some theorists of governance rightly emphasize that governance takes place in the shadow of hierarchy, this should be understood in terms of a democratically accountable, socially inclusive hierarchy organized around the problematic of responsible metagovernance rather than unilateral and top-down command. This places issues of constitutional design at the heart of debates on the future of governance and metagovernance.

This is why 'good governance' is so crucial, both as a theoretical paradigm and as a policy paradigm. In the terms presented above, we can see good governance, both as a theoretical paradigm concerned with the self-reflexive organizational, institutional and constitutional design of metagovernance (not just individual modes of governance) premised on a commitment to 'romantic public irony', and as a policy paradigm that has distinctive functions in the overall cycle of governance success and failure. It can be seen as a discursively mediated policy response to the failures of statism and neoliberalism that has been articulated in the broader economic, political and ideological project of a globalizing neoliberalism. It is important to disambiguate these different paradigms, otherwise we will be led to reject best practice in metagovernance (the theoretical paradigm) because of the way in which 'good governance' has been mobilized discursively behind a neoliberal project which serves to disguise governance failure (the failure of the neoliberal project to deliver on its promises, as opposed to its profits). To conclude, building on preceding arguments in Chapters 1 and 2, I offer four observations. First, contingent necessity and complexity are inevitable features of the real world and face any agent with problems of how to reduce and structure that complexity. This is partly a question of cognition and partly a question of self-organization. To repeat an earlier argument, it involves:

- Simplifying models and practices that reduce the complexity of the world but are nonetheless congruent with real world processes and relevant to the objectives of the actors concerned.
- Developing the capacity for dynamic social learning about various causal processes and forms of interdependence, attributions of responsibility and capacity for actions, and possibilities of coordination in a complex, turbulent environment. This is enhanced when actors are able to switch among different modes of governance to facilitate more effective responses to internal and/or external turbulence.
- Building methods for coordinating actions across different social forces with different identities, interests and meaning systems, over different spatio-temporal horizons, and over different domains of action. This depends on the self-reflexive use of self-organization to sustain exchange, negotiation, hierarchy or solidarity as well as on the specific nature of the coordination problems engendered by operating on different scales and over different time horizons.
- Establishing both a common world view for individual action and a system of metagovernance to stabilize key players' orientations, expectations and rules of conduct. This allows for a more systematic review and assessment of problems and potentials, of resource availability and requirements, and the framework for continued commitment to negative and positive coordination.

Obviously, the specific forms of governance will vary with the nature of the objects to be governed: effective governance of local economic development, hypermobile financial capital, international migration, universities, medical practice, the nuclear power industry and cyberspace, for example, would entail very different sets of partners and practices. Equally obviously, the relative success of attempts at governance will also depend on the nature of the objects of governance.

Second, self-organization and its resulting operational autonomy cannot eliminate social, material and spatio-temporal interdependence with the environment and its ecology of systems. It is the management of reciprocal interdependence that provides the basis for attempts at governance, that is, the heterarchic coordination of operationally autonomous systems. Attempts to establish any particular institutional logic as the dominant principle of societalization (as the axial principle of social organization) are conditioned by functional linkages between different systems that work 'behind the backs' of those involved as well as by capacities for strategic coordination. Thus, the role of governance mechanisms in securing the subordination of other institutional orders or functional subsystems to capital accumulation is necessarily constrained by the contradictory logic and strategic dilemmas with which the capital relation is associated. Crisis plays a key role in guiding this process, but does so by providing turbulence (noise) that must then be interpreted in ways favourable to the reimposition of the logic of capital rather than that of some other institutional order. It is in this context that particular attention needs paying to the strategic selectivity of different metagovernance mechanisms.

Third, although there is no master subject able to govern the intersection of all possible governance arrangements, there is scope for metagovernance attempts to conform and coordinate several sites and objects of governance. The SRA adopted here implies that the very processes of governance help to constitute the objects that come to be governed: these objects do not fully pre-exist the process of governance. This highlights the need to study struggles over the constitution of such objects, the necessary failures or incompleteness of their governmentalization, and the conditions in which, against all odds, the improbable occurs and attempts at governance succeed. This improbability is nonetheless evident in the fact that successful governance is always provisional, localized and partial, and always has unintended consequences that operate to the detriment of other subjects, interests and projects, and may eventually prove counter-productive, even for those who instituted the governance mechanisms and projects in question.

Finally, while Hayek is wrong to suggest that the free market based on the price mechanism provides the best long-run solution to many problems of governance (subject to the metagovernance of the market through a liberal constitutional order), there is still a rational kernel to his argument. Since there can be no master metagovernance subject, the evolution of governance mechanisms depends on contingent evolution. Certain governance mechanisms that emerge from chance discovery or random variation will prove more adaptable than others. But the incompleteness of governance and turbulence in the environment mean that no single governance mechanism can be perfectly adapted to its environment. It follows that a plurality of governance mechanisms is needed to ensure requisite variety and flexibility in managing the manifold forms of unstructured complexity. Such plurality cannot be guaranteed from above, but depends on the scope for initiative from below.

4

Semantic, institutional and spatio-temporal fixes

This chapter explores three interrelated aspects of governance. Actors must reduce the complexity of the natural and social world to 'go on' within it, whether as participants or observers, by selecting some aspects as more meaningful or important than others. *A fortiori*, this holds for the complexity of geophysical and sociospatial relations with the result that actors are forced (usually unwittingly) to approach them through spatial imaginaries that frame their spatial understandings, projects and experiences or at least, through other kinds of social imaginary that have significant spatial presuppositions and implications (cf Lefebvre, 1991 [1978] on the dialectical relations among conceived, perceived and lived space). I first introduce the idea of semantic fixes and then consider institutional and spatio-temporal fixes. The latter two have three aspects – one concerns space and time as direct objects of governance, the second addresses the task of governing the spatio-temporal dimensions of other substantive objects of governance, and the third deals with governing or compensating for the uneven spatio-temporal effects of governance, as seen in the potentially unintended consequences of governance. My analysis draws on previous work on conjunctural analysis, cultural political economy (CPE), institutional fixes and spatio-temporal fixes, but I relate them directly to governance in its various guises. Combining these approaches facilitates the study of how the inherent contradictions and antagonisms of the capital relation are governed through a historically variable set of institutional, spatio-temporal and semantic fixes.

Discourse and semantic fixes

While institutional fixes and spatio-temporal fixes are increasingly familiar terms in CPE, 'semantic fix' merits a brief definition in CPE terms. It refers to the sedimentation of a social imaginary that is naturalized as an appropriate object of observation, calculation, management, governance or guidance, and that thereby frames the competition, rivalries and struggles that occur within its parameters. Such fixes are never fully closed or sedimented, of course: even hegemonic imaginaries are contested from within the power bloc, often depend on complementary subhegemonic imaginaries with different sociospatial bases of support and are vulnerable to counter-hegemonic economic imaginaries. Like institutional and spatio-temporal fixes, semantic fixes are partial, provisional and temporary. They work best when they connect different spheres, scales and sites of social action and have in-built sources of redundancy and flexibility that can be mobilized in the face of instability or crisis (for the general analytical framework, see Sum and Jessop, 2013).

Since its inception in the 19th century, sociology has taken 'society' and its reproduction as its privileged object(s) or at least, as its ultimate horizon of analysis. Yet society is a deeply problematic notion, and recent sociological contributions have questioned whether it should, or indeed can, remain the central focus of the discipline (see, for example, Luhmann, 1992; Urry, 1999). If sociology can no longer take the existence of 'society' for granted, is there an alternative theoretical object at a similar level of generality that does not assume fixed boundaries and that offers more scope for analysis across different sites and scales? One candidate is societalization (*Vergesellschaftung*, or societal organization) and societal projects. Whereas societalization denotes the social processes through which 'society effects' are produced, societal projects refer to the competing social imaginaries that envision different principles of societalization and different ways to achieve 'society effects'.[1]

This implies that, to the extent that 'society' exists, it is constituted and reproduced through social processes and practices that articulate diverse social relations in ways that produce macro-social order. For example, against the still common 'methodologically nationalist' equation of society with the national territorial state (or, less persuasively, the nation-state and its imagined community), the alternative approach proposed here claims that the rise of modern (national) societies simply reflects the hegemony or domination of one, time-and-space-bound, principle of societal organization. Earlier (and still current) principles include segmentation, centre–periphery relations and diverse projects that either prioritize the codes and programmes of one or another 'functional system' (or institutional order), or, conversely, privilege the dominance of one or another social identity or category that is transversal to these codes (on principles of societalization, see Luhmann, 1992, 1996; on the transversal character of social identities such as ethnicity, gender, generation, nation, place, 'race', region, and so on, see Jessop, 2010b).

The nature of any particular 'society' depends on its hegemonic or dominant principle of societalization and its collective identity (or self-description), if any; on how this principle is articulated with others; and on how the production of the corresponding 'society effects' is secured despite its specific contradictions, crisis tendencies and conflicts. A successful societalization project typically emerges from, and is based on, a more extensive substratum of social relations that includes many more elemental relations than those that are actually combined as moments of a structurally coherent configuration to form these 'society effects'. There are always interstitial, residual, marginal, irrelevant, recalcitrant and contradictory elements and, in so far as alternative societies are possible, there is clearly scope for conflict over rival 'societal projects' as well as contradictions among competing institutional logics.

Competing social forces try to establish one or another societal project and its associated principle of societalization as the hegemonic or dominant 'frame' in a given context and/or to foster complementary (subhegemonic) or opposed (counter-hegemonic) projects. Given the existence of competing societal projects, each with its own social bases and organizational principles, societalization is always incomplete. There are no societies (not even fully closed 'total institutions')[2] in which only one project prevails and achieves closure. In addition, and equally importantly, not only can social interaction and organizational life occur in the absence of societies, but much of social life occurs without regard to their existence, if any, and on these grounds, there is no reason to privilege 'society' as a unit of analysis.

In these terms, the analysis of societalization does not entail a totalizing view of 'society' as a fully formed, internally coherent, externally closed system but rather, a concern with the relative weight of competing societalization projects and their always partial, contrary and permeable 'society effects'. An important question for the nature of the 'social' and 'society' in this regard concerns the importance of different axes of societalization: economic, political, legal, scientific, educational, religious, moral, artistic, and so on. Whereas Luhmann and his adherents tend to regard all functional systems as equal, I am less inclined, for reasons elaborated elsewhere,[3] to accept this systems-theoretical postulate. On the contrary, to paraphrase George Orwell's fable of *Animal Farm* (1945), some systems are more equal than others. Which system is paramount in a given set of spatio-temporal parameters is not pre-determined (not even by some logic of 'the last instance that never comes') but is contingent on the prevailing societal project and structuring principles and the capacities of its associated institutional and spatio-temporal fixes to displace and/or defer problems beyond these parameters.

For present purposes, societal projects can be understood as instances of the broader notion of social imaginary. Imaginaries exist at different sites and scales of action – from individual agents to world society (Althusser, 1971; Taylor, 2001). There are many imaginaries, and most are loosely bounded and have links to others within the broad field of semiotic practices. Without them, individuals cannot 'go on' in the world and collective actors (such as organizations) could not relate to their environments, make decisions or engage in strategic action. In this sense, imaginaries are an important *semiotic* moment of the network of social practices in a given social field, institutional order or wider social formation (Fairclough, 2003). Imaginaries have many of the same features as discursive relations more generally. They are polysemic and heteroglossic, that is, they have alternative meanings and involve different voices and agents. This is both a source of the discursive power of societal projects (their capacity to mobilize different social forces in an unstable equilibrium of compromise) and a source of vulnerability (their susceptibility to critique and rearticulation into rival projects). This is another way of restating the paradox that provides the theme of this book. Where a societal project is hegemonic, it leads to the *sedimentation* of the resulting society effects, that is, to relative stability. But hegemony is continually liable to *repoliticization* of what is only ever provisionally taken for granted (cf Glynos and Howarth, 2007).

Imaginaries are most powerful where they operate across many sites and scales and can establish and connect local discourses and practices into a more encompassing hegemonic project.[4] In this sense, they become societal projects. They will be *retained* (discursively reproduced, incorporated into individual routines and institutionally embedded) when they reorganize the balance of forces and guide supportive structural transformation. Although any given societal project is only ever partially realized, those that succeed, at least in part, have their own performative, constitutive force in the material world, especially when they correspond to (or successfully shape) underlying material transformations, mobilize key social forces to form a ruling bloc, organize popular support, disorganize opposition and marginalize resistance.

This argument is closely linked to a second aspect of societalization. This concerns the emergent pattern of social interactions, including direct or indirect human interactions with the natural world. Structuration establishes possible connections and sequences of social interaction (including interaction with the natural world) so that they facilitate routine actions and set limits to path-shaping strategic actions. Whereas structuration refers to a complex, contingent, tendential process that is mediated through action but produces results that no actors can be said to have fully willed, structure refers to the contingently necessary outcome of diverse structuration efforts. In this sense, structuration creates a complex assemblage of asymmetrical opportunities for social action, privileging some actors over others, some identities over others, some ideal and material interests over others, some spatio-temporal horizons of action over others, some coalition possibilities over others, some strategies over others, and so on (Jessop, 2007c). Structural constraints always operate selectively: they are not absolute and unconditional but temporally, spatially, agency- and strategy-specific. Conversely, so far as agents are reflexive, capable of reformulating within limits their own identities and interests and can engage in strategic calculation about their current situation, there is scope for strategic action to alter the strategic selectivity of current structural configurations and thereby modify strategically selective constraints.

Where semiosis and structuration as forms of complexity reduction are complementary, they transform meaningless and unstructured complexity into meaningful and structured complexity. The social and natural world becomes relatively meaningful and orderly for actors (and observers) insofar as not all *possible* social interactions are *compossible* in a given set of spatio-temporal parameters. While there is usually massive scope for variation in individual transactions, the medium- to long-term semiotic and material reproduction demands of meso complexes and macro-social orders narrow this scope considerably. In a complex world there are many sites and scales on which such processes operate; for present purposes, what matters is how local sites and scales come to be articulated to form more encompassing sites and scales and how the latter, in turn, frame, constrain and enable local possibilities. If these are not to be random, unpredictable and chaotic, possible connections and sequences of action must be limited. This poses intriguing questions about the articulation of micro-social diversity to produce relatively stable macro-social configurations (Foucault, 1979b [1981]; Wickham, 1983; Bourdieu, 1990; Luhmann, 1992, 1996; Jessop, 2007c).

Recursive selection of semiotic practices and extra-semiotic processes at these scales tends to reduce inappropriate variation and thereby secure the 'requisite variety' (constrained heterogeneity rather than simple uniformity) that supports the structural coherence of a stable social order. Many other meanings are thereby excluded and so are many other possible social worlds. Stable semiotic orders, discursive selectivities, social learning, path dependencies, power relations, patterned complementarities and material selectivities all become more significant, the more that material interdependencies and/or issues of spatial and intertemporal articulation increase within and across diverse functional systems and the lifeworld. This does not exclude competing imaginaries for different scales and fields of social action or indeed, rival principles of societalization more generally. All it means is that they are marginalized, subject to a logic of negative integration (not 'rocking the boat') and persist as useful sources of irritation and flexibility. Just stating the conditions for macro-social order reveals the fragility and indeed, improbability of the smooth reproduction of complex social orders. Yet they do exist.

Institutional fixes

Two key concepts that note the role of agency and strategy in resolving contradictions and dilemmas are 'institutional fix' and 'spatio-temporal fix'. These both emerge, to the extent that they do, in a contested, trial-and-error process, involving different economic, political and social forces and diverse strategies and projects, and they typically rest on an institutionalized, unstable equilibrium of compromise.

An institutional fix is a complementary set of institutions that, via institutional design, imitation, imposition or chance evolution offer (within given parameters) a temporary, partial and relatively stable solution to the coordination problems involved in securing economic, political or social order. Nonetheless, it is not purely technical but rests, at best, on an institutionalized, unstable equilibrium of compromise and at worst, on the open use of force. Rather than providing a post hoc solution to pre-given coordination problems, it is partly constitutive of this order. Such a fix can also be examined as a spatio-temporal fix (or STF), and vice versa (the following definition differs from that offered by David Harvey, 1982; see Jessop, 2006).

STFs set spatial and temporal boundaries within which the always relative, incomplete and provisional structural coherence (and hence the institutional complementarities) of a given order are secured, in so far as this ever occurs. One of their key contributions is to externalize the material and social costs of securing such coherence beyond the spatial, temporal and social boundaries of the institutional fix by *displacing* or *deferring* them (or both) in more or less complex sociospatial ways that can be analysed using the territory, place, scale, network (TPSN) schema. Such fixes delimit the main spatial and temporal boundaries within which relative structural coherence is secured and displace certain costs of securing this coherence beyond these boundaries. The primary sociospatial moments and temporal horizons around which fixes are built and their coherence vary widely over time. This is reflected in the variable coincidence of different boundaries, borders or frontiers of action and the changing primacy of different scales in complex configurations of TPSN relations.

Institutional fixes work in part because, in strategic-relational terms, institutions have distinctive discursive-material selectivities, favouring some actors, alliances, identities, interests, projects, spatio-temporal horizons, and so forth, over others; they are linked with specific technologies of governance; and they are articulated into specific institutional orders and ensembles that create specific forms of domination (Jessop, 2007c). In this sense, institutions matter. Different modes of societalization may have their own institutional fixes that provide the strategically selective framework in which their respective hegemonies or domination may be secured. Here we focus on the case of capitalist societalization. While many institutions that belong to an institutional fix are related to the fundamental categories of the capital relation noted above (and further explored below), their specific forms and logics, their particular patterns of selectivity and their most likely points of rupture and fragility are irreducible to these basic categories. This requires a more detailed institutional analysis, but one that does not forget that these are institutional fixes tied to capitalist societalization and not to the production of 'society effects' in general.

Spatio-temporal fixes

An institutional fix can also be examined as an STF, and vice versa. The notion of *spatio-temporal fix* is an important complement to (or better, a dimension of) *institutional fixes* insofar as they partly overlap. STFs establish spatial and temporal boundaries within which the always relative, incomplete and provisional structural coherence (and so, institutional complementarities) of a given order are secured – to the extent that this is ever the case.[5] A key contribution of STFs is externalizing the material and social costs of securing such coherence beyond the spatial, temporal and social boundaries of the institutional fix by *displacing* and/or *deferring* inherent or contingent problems elsewhere and/or into the future. These fixes externalize the material and social costs of securing coherence beyond specific spatial, temporal and social boundaries, such that zones of relative stability depend on instability elsewhere. Even within 'internal' boundaries, some classes, class fractions, social categories or other social forces located within these spatio-temporal boundaries are marginalized, excluded or subject to coercion. This can be analysed inter alia from the viewpoint of civic stratification (Lockwood, 1999). STFs thereby only *appear* to harmonize contradictions, which persist in one or another form. Such regimes are partial, provisional and unstable, and attempts to impose them can lead to 'blowback' at home as well as abroad.

Each sociospatial organizing principle has its own forms of inclusion–exclusion and entails differential capacities to exercise state powers. This opens a strategic field in which social forces seek to promote different modes of sociospatial organization to privilege their ideal and material interests. Regarding the state in its narrow, juridico-political sense, examples include gerrymandering constituency boundaries, voter suppression, promoting or weakening place-based uneven development and centre–periphery inequalities, reordering scalar hierarchies and scale jumping, and organizing parallel power networks that crosscut formal vertical and horizontal divisions of power within and beyond the state.

These distinctions are useful in exploring how institutional and spatio-temporal fixes contribute to the overall *régulation*-cum-governance of the capital relation. Specifically, contradictions and their associated dilemmas may be handled through:

- *Hierarchization*, treating some contradictions as more important than others.
- *Prioritization* of one aspect of a contradiction or dilemma over the other aspect.
- *Spatialization*, relying on different scales and sites of action to address one or another contradiction or aspect or displacing the problems associated with the neglected aspect to a marginal or liminal space, place or scale.
- *Temporalization*, alternating regularly between treatment of different aspects or focusing one-sidedly on a subset of contradictions, dilemmas or aspects until it becomes urgent to address what had hitherto been neglected.

Different patterns of societalization can be distinguished, based on the weights attributed to different contradictions and dilemmas (hierarchization), the importance accorded to their different aspects (prioritization), the role of different spaces, places and scales in these regards (spatialization), and the temporal patterns of their treatment (temporalization). In all cases, because the societal order is reproduced – when it is – through social agency and entails specific forms, stakes and sites of conflict and struggle, the relative importance of contradictions and dilemmas is not structurally inscribed or strategically pre-scripted.

Last, but not least, because the basic contradictions and dilemmas are incompressible, even if modified in specific stages and/or varieties of capitalism, all fixes will be incomplete, fragile and impermanent. When the circuit of capital breaks, for whatever set of causes, space opens for struggles over different trajectories.

An important caveat is needed here. To paraphrase Marx in the 1857 'Introduction' to the *Critique of Political Economy*, 'there is no contradiction in general, there is also no general contradiction' (1973b).[6] Continuing the paraphrase, each contradiction has its own aspects and is actualized in its own ways in particular institutional and spatio-temporal contexts, giving rise to a complex, overdetermined, contradictory and multiply dilemmatic ensemble of social relations. These arguments imply that no regime has just one (fundamental) contradiction that must be regulated and/or governed appropriately to ensure continuing accumulation. The relation among contradictions and dilemmas is not mechanically additive but reciprocally, albeit asymmetrically, overdetermined: they are not simply aggregated as 'so many potatoes in a sack' but modify each other in distinctive ways. Their significance varies, posing differently configured sets of *régulation*-cum-governance problems at different sites and scales (cf Gough, 1991, 2004). The asymmetries can be analysed by deploying three key concepts elaborated by Althusser, inspired by Mao Zhe Dong: (1) the distinction between the *principal contradiction* and other, *secondary contradictions* in a given social order, with their articulation being complex and overdetermined rather than simple and set exclusively by the principal contradiction; (2) the distinction between the *primary* aspect and the *secondary* aspect of a given contradiction in a given conjuncture, that is, which of its poles is more problematic for expanded reproduction; and (3) the *uneven development* of contradictions, that is to say, changes in the principal and secondary contradictions and their primary and secondary aspects (Althusser, 1965).

The prevailing strategies modify each contradiction, with the result that they are mutually presupposed, interiorizing and reproducing in different ways the overall configuration of contradictions. Different configurations can be stabilized based on the weights attached to (1) different contradictions and dilemmas and their dual aspects, (2) the counterbalancing or offsetting of different solutions to different contradictions and dilemmas, (3) different patterns of social conflict and institutionalized compromise, (4) differences in the leading places and spaces for accumulation, and (5) the changing prospects of displacing and/or deferring problems and crisis tendencies. The complex structural configuration of a given accumulation regime depends on institutional and spatio-temporal fixes that *establish* the primacy of one or more contradictions and assign a primacy for governance to one rather than another of its aspects. Other contradictions are regularized or governed according to how they complement the current dominant contradiction(s). Nonetheless, these fixes are not 'magic bullets': they cannot eliminate contradictions and dilemmas and, whatever their capacity to temporarily 'harmonize' or reconcile them, they create the conditions for the next crisis.

Neither institutional nor spatio-temporal fixes are solely concerned with the state system or with state powers or governance more generally. They are nonetheless fundamental features of the state in its narrow and integral senses, and in addition, the state system and the activation of state powers shape institutional and spatio-temporal fixes more generally. The same holds for the modalities of governance.

Multispatial metagovernance

An important aspect of governance success (or more precisely, conveying the impression thereof) is the discursive and institutional framing of specific STFs within which governance problems appear manageable because certain ungovernable features manifest themselves elsewhere. Two corollaries are that *current* zones of *stability* imply *future* zones of *instability* and that zones of stability *in this place* imply zones of instability *in other places* – including within a given zone of stability that is internally differentiated and stratified. Indeed, capacities to defer and displace problems were one source of 'steering optimism' in early governance and metagovernance literatures, especially when reinforced by the ability to engage in a *fuite en avant* by producing new fixes to escape the consequences of past failures. These attempts may not work and can cause 'blowback'.

While contradictions, dilemmas and antagonisms cannot be reconciled permanently, they may be moderated – partially and provisionally – through mechanisms and projects that prioritize one aspect of a contradiction, one horn of a dilemma, or just some interests over others with resulting asymmetrical effects. This can be achieved 'ideally', at least in the short run, by successfully presenting specific, necessarily selective solutions as the expression of an (always illusory) general interest. In other cases, the 'resolution' will involve more visible, even forceful, strategies and tactics.

This is a contested process, involving different economic, political and social forces and diverse strategies and projects and this, in turn, is one source of the instability of institutional and spatio-temporal fixes that are consolidated, if at all, only provisionally and partially, and that are always the product of a temporary unstable equilibrium of compromise. It is also fractal. That is, at whatever scale of analysis we adopt, we find competing, contrary and contradictory attempts to establish organizational, institutional and spatio-temporal fixes on many sites, with alternative targets of government and/or governance, using different kinds and combinations of sociospatial organizing principles and strategies, intended to serve different kinds of ideal and material interests, and reflecting different sets of social forces.

This poses a series of challenges, for actors as well as observers, on how to reconcile micro-social diversity and a contingent macro-social order. If a strategic line rather than chaos can be discerned, this may be related to relatively successful metagovernance practices pursued in the context of specific institutional and spatio-temporal fixes that privilege some interests and strategies over others and, for a time, displace or defer the conflicts, contradictions and crisis tendencies associated with these fixes.

Metagovernance in the shadow of hierarchy

Combining Gramscian and Foucauldian perspectives with the polity–politics–policy distinction, I suggest that state power can be analysed as 'government + governance in the shadow of hierarchy' (see Chapters 6 and 7). It shifts attention from the state as a juridico-political apparatus formally at the heart of the polity to the various modalities of state power considered in broader, integral terms. This shift also requires attention to politics and policy. Overall, this reinterpretation implies that state power: (1) extends beyond coercion, imperative coordination and positive law to include other ways in which the state can mobilize active consent or passive compliance from forces situated and/or operating beyond the state in its narrow juridico-political sense; and (2) includes efforts by the state to strategically rebalance modes of government and governance – including their spatio-temporal aspects – to improve the effectiveness of direct and indirect direct state intervention in and across different social fields.

Metagovernance practices may develop in response to the tendency of all forms of governance and associated policies to fail (market failure, state failure, network failure or collapse in solidarity), leading to attempts to redesign them, or it may occur because certain social forces wish to rebalance modes of governance. Metagovernance occurs at many sites and scales as governance problems or the shifting balance of forces prompt efforts to improve governance or change its strategically selective impact on ideal and material interests.

Because governance and government mechanisms coexist in a complex sociospatial matrix, success in regard to political redesign, politics or policies in one dimension of this matrix may depend on practices and events in other dimensions. Different government and governance mechanisms may also have different temporal horizons with a corresponding potential for disjunctions that may undermine the viability of any given mechanism.

Building on these ideas, we might argue that governance (in its narrow sense of heterarchy) and metagovernance depend on the organization of reflexive self-organization among multiple stakeholders across several scales of state territorial organization and indeed, in diverse extra-territorial contexts. In this context, the state's role (at any scale) is that of *primus inter pares* in a complex, heterogeneous and multilevel network rather than that of *the* sovereign authority in a single hierarchical command structure. Further, its primary contribution is as one actor-cum-stakeholder among others that can contribute distinctive resources to governance arrangements and projects that may originate beyond the state. In this context, formal sovereignty is better seen as a series of symbolic and material state capacities than as an overarching, dominant resource. Other stakeholders contribute other symbolic or material resources (for example, private money, legitimacy, information, expertise, organizational capacities or the power of numbers) to be combined with states' sovereign and other capacities to advance collectively agreed (or accepted) aims and objectives. Thus, states' involvement in MLG thereby becomes less hierarchical, less centralized and less directive and, compared to the clear hierarchy of territorial powers theoretically associated with sovereign states, it typically involves tangled hierarchies and complex interdependence. In addition, work on MLG and the network polity poses fundamental issues about how far a network polity will remain tightly anchored in territorial terms (as opposed to being necessarily territorially embedded) despite its highly pluralistic functional concerns and its equally variable geometries. Scalar-specific regulations also act as buffers to reduce conflicting articulation among different geographical production/reproduction systems.

Three further sets of remarks will help to put governance and metagovernance in their place within an SRA. First, governance is certainly not a purely technical matter limited to specific problems defined by the state (or other social forces) that can be solved by experts in organizational design, public administration and public opinion management. This is not only because of the 'wicked problems' generated by a complex world, but also because governance (and, *a fortiori*, metagovernance) practices involve not only specific political and/or policy outcomes in particular political and policy fields but also have broader effects on state capacities. They modify the available mix of government and governance techniques and change the balance of forces. Indeed, those engaged in metagovernance may redraw the inherited public–private divide, alter the forms of interpenetration between the political system and other functional systems, and modify the relations between these systems and civil society in light of their (perceived) impact on state capacities.

Second, while collibration is a core meta-political activity of states, it is often hotly contested because of competing metagovernance projects and competing interests mobilized behind them. This requires some flexibility in the exercise of state powers in terms of particular functions and the impact of state intervention (or non-intervention) on partisan and global political advantage. This is related in the last resort to the declaration of states of emergency, which give extraordinary powers to state officials to reorder government and governance arrangements.

Third, Offe once noted that modes of policy-making are better for some purposes than others and that, as policy objectives change, so would the best mode (Offe, 1975b). Nonetheless even appropriate forms have their own problems and generate others in turn. Offe asked how the state apparatus survives in the face of these tendencies towards policy and state failure. His answer was that it does so through a continual *fuite en avant*. In other words, it escapes from an emerging crisis in one mode of policy-making by moving to another, even though that is also likely to fail. His argument can be extended to modes of governance and hence, to the need for specific institutional and spatio-temporal fixes that provide temporary, provisional and partial solutions to these challenges.

These remarks remain underdeveloped at two levels. First, the general remarks still require development in terms of other modes of societalization, that is, in relation to the fragility of segmentation and core–periphery relations as bases of societalization, as well as in relation to hybrid forms of societalization. Second, my observations on capitalist societalization imply that modern societies (social formations dominated by functional differentiation) are not necessarily organized in terms of a capitalist logic. But this is not elaborated, and it would be important to explore the nature and conditions of other principles of societalization, such as national security, juridification, religion, or crosscutting functional systems, a social order based on ethnic or 'racial' stratification (such as an apartheid regime). This, in turn, poses the problem of whether all possible modes of societalization are equal or some are more equal than others.

Concluding remarks

This chapter concludes Part I of the presentation, and has introduced the modalities of governance, forms of governance failure, metagovernance and modes of metagovernance failure. It took a contrarian position that posited the failure of different forms of governance rather than assuming that any and all of them work. Different forms fail in different ways that reflect the respective logics of governance and make it possible to believe that another mode will solve the respective problems of a given mode. Often this means that the new mode seems superior to the replaced mode when judged by the latter's logic but may not prove superior when judged by the criteria of the new mode. It takes time to learn the problems of new modes. These are problems that may appear to be solved at a local level and are the basis for 'steering optimism' because there may be discursive and semantic, institutional and spatio-temporal fixes that makes local modes viable. The problems arise when one considers the compossibility of different modes over different scales, terrains and interests, and the prospects of securing compatibility among these when so many actors have stakes in designing macro-social order, whether at the national level or on a wider scale. We now turn to the WISERD project which is concerned mainly with specific instances of governance in the spatial framework of Wales and comparisons with other countries in the UK, in European space, and more generally. This is why Part I focused on more general issues of governance, governance failure, metagovernance and metagovernance failure. This will enable readers to locate the weaknesses as well as strengths of the WISERD Civil Society programme during its development.

PART II

Locating civil society as a mode of governance

5

Locating the WISERD Project: Public policy governance towards common good

Governance is said to be one of the public–private spheres of activities that are essential for the flourishing of a stronger civil society. It is seen to comprise new forms of relationship that can transform an arena of 'unstructured complexity' that covers the corporate and public spheres (Osborne, 2010: 6) into more structured complexity. This is the form of meta-heterarchy discussed in Part I of this book, which is concerned to reorder networks, reorganize the conditions of self-organization and promote new forms of dialogue. This reorganization can allow the formation of public governance that is more concerned with the creation and governing of public policy and initiatives. Its first-order roles are to address societal problems and enhance policy opportunities (Osborne, 2010: 80) for the building of possible common goods and to enlarge civil society.

Origins of WISERD

The Wales Institute for Social & Economic Research Data & Methods arose from a series of long-standing and distinctive research collaborations within Wales. Its origin was an earlier bid for a Wales Institute of Economic and Social Research (WISER), which aimed to build capacity around usage of Welsh data and to conduct research into geography and locality, regeneration and Welsh governance. Following advice from the Higher Education Funding Council for Wales and the Economic and Social Research Council (ESRC), the proposal was revised to include colleagues with significant quantitative experience and to consider ways in which joint funding could be awarded through integration of the WISER bid with a continuation of the methodological and research capacity-building work of the existing Cardiff-based unit, QUALITi, funded from 2005–08 by the ESRC as a Node of the National Centre for Research Methods (NCRM). QUALITi was a research unit at Cardiff University that focused on innovation, improvement and impact in qualitative research methods, especially concerning the social contexts in which research methods and methodologies are situated. By bringing QUALITi and WISER together, WISERD was created as a collaborative venture between the research-intensive universities of Aberystwyth, Bangor, Cardiff, South Wales and Swansea.

Its aims can be described as:

- To build and develop existing expertise in quantitative and qualitative research methods and methodologies
- To develop and integrate a coherent set of research data relating to Wales
- To build networks of researchers and research capacity across Wales in the economic and social sciences, as well as contributing to UK-wide research capacity building
- To explore the relationships between research data, research methods and the development and understanding of policy
- To develop a sustainable increase in the quantitative research base across the social sciences in Wales through academic appointments and training
- To increase collaborative interdisciplinary research grant applications and interaction with policy-makers and the private sector through consultancy.

The research agenda of the first phase of WISERD was made up of five independent but interconnected research programmes: knowing localities and local knowledge in context; quantitative research; data integration and management; training and capacity building; and policy analysis and evaluation (cf Beynon, 2016: xvi).

WISERD's Civil Society programme emerged later, initially for 2014–19. It was an ESRC research centre that undertook a five-year, multidisciplinary programme of policy relevant research addressing civil society in Wales, the UK and internationally. It was renewed for a further five years in 2019–24 with the remit to develop and extend the policy-relevant research from the first Civil Society programme. It was to undertake a new programme of work to transform understanding of how civil society is affected by forms of civil exclusion and expansion, civic loss and gain and the potential for civil society organizations (CSOs) to play a key role in civil repair. This is reflected in the Centre's name for the second period: WISERD Civil Society Centre: Civic Stratification and Civic Repair. The Centre's research aims to produce new evidence on the changing nature of civil society at local, regional, national and international levels. In addition, the programme aims to describe and explain the impact of social change on local forms of civil society and CSOs, and to examine what this means for social cohesion and wellbeing.

WISERD Civil Society extends to co-investigators from 12 UK universities as well as international collaborators in Europe, North America, China, India and Australia. It also works in close partnership with colleagues from the public, private, policy and third sectors (WISERD ESRC Centre on Civil Society, 2014: passim).

The first phase of the Civil Society Centre included a suite of 23 research projects, addressing four key thematic areas:

- Locality, community and civil society
- Individuals, institutions and governance
- Economic austerity, social enterprise and inequality
- Generation, life course and social participation.

The projects explore a series of policy- and practice-relevant themes that impact on civil society at local, regional and national levels. These include education, volunteering, wellbeing, ageing, governance and diversity:

> WISERD/Civil Society research will aim to inform our understanding of the changing nature of civil society in the context of devolved government and processes of profound social and economic change. Furthermore, because of its size and devolved government, Wales offers a unique context for studying these issues. Viewing Wales as a "laboratory for social science", the centre will build on existing networks of researchers who have a wide range of expertise and skills. (Professor Ian Rees Jones, WISERD Director, cited in WISERD, 2014)

Ian Rees Jones said of the second phase of the Centre:

> One of our key strengths is the ability to jointly undertake research with civil society partners, such as charities and our local communities. This award gives us the opportunity to further strengthen these partnerships and networks, in the UK and internationally, and deliver an exciting and accessible knowledge exchange programme over the next five years. (cited in WISERD, 2019)

A WISERD Civil Society Centre launch pamphlet reports that the second phase programme:

> Through the production of new empirical evidence and analysis ... will address many of the key challenges facing society, such as social and economic inequality, political polarisation and disengagement, migration and multiculturalism, the changing dynamics of work and the gig economy, and the impact of new technological innovations. (WISERD Civil Society, 2020: 3)

The second phase includes projects conducted under four key themes concerned with civic stratification and civic repair:

- Frontiers of civic exclusion and expansion
- Polarization, austerity and civic deficit
- Contentious politics of civic gain
- Material resources, social innovations and civil repair.

It also includes a separate crosscutting theme to address data infrastructure and data integration.

The first four themes in the second phase of the Civil Society Centre are concerned with civic stratification, a concept that derives from David Lockwood (1999) and builds on T.H. Marshall's concept of citizenship (1950). It focuses on how the structuring of life chances and social identities is the direct or indirect result of the institutionalization of citizenship under conditions of social and economic inequality (Lockwood, 1999: 532):

> Because the ethos of citizenship engenders expectations of equality and participation in public affairs that out-run its momentary practice, it seems appropriate to refer to action that is oriented to this realm of citizenship potential as "civic expansion", and to those seeking to establish new rights of citizenship as "civic activists".

While civic stratification is heavily influenced by the structure of social inequality, citizenship can be seen to exert a forcefield of its own. Four main types of civic stratification are distinguished by reference to citizens' differing enjoyment of rights, and abilities to exercise them, their social categorization by the rights they already hold and by their motivation to extend and enlarge them. The four types are civic exclusion, civic gain and deficit and civic expansion (Lockwood, 1999: 531):

> Civic gain refers to the various ways in which legal, formally universal entitlements confer unequal benefits on citizens according to their ability to make use of them; just as civic deficit refers to a lack of capacity in this respect.... An example of a power gain in the field of civil rights is that only the very wealthy can risk undertaking libel actions; the corresponding deficit being that only the very poor are eligible for legal aid. (Lockwood, 1999: 541)

Lockwood distinguishes three types of civic deficit: power deficit, stigmatized deficit and fiscal deficit. Power deficit refers to someone's inability to exercise rights because of an unequal distribution of capacities to do to. Stigmatized deficit occurs when citizens are deprived of their rights because of ascribed personal qualities that inhibit unified action. Fiscal deficit is illustrated by the poverty trap in social security, where high marginal tax rates means disproportionate losses when income rises (Lockwood, 1999: 537, 542, 545–6):

> Thus inspired, the research programme aims to transform our understanding of how civil society is affected by, responds and contributes to, forms of civil exclusion and expansion, civic loss and gain, and the potential for civil society organizations to play a key role in repairing the fabric of civil life. It addresses many of the key challenges facing society, such as social and economic inequality, political polarization and disengagement, migration and multiculturalism, the changing dynamics of work and the gig economy, and the impact of new technological innovations. (WISERD Civil Society, 2020: 3)

Civil society and common good

There has been a growing interest in civil society and its enlargement in recent decades Despite the growing literature, however, there is no definitive answer of what constitutes civil society. The term usually generates some positive feelings or images. Neera Chandoke (2009) called it a 'hurrah word' (or buzzword) that denotes a vibrant and harmonious sphere of society outside the state. These images date back to the 18th century to a period that Fred Powell called 'Enlightenment humanism' (2013). Building on a long history with its classical origins in Greek communal life of the *polis*, Enlightenment humanists raised the idea of civil society as a motor for democracy.

It focuses on the Scottish thinkers such as Adam Ferguson, whose *An Essay on the History of Civil Society* (1995 [1767]) sees civil society as crucial for maintaining a good society. It is an important site of societal change that can also bring about democracy. This site allows citizens to pursue personal and social good that is regulated by law and moral sentiments. With deliberation and association, diverse civil society groups can come forward and construct a public space within which they can pursue their interests in harmony with common goals (Jensen, 2011: 31).

These Enlightenment ways of thinking coexisted with more communitarian and left-leaning interpretations. For instance, in the field of communitarian thinking regarding welfare policies, civil society and its associations are crucial in keeping communities and societies together amidst complex social transformation (Powell, 2013). In the field of left-leaning social movement studies, civil society can deliver the radical task of driving society beyond neoliberal market-based modes of governance (della Porta and Diani, 2010). These idealistic views of civil society are criticized, for example, by Marx, as being an illusion that needs to be unmasked (see Chapter 6).

Despite its diverse meanings, the civil society concept maintains its buzzword status well into the 21st century with newly invented terms such as 'Big Society', social capital, social innovation, stakeholder engagement, partnership, social participation, community capacity, resilience, solidarity and the like, that cut across the right–left divide.

Public policy governance and the 'little platoons' of the WISERD project

Fred Powell's insights can be deployed to examine the nature of the WISERD project, especially its civil society dimension. For Powell, civil society is the nurturing of a public sphere for the common good with a policy-relevant dimension in the building of civil society. Contextually, the WISERD project is located in the conjuncture of global neoliberal changes, the development of national austerity and Westminster's devolutionary policy in Wales, Scotland and Northern Ireland. Devolution provides policy opportunities for the third sector to expand its role as a welfare provider in Wales. This sector is increasingly motivated by 'rights-driven' and interest-driven social groups, manifested in phenomena such as popular participation, assertive ethnicity, regionalism and issue networks (Conteh, 2013a). This rise in social involvement raised issues concerning the coproduction arrangements with citizen groups, subnational identities and transnational changes. Against this backdrop, WISERD is one such public policy governance project to (re)think and (re)map subnational-regional and civil society, especially on issues related to the policy delivery of health, education and welfare as well as policy questions of inequalities therein and beyond.

WISERD proactively develops multilevel connections with orders of government, five research-intensive universities in Wales, diverse third sector organizations (for example, the National Museum of Wales, Age Cymru, the Wales Council for Voluntary Action and the Council for Wales of Voluntary Youth Services) and national and overseas research and funding bodies. Given the complexity of the political and economic environment in which it operates, it institutionalizes a network governance framework to harness its civil engagement towards common good. Public policy governance of this kind navigates institutional boundaries to make connections across levels of government and to create and share ideas and resources with public and non-state actors (Conteh, 2013b). Its network governance framework allows the coproduction of expertise on regional knowledge (in comparative contexts) that is mapped via a multidisciplinary body of research that covers diverse themes on civil society in Wales and elsewhere. In order to navigate and span the boundaries between diverse institutions, actors and knowledge areas, it runs events, conferences, seminars series, workshops, newsletters and blogs to bring together academics, CSOs and other groups to come forward with critical knowledge and practices that are conducive to the building of Welsh social goods and wellbeing in the contexts of its devolutionary and global–regional changes.

This public knowledge sphere becomes an arena for multilevel public engagement, policy discussions and community participation. Its knowledge- and practice-building were four 'little platoons' with its main themes, subthemes and reviews (see Table 5.1) that explore the sociospatial and temporal processes associated with local community development, political engagement, social policies, welfare provisions, and so on. Together they facilitate the making of the organization of social space in which stakeholders can learn, coordinate and advocate policies related to the current devolutionary processes related to areas such as local community development, higher education, welfare provision, an ageing population, migrant engagement, inequalities, and so forth.

Let me explain the significance of some of these research themes in the first Civil Society research programme and then turn to projects scheduled for 2010–24.

Table 5.1: The four 'little platoons' of Phase 1 of the WISERD Civil Society research programme, 2014–18

Four 'little platoons' and their themes	Sub-themes and work packages	Examples of investigation
Theme 1: Locality, community and civil society	**Work Package 1.1 (2014–17)** *Researching civil partnership in Wales in place and over time*	Bowling together? Local civil society in a North East Wales village (2016)
	Work Package 1.2 (2014–17) *Redefining local civil society in an age of global interconnectivity*	Reconceptualizing comfort as local belonging (2016)
	Work Package 1.3 (2015–17) *Migrants, minorities and engagement in local civil society*	Research on A8 migrants in Welsh civil society, The city-region chimera (2016)
	Work Package 1.4 (2015–18) *Spaces of new localism: Stakeholder engagement and economic development in Wales and England*	
Theme 2: Individuals, institutions and governance	**Work Package 2.1 (2014–17)** *Higher education in civil society*	Giving something back? Sentiments of privilege and social responsibility among elite graduates from Britain and France (2016)
	Work Package 2.2 (2016–19) *Territoriality and third sector engagement in policymaking and welfare provision*	Gendered political space (2016)
	Work Package 2.3 (2016–19) *Education, language and identity*	Promoting a 'Welsh dimension' within education in Wales (2018)
	Work Package 2.4 (2016–19) *Building trust? Institutions and interactions of multi-level governance in the UK, Germany and France*	Political trust in France's multilevel government (2018)

(continued)

Table 5.1: The four 'little platoons' of Phase 1 of the WISERD Civil Society research programme, 2014–18 (continued)

Four 'little platoons' and their themes	Sub-themes and work packages	Examples of investigation
Theme 3: Economic austerity, social enterprise and inequality	**Work Package 3.1 (2014–16)** *Social enterprise in Wales, the UK and Europe*	Do social enterprises mean business? (2018)
	Work Package 3.2 (2016–18) *Implications of spatial and temporal variation in service provision for inequalities*	Investigating spatial variations in access to childcare provision using network-based Geographic Information System models (2018)
	Work Package 3.3 (2016) *Trade union membership: Associational life and wellbeing*	Trade union membership among the migrant community (2016)
	Work Package 3.4 (2016–18) *Equality, diversity and third sector welfare*	Research shows disability has lasting negative effect on employment (2017)
	Work Package 3.5 (2016–18) *Wellbeing, deprivation and social cohesion*	Regional pay? The public/private sector pay differential (2017)
Theme 4: Generation, life course and social participation	**Work Package 4.1 (2015–17)** *Generativity, social participation and later life*	*Continuïteit in familiebanden* [Continuity in family ties] (2015)
	Work Package 4.2 (2016–18) *The transmission of intergenerational capital in Wales: Language, religion and community*	Young people, family relationships and civic participation (2018)
		Engaging with the voluntary sector at gofod3 (2018)
	Work Package 4.3 (2016–18) *Ageing, serious leisure and the contribution of the grey economy*	What are the barriers to older people's participation in civil society? Grand parenting and the early years (2017)
	Work Package 4.4 (2017–18) *Social and cultural capital in later life*	
	Work Package 4.5 (2016) *Involvement of grandparents in the early years: A geographical comparison*	

Source: WISERD ESRC Centre on Civil Society (2014); WISERD (2015)

Research in the first research programme

Researching civic participation in Wales, in place, and over time (2014–17)

This project examined experiences of participation at the local level and changing patterns of mobilization in particular places in Wales. Fieldwork took place in the largely rural and Welsh-speaking area of North West Wales and in industrial South Wales in three stages: the research mapped local-level civil society groups; used life history/ narrative interviews to capture the experiences and biographies of key individuals who run local associations and who work to involve others; and engaged in participant observation of activities at each site. Particular attention was paid to trust in social organizations and how social identities and inequalities shape local civic relations. The project asked: what kinds of local civil society activities exist and what are their social and demographic determinants? How do civil society actors and organizations relate to communities experiencing structural inequalities? Why do some types of activity flourish and others are in decline? Do such types have discernible pathways? What has happened to those groups less suited to the contemporary period, and have others replaced them? (See, for example, Mann, 2016.)

Migrants, minorities and engagement in local civil society (2015–17)

Collective action is mobilized within places because they offer an appropriate scale at which regular direct participation by volunteers can be organized, and shared interests and identities defined. While new civil society groups may be formed, localities have also commonly an established cohort of civil society groups with dispositions towards humanitarian action, such as churches and trades unions, whose resources and networks may be enrolled. They may also connect to local government institutions, with civil society groups lobbying authorities to act practically or symbolically. Further, civil society groups may be mobilized to fill gaps in local government provision or response, for instance by directly sponsoring refugees. The three case study locations – Aberystwyth, The Mumbles and Splott – were chosen to indicate different geographical contexts, socioeconomic profiles and histories of civic and civil society activity, but not initially with specific regard for questions of refugees and asylum-seekers. Local civil society mobilizations for refugees developed networks of support and mutual exchange of advice informally and through organizations such as CitizensWales and Cities of Sanctuary Wales, as well as by working with national civil society groups such as the British Red Cross, while translocal support was also engaged through social media, with Bloom, for instance, reporting receiving donations from fundraising by churches in London (Guma et al, 2019: 98–9, 102).

Spaces of new localism: Stakeholder engagement and economic development in Wales and England (2015–18)

This project utilized a series of interviews and documentary analysis to explore the notion of stakeholder involvement in Local Enterprise Partnerships (LEPs), Enterprise Zones (EZs), City Deals and City Regions. Fieldwork occurred in four City Regions, two within Wales and two within England. One hundred semi-structured interviews were conducted. Two case study locations were selected in Wales, building on WISERD Phase 1 and on the localities research paradigm developed by geographers. These were the Cardiff and Swansea City Region and North East Wales to give a geographical comparison. Two case study locations were selected in England: Greater Manchester and Sheffield. Stage one involved desk-based analysis of national and local documentation on the 'new localism' and focused on LEPs, City Deals, EZs and City Regions. Stage two looked at the new localism in action in the four case study locations. Stage three connected to the academic and policy debates on the new localism and new localities: what policy, strategy and institutional changes have taken place, and are currently taking place, in the landscape of economic development since 2010 in England and Wales? What are the connections between LEPs, EZs, City Deals and City Regions? What narratives of devolution and community engagement are mobilized in these four types of locality? How are they worked into policies and procedures for stakeholder engagement? Who is involved in the new localism? What are the compositions of LEP, EZ, City Deal and City Region boards, and their subgroups and other structures of engagement? How successful is the new localism in realizing its objectives of economic and social empowerment? (See Beel et al, 2016, 2017, 2018a, b, 2019; Etherington and Jones, 2016; Jones et al, 2016.)

The research was sensitive to governance failure in its broad sense. Thus, Martin Jones writes:

Instances of regulatory failure across cities and regions, though, are becoming apparent, as state policy-making constantly switches economic problems in concerns of state rationality that can be more easily addressed through public policy. State actors appear to be continually reinventing policy initiatives, often in response to the problems and contradictions caused by previous rounds of state intervention, in a search to get things right. (Jones, 2019: 34)

He also noted a 'discernible shift' in the STFs in his case studies. This involved the path-dependent legacy of place-place state spatial strategies of the Victorians' localist era as it was replaced by the territory-place strategies of the spatial Keynesian welfarist era. Later, place-network and scale-network forms of neoliberal state intervention were dominant in the new localism and new regionalism. Network-place state spatial strategies seem to have become the preferred face of the new localism (Jones, 2019: 37).

Higher education in civil society (2014–17)

This project explored the relationships between participation in higher education (HE) and engagement in civil society, especially at the local level. More specifically, it examined the extent to which the institutional shift from an elite system of HE (up to the mid-1970s) to a mass system of HE (from the 1990s) has affected the roles that graduates play in the institutions of civil society. It also analysed the extent to which distinctive national (or more local) patterns in these relationships can be distinguished in the constituent countries of the UK. The project required a longitudinal design that compared the character of participation in (local) civil society for participants and non-participants in HE. Hence, there were four samples, which were derived from the British Household Panel Survey (BHPS) and Understanding Society, which is a systematic longitudinal study of people living in 10,000 households across the different countries in the UK. Semi-structured interviews with taken with two groups of graduates, one from the elite system and the other from the mass system. Supplementary analysis included analysis of the interviews conducted by WISERD (and others) with a subsample of National Child Development Study respondents (who entered HE in the mid-1970s) and reanalysis of the data generated by the major official reports on HE (see, for example, Power et al, 2016, 2018).

Territoriality and third sector engagement in policy-making and welfare provision (2016–19)

This project had three components. The first two combined archive work, case studies and interviews to investigate how the postwar territorial administration of the third sector in Wales has changed in response to shifting patterns and processes of governance, and how this has affected how third sector organizations shape and deliver new social welfare delivery models to implement the Social Services and Wellbeing (Wales) Act (2014). This legislation promoted third sector organizations in contrast with the equivalent English Act, which was more neoliberal and market-friendly. Results were published in the Ministerial Briefing Paper, 'Delivering Transformation in Wales: Social Services and Wellbeing (Wales) Act, 2014' (see Rees et al, 2017). The third component explored civil society's role in advancing human rights in the delivery of social welfare and other areas of public policy across a broad range of countries in Europe, Asia and Africa. It used discourse analysis to examine CSOs' critical views of state practices, as submitted to the United Nations (UN) Universal Periodic Review (see, for example, Chaney, 2016a, b).

Education, language and identity (2016–19)

The project used interviews and questionnaires to investigate the types of civic participation and conceptions of language and identity promoted within the statutory education system, and within CSOs working with young people, in both Wales and Scotland. After an inquiry with national-level elite policy-makers, a total of 120 follow-up interviews were undertaken – 60 in each country, drawn from the people who replied to a questionnaire. In addition, as part of fieldwork visits, the researchers undertook 20–25 interviews with teachers in schools and local leaders of CSOs to which young people belong. The research aimed to identify what understandings of cultural identity, especially linguistic identities, young people acquired from statutory and voluntary educational institutions: how, if at all, does the history of civic institutions impinge on young people's identities today? What is the relative importance of statutory and non-statutory institutions in shaping young people's identities? What role, if any, do devolved political institutions play in shaping young people's identities? How do the answers to all these questions vary by other factors that affect young people's identities – for example, gender, ethnicity, religion, place of residence and place of origin?

Building trust? Institutions and interactions of multilevel governance in the UK, Germany and France (2016–19)

The core research question was how far a pan-European convergence in norms of trust has emerged and its relationship to transparency. The research examined the interplay of trust and transparency within and between three EU states: the UK, France and Germany. The project focused on one region with a strong identity and one 'instrumental' region within each state to explore the impact of factors such as varying identities, institutional configurations and resource profiles on trust and transparency. Interviewees in Wales, Saxony, Brittany, South West England, Île-de-France and Hesse were drawn from functionally equivalent panels. Focus groups allowed for visual and oral comparisons of observable interactions in similar conditions in these regions: is there a pan-European convergence in norms of trust? Are certain types of democratic polity or national systems of multilevel governance (MLG) better equipped to retain trust than others? Are trusting relationships related to national systems of MLG, and the emphasis they place on the scale of governance or the proximity of decision-making? Does Europeanization engender more distant relationships across the policy spectrum? Or are these sentiments played out differentially according to the field of policy intervention? (See Chaney and Sophocleous, 2018; Cole, 2018.)

Social enterprise in Wales, the UK and Europe (2014–16)

This project used a range of econometric approaches to analyse entrepreneurial activity, the growth in social enterprise and the changing role of the third sector. Research focused on the early stages of entrepreneurial activity and on the survival and performance of small businesses in Wales (and beyond) to contribute to economic growth and, more widely, wellbeing. It looked at the survival of firms by using the Small Business Survey, aiming to differentiate between social enterprises and other start-ups, and used the Business Structure Database to examine job creation and job destruction and also productivity decompositions for Wales (compared with other UK regions): what sort of enterprise is displaying particularly significant birth or growth? To what extent are social enterprises increasing in Wales, and what are their characteristics? What determines the survival of small and medium enterprises in Wales compared to other regions of the UK, and are social enterprises more or less likely to survive? What is the scale of the contribution of these different forms to the nature and growth of employment and productivity? (See, for example, Clark et al, 2017.)

Implications of spatial and temporal variation in service provision for inequalities (2016–18)

The study analysed secondary sources of quantitative data (large-scale government social surveys) to investigate levels of social capital within communities in relation to changing levels of provision of key public services. A subset of these data was used to further investigate potential associations with small area variations in accessibility to services. The research questions were: which communities have high levels of social capital that could be harnessed to substitute for government or private provision and run services through community-based initiatives or help save facilities at risk of closure? Which areas have lower levels of social capital where existing levels of voluntarism or self-help are insufficient to respond to changes in provision leading to the possibility of increased spatial and social inequalities in accessibility to services? (See, for example, the database at Page et al, 2020.)

Trade union membership, associational life and wellbeing (2016)

This project built on previous WISERD research into geographical variations in trade union membership in Wales, which suggested that, in South Wales, collective understandings, rooted in an earlier period of unionization, are spilling over into the contemporary period (Beynon et al, 2012). The follow-up study investigated the concept of 'spillover' and whether geographical variations in membership levels are due to differences in the nature and activities of trade unions and the attitudes of employers and workers. It also considered how mechanisms of intragenerational and intergenerational transmission and geographical mobility relate to variations of trade union membership. The project examined how trade unions (and their form) contribute to other dimensions of social capital, and whether there is geographical variation in this. It studied 'spillover' in relation to three distinct groups: (1) rank-and-file trade union activists based in both the public and private sectors; (2) non-unionized young workers employed on 'non-traditional' labour contracts in retail, hospitality, food and drink (exploring the influence of the changing nature of the economy and work organization in establishments with a history of low trade union recognition and membership); and (3) migrant workers (in terms of how unions are adapting their structures and strategies to engage with this group).

The research asked: where in the UK are levels of trade union membership higher or lower than they expected after taking account of industrial structure and the composition of the workforce? Can differences in membership levels be attributed to differences in the trade unions (such as levels of activity, recognized versus non-recognized unions, the presence of shop stewards)? Can these differences be attributed to differences in the attitudes of employers to unions (for example, favourable attitudes towards unions)? What is the contribution of intragenerational and intergenerational transmission to explaining regional variations in trade union membership, what form does this take, and does the strength of these mechanisms vary geographically? What affect does geographical mobility have on trade union membership – does membership behaviour travel with the individual or is it shaped by the locality to which they move? Is trade union membership correlated with other measures of social capital and associational life, and does geographical variation in union membership contribute to geographical variations in associational life and social capital? (See, for example, Blackaby et al, 2018; Blakeley and Moles, 2019; Bryson and Davies, 2019.)

Equality, diversity and third sector welfare provision (2016–18)

This project used a mixed-methods approach, combining secondary analysis of existing datasets, case studies, documentary analysis and a series of interviews to investigate the impact of faith-based welfare provision on social cohesion. Primarily it used the British Crime Survey and data from faith groups and local government on levels of voluntarism and involvement of faith-based organizations (FBOs) in welfare delivery to help create a map of cohesion levels across Wales. The qualitative component involved a three-site case study using different locations in Wales to explore the role of FBOs in service delivery. The case studies combined semi-structured interview surveys with documentary analysis and secondary analysis of published data and reports. The semi-structured interview survey(s) added the perceptions of the relevant actors about any potential or perceived gaps between expectations and outcomes (see, for example, Johns et al, 2019).

Wellbeing, deprivation and social cohesion (2016–18)

This project used diverse econometric techniques to explore the relationship between the domains of individual subjective wellbeing, individual and household characteristics, work–life circumstances and a range of indicators related to the measurement of social cohesion and civil society. It considered the spatial diversity of subjective measures of wellbeing in the UK and how these have evolved. The aim was to develop a spatial index of social cohesion comprising distinct domains that include a measure of social capital, civil society and social exclusion. It modelled different domains of subjective wellbeing and considered how far different domains contribute to an overall measure of life satisfaction or wellbeing. It considered the effect that spatial measures of social cohesion and civil society have on subjective measures of wellbeing and their development over time. It examined the part played by 'people' or 'places' in explaining spatial variation in wellbeing and the extent to which measures of social cohesion and civil society mitigate the effects of personal circumstances typically associated with lower levels of subjective wellbeing (for example, deprivation measures including income, health and work poverty).

The transmission of intergenerational capital in Wales: Language, religion and community (2016–18)

This WISERD project explored the role of family in people's accounts of civic engagement, focusing on the values and behaviours that get shared between different generations. The project drew on survey data from three generations of participants from across South and West Wales to identify patterns of political, religious, social and environmental engagement. The research also incorporated a family tree-mapping exercise during qualitative interviews with a subsample of participants to explore the role of family in people's accounts of civic engagement. The result of the EU Referendum and perceptions of a 'generational divide' emerged as a prominent theme in participant interviews. These perceptions were linked to familial influences on young people's political engagement in relation to education and engagement with different medias (see Power et al, 2016, 2018; Fox et al, 2019; Muddiman et al, 2019; Taylor et al, 2019).

Ageing, serious leisure and the contribution of the grey economy (2016–18)

This project utilized a mixed-methods approach, combining a strategic review of existing survey data with ethnographic observation and interviews to make an original contribution to understanding the benefits of 'serious leisure' in retirement for the individual and for the wider communities of which they are part. The setting for the research was in Mid Wales. Four case studies were selected to represent a range of spaces (territorial and functional) in which serious leisure is variously engaged with by the over-60s: what value do non-working or retired people over 60 (as a heterogeneous) group attach to, and extract from, serious leisure pursuits as individuals and members of communities of interest? How do the varied trajectories of serious leisure engagements express and institute relations of social class? What is the value of serious leisure pursuits as part of the social and economic fabric of the communities and localities that play host to these pursuits? (See, for example, Doheney and Milbourne, 2017.)

Social and cultural capital in later life (2017–18)

This Work Package explored the importance of ageing and intergenerational relations for social participation and civil society. It used the lens of crime across the life course and the extent to which this, and the fear of crime, influence the ways in which older people are involved in their communities. It drew on critical writings challenging the 'myths surrounding ageing' to situate the debate surrounding the age fear-of-crime link. It undertook extensive secondary data analyses of several large-scale national surveys as well as relevant qualitative data sources. The research was underpinned by a 'life-span methodological framework' aiming to distinguish between age effects, cohort effects and period effects. This theme was explored with data at a Wales-wide level and compared with England and in the EU. The research asked: what do existing data sources tell us about ageing, social participation and civil society? How do narratives about active ageing influence narratives about barriers for participation? What are the barriers to older people's participation in civil society? Specifically, do perceptions of crime, in particular fear of crime, and the perceptions of young people influence older people's involvement in their community? How does ageing influence perceptions of young people, levels of fear of crime, levels of crime, social trust and views and expectations of the criminal justice system? Are expectations and attitudes linked to the life course or other factors such as place, health, status, levels of deprivation, transition into retirement, crime levels, and so on? Do existing theoretical frameworks for ageing have the capacity to account for social participation in civil society? (See, for example, Feilzer and Jones, 2015.)

Involvement of grandparents in the early years: A geographical comparison (2016)

This project utilized two key large-scale secondary datasets in order to undertake detailed analysis of what impact grandparents can have on their grandchildren's cognitive, social and emotional development. The Millennium Cohort Study is a study of children born in the UK in 2000–01. The sample in this study is over-represented with children from disadvantaged backgrounds and from the smaller countries of the UK. The other dataset was Understanding Society. Through this analysis, the project attempted to explore the complex relationships between social mobility, spatial mobility and intergenerational transmission. These datasets also allowed a comparison of urban and rural influences on grandparent involvement. The research examined: what are the interrelationships between grandparent involvement in the early years and other social, economic and geographical contexts? What association is there between the involvement of grandparents and early child development (cognitive and behavioural) at age three after controlling for other factors? What advantages and disadvantages are there to a child's development? What impact does grandparent childcare have on child development (cognitive, behavioural and wellbeing) after the age of five? How far do any advantages or disadvantages outweigh one another later in the child's life? Does the involvement of grandparents in the early years vary geographically? How does country and locality influence the involvement of grandparents in the early years? What are the policy implications of this analysis for early years interventions? (Chris Taylor and Jennifer May Hamilton conducted the research.)

Research in the second research programme

The second work programme is specified in a pamphlet issued by WISERD Civil Society Centre in 2020, organized by themes and subthemes.

The first theme, 'Frontiers of civic exclusion and expansion', will examine factors shaping civil society engagement with migration and forms of bordering through comparative international case studies and place-based ethnographies. It will also explore how civil society groups articulate social boundary activation mechanisms. In addition, it will examine new arenas for civic expansion by undertaking cross-national qualitative research to explore what factors shape individualism, and human and non-human relations in civil society, with reference to animal rights and welfare and artificial intelligence (WISERD Civil Society, 2020: 2)

The second theme explores 'Polarization, austerity and civic deficit'. Research on this theme focuses on formal and informal constructions of citizenship and utilizes an international comparison of the civic expansion of children's rights in four Western countries (including Wales), and how this can rebalance the civic deficits associated with childhood. A second subtheme focuses on identity and civic divides in the UK by examining the relationship between different forms of identity (disability, sexuality, religion) and political participation and wellbeing. It will consider whether identity groups experience differential abilities to exercise rights, and possible explanations for any differences (WISERD Civil Society, 2020: 3). In addition, there will be research on inequalities, civic loss and wellbeing using innovative methods to compare place-based and individual measures of accessibility and to explore how changing patterns of civic loss and gain relate to measures of health and wellbeing. This theme considers the impact of austerity and increasing economic and political polarization on different forms of civic loss (WISERD Civil Society, 2020: 3–4).

The third theme considers populism, conflict and political polarization by examining the links between shifting political behaviours and changes in employment structures, as well as how populist politics are fostered within places and how civil society can act to address this. Topics include systems of patronage within civil society and the connections between civil society, civic stratification and elite formation. What are the origins and destinations of patrons in CSOs and institutions, and what significance do different educational institutions and occupational profiles have in giving privileged access to elite positions within civil society (WISERD Civil Society, 2020: 5)?

A linked project explores trust, human rights and civil society within different territorial welfare mixes in China and the UK (WISERD, 2020: 5). And another project will study shifting forms of governance and the grassroots politics of separatism by comparing case studies in regions where separatist movements are in flux, to understand perceptions of and engagement in separatist conflicts from the bottom up. How do established structures and processes of governance get challenged by new civic demands and forms of mobilization as articulated through civil society (WISERD Civil Society, 2020: 4–6)?

The fourth theme involves the 'Contentious politics of civic gain' and social mobilization. Shifting dynamics of civic stratification and the marketization of social justice in the energy transition utilizes comparative case studies in the UK and Australia to explore how new, technologically enabled, transnational repertoires of social mobilization contribute to the shifting dynamics of civic stratification in the present age of uncertainty (WISERD Civil Society, 2020: 6).

Likewise, a study of trade unions, grassroots activism and solidarity uses case studies from Europe, India and the UK to examine forms of worker representation that are directly related to the changing role of women in work and society, and associated issues of civic gain and expansion. And another study will explore experts, expertise and citizen science by investigating the role of citizens and experts in democratic debates relating to science and the environment in a case study of air quality monitoring (WISERD Civil Society, 2020: 7).

Relatedly, there will be a study of the foundational economy, citizenship and new forms of common ownership. This explores place-based solutions and experiments with social mechanisms and new institutional forms that provide the material basis for citizenship to consider how the foundational economy approaches can promote civic gain and address contemporary social and economic policy concerns at regional and local levels, focusing on food, care, housing and the environment (preliminary results are published in Barbera and Jones, 2020). In addition, a project on 'Machines, platforms and capabilities' uses mixed methods to examine the significance of different sectors of the gig economy within local labour markets, and includes the study of cooperative alternatives to more dominant forms of platform capitalism (WISERD Civil Society, 2020: 8).

Also included in this fourth topic is research on place-based social innovation strategies for sustainable development drawing on regional policy studies in Wales, the UK and Europe, and action research in specific foundational sectors. It considers how far regional growth policies focus on foundational sectors and address inclusive growth through social innovation (WISERD Civil Society, 2020: 9).

Concluding remarks

At the time of writing (2019–20), many studies from the first phase of the research were still in press and not all segments of the first phase of research were conducted. The second phase of research on civic stratification and repair marked a shift in focus to the dynamic of class inequality and citizenship rights in liberal bourgeois democracies. The limited theoretical scope of the research to date is recognized in the concern with local studies that had a strong policy orientation and focused on the behaviour of individuals and households and cooperation with CSOs. Much of the first phase research involved secondary analysis of large datasets and/or semi-structured interviews. There was little engagement with the issues of metagovernance raised in Part I except insofar as attempts were made to use soft steering techniques to improve policy and its implementation within a Welsh context (Røiseland, 2007: 3).

Network governance can help to produce a political space that empowers citizens and enhances active citizenship in the expansion of democratic civil society. This citizenship-based mode of ethical governance is where democracy, equality and solidarity flourish, and these concerns are reflected in the second stage of the WISERD Civil Society programme. It can enhance alternative communities and even promote counter publics in the sociopolitical arena (Powell, 2013: 58–61) that may find themselves at odds with the public policy governance regime. The latter may not be free from the micro-political disciplinary and governmental powers that are discussed in Foucault and Foucauldian work (see Chapter 7 of this book). In addition, this form of more contestatory citizenship and related hegemonic discourses of 'governance' 'partnership' and 'empowerment' (Geoghegan and Powell, 2009) can be found in the more structural contexts in the remaking of neoliberal capitalism. This will be discussed in Chapter 6 on Marx's and Gramsci's work on civil society.

6

Locating civil society in Marx and Gramsci

Here I introduce the political economy of governance by sketching Marxian and Gramscian perspectives. This reflects the fact that Part I was primarily a sociological perspective in critical governance studies, that Chapter 5 presented a political and policy perspective, and that it is now time to present a radical perspective grounded in recognition of the capitalist character of the contemporary concept of civil society. This perspective was influential in Lockwood's critique of a class-based analysis as he showed the way in which citizenship played an independent role as a forcefield in civil society dynamics.

In Hegel's work civil society was presented as a *bürgerliche Gesellschaft* (bourgeois society) and saw its *bourgeois* (economic agent) character as dominant over the *citoyen* (citizen). For Hegel, the political consolidation of bourgeois society involves the subsumption of social struggle under an administrative form organized by the state (Neocleous, 1996: 14). Indeed, the police and corporations represent the penetration of the state into civil society, while the Estate assembly (comprising members of the Estates) represents the penetration of civil society into the state. This interpenetration of state and civil society follows from Hegel's understanding that the system of needs does not and cannot exist in a vacuum free from any 'interference' by public authority (Neocleous, 1996: 3).

This was criticized by Marx who saw the conflict between *bourgeois* and *citoyen* as requiring resistance to the state and by Gramsci who saw that civil society became more important in the 1870s as the masses gained the vote in their campaign for political rights. For both Marx and Gramsci, the separation between the economic and political spheres was a key feature of bourgeois societies. They argued that democracy could not be restricted to the political sphere but should also involve economic democracy. This has been called into doubt by the expansion of the world market and survival of national states.

The relevance of Marx

In introducing his 1859 Preface to the *Contribution to the Critique of Political Economy*, Marx wrote:

> My inquiry led me to the conclusion that neither legal relations nor political forms could be comprehended whether by themselves or on the basis of a so-called general development of the human mind, but that on the contrary they originate in the material conditions of life, the totality of which Hegel, following the example of English and French thinkers of the eighteenth century, embraces within the term "civil society"; that the anatomy of this civil society, however, has to be sought in political economy. (Marx, 1987: 262)

This poses the vexed question of the correct rendering of *bürgerliche Gesellschaft*: 'civil society' or 'bourgeois society' must be chosen according to context. Marx was discussing the views of Smith, Ricardo and their 18th-century predecessors about a 'society of free competition' (Marx, 1973b: 83). They referred to this as 'civil society', not 'bourgeois society', because they presented it ideologically as the creation of 'free' and 'equal' individuals having rights to their minds and bodies and possessions. Marx wrote mostly in German, and 'bourgeois society' is translated in 'scare quotes' indicating the term is somewhat problematical. The scare quotes indicate that, with *bürgerliche Gesellschaft*, Marx followed the standard German translation of the English term 'civil society' (cf Arthur, 2008: 253–4).

As George McCarthy observes, Marx worried that, in a society founded on two contradictory premises and systems of rights – the practical rights of the community and political participation on one hand, and the economic rights of property, egoistic liberty and maintenance of the class system (security) on the other – the latter will always prevail and destroy the former. The two systems of rights contradict each other and reflect the contradictions between human as a species being and 'citizen' and human as a bourgeois member of civil society. McCarthy (1990) argued that:

> One view of rights leads to the inclusion of people in the decisions that affect their daily lives, the development of their personalities and their own subjectivity, and the social constitution of themselves through the creation of their own laws and the furtherance of their own moral and political

education in the public sphere. On the other hand, with the natural rights of the private sphere, the citizens are stripped of any rights to participation, equality, and moral self-development – for these are reserved for the privileged few owners of private property and become impossible, given the imperatives of civil society. Thus, there seems to be a major conflict within the social system between competing rights. (McCarthy, 1990: 183)

Where Hegel's *Bürger* skillfully combines the bourgeois and the citizen, Marx reveals a "fundamental division" between the two. He separates the different features, pits them against each other, and finally demonstrates that the *citoyen* is treated as the "servant" of the egoistic *bourgeois,* while the "sphere in which man acts as a communal being" is degraded to the sphere in which he acts as a partial being.... What Marx "negates" is precisely not the *citizen,* but his/her degradation and subordination to the *bourgeois.* His target is not *civil* society, but *bourgeois* society. (Rehmann, 1999: 6; original emphasis)

Marx's views on the state were shaped by his critique of Hegel's *Philosophy of Right* in the 1840s and by his analysis of the separation within bourgeois society between the economic and political terrains. Hegel identified civil society as the sphere of bourgeois rights based on private property and juxtaposed this to the family and the state. The family was patriarchal and the state monarchical. Civil society was politically represented through corporations. Marx criticized this conception of the mediations in the modern state and emphasized the role of a free information press in developing a sense of public opinion: 'Thus, the free press becomes the organizing centre of the national or popular historical bloc in its struggle for cultural and political hegemony against the forces supporting the *ancien regime*' (Kouvelakis, 2008: 264). In this context, as Marx moved from liberalism to socialism, he came to understand that democracy should be extended from the political to the economic sphere. He did not reject the call to democratize the state, but argued that political democracy was a necessary, not sufficient, condition for freedom. The economic sphere must also be democratized. In 1843 and 1844, 'Contribution to the Critique of Hegel's *Philosophy of Law*' (1975a), 'On the Jewish Question' (1975d) and finally, in the 'Economic and Philosophic Manuscripts of 1844' (1975c) he confronted these problems.[1]

In the 'Contribution to the Critique of Hegel's *Philosophy of Law*' (1975a), Marx proposed that democracy is a politics rooted in the agency of citizens: 'In democracy the constitution, the law, the state itself, insofar as it is a political constitution, is only the self-determination of the people, and a particular content of the people' (Marx, 1975a: 31). He added that the '[t]he abstraction of the *state as such* belongs only to modern times, because the abstraction of private life belongs only to modern times' (Marx, 1975a: 32, original emphasis). In 'On the Jewish Question' (1975c), Marx extended these views. Here he emphasized that, while citizens are politically equal, inequalities in civil society undermine the possibility of autonomous action for most citizens. Marx argued: 'In the *political community* he [the citizen] regards himself as a *communal being*, but in *civil society* he is active as a *private individual*, treats other men as means, reduces himself to a means, and becomes the plaything of alien power' (Marx, 1975c: 154, original emphasis, cited in Mostov, 1989: 201).

Marx identified a fundamental contradiction between the political community, which pursues the common good, and civil society, where individuals pursue their self-interests. He concluded that inequalities in civil society undermine the possibility of democratic agency for citizens. Commenting on the French *Declaration of the Rights of Man*, he noted that the rights of man really simply protect private property; they create man as an 'isolated monad' whose competition makes cooperation for the common good become impossible (Marx, 1975c: 162-4). Social existence under liberal capitalism thus undermines the possibility of a genuine public life. None of the rights of man [sic] go beyond egoism. And the state is simply a means to private life (Marx, 1975c: 165–6). Thus, despite the language of the common good in liberalism, the liberal state ends up securing egoism. The right of private property cannot be generally enjoyed, so social cooperation becomes impossible, and the agency of citizens is undermined (Mostov, 1989: 201; Kouvelakis, 2005: 710). It follows that giving Jews the vote would not enable them to escape the domination of hierarchical social relations. Nonetheless, Marx never abandoned the position that political democracy is a necessary, although insufficient, aspect of his conception of freedom.

The 'Economic and Philosophical Manuscripts of 1844' (1975c) completed this democratic transformation in 1843–44 by providing a political economy analysis of civil society. Marx concluded that capital or property is a relationship, and that human emancipation requires that workers must be emancipated from capitalist production relations: 'The problems of alienation, poverty, and the lack of democracy for the working-class during the industrial revolution could only be solved by altering the economic – and thus the sociological – structure of society' (Niemi, 2011: 45). While this constituted Marx's break with liberalism, it did not mean a break with democracy. Later in his career, from *The Manifesto of the Communist Party* onwards, he would argue that collective (that is, democratic) control over the means of production would also be a necessary condition of freedom (Wolff, 2000: 113–15).

Marx on democracy and freedom

We can now interpret some of Marx's most famous passages, as found in *The German Ideology* (Marx and Engels, 1975) and *The Manifesto of the Communist Party* (Marx and Engels, 1976), about the relationship between democracy and freedom. Marx would argue that freedom involved a democratic alteration of the relations of civil society such that life opportunities were not to be determined by the hierarchical structure of civil society, production relations or alien market forces, but would be the product of social regulation aimed at human development. Hence, 'the first step in the revolution by the working-class is to raise the proletariat to the position of ruling class, to win the battle of democracy' (Marx and Engels, 1976: 504). This would be a step toward 'an association, in which the free development of each is a condition for the free development of all' (Marx and Engels, 1976: 506).

At this point, Marx embraced socialism through the recognition that democracy as a form of state governance was an inadequate shell for democracy. In the context of the Industrial Revolution, Marx observed liberal political theory as ignoring its own sociological preconditions – a theory that was incapable of assessing the problems associated with the consequences of its own civil society. The hierarchies of civil society made political democracy a mere 'lion's skin',[2] and prevented human development by liberalism's own standards. Such conclusions also informed Marx's political practice and interpretation of the significance of political practices.

Karl Marx and democratic practices

Workers must carry equal weight as citizens for their citizenship to enable meaningful, effective action (Mostov, 1989: 197). This necessarily involves a certain kind of civil society: the creation of an economic and social structure that would allow for autonomous action and equal opportunity for human development. As Marx put it in *The Civil War in France*, 'They [the working class] have no ready-made utopias to introduce *par décret du peuple*' (Marx, 1986b: 335). This would have to be worked out in practice. Nevertheless, Marx did articulate his views on democratic practices in at least two contexts that demonstrate the understanding of democracy argued for here: his essay, 'The Civil War in France' (1986b), and his writings about the operation of the International Workingmen's Association (IWA).

'The Civil War in France' (1986b) was Marx's history of the Paris Commune from the French Revolution of 1870–71. He viewed this as an example of working-class (and democratic) government, although he was disappointed that the Commune did not strike decisive blows. What did it do? It had a democratic structure based on decentralized governance: 'It was essentially a working-class government, the produce of the struggle of the producing classes against the appropriating class, the political form at last discovered under which to work out the economic emancipation of labour' (1986b: 334). Officials were elected based on universal [male] suffrage – 'elective, responsible, revocable' (1986b: 332). And he noted that they would be paid workmen's wages, in contrast to the pre-existing public agents of the 'parasitic' state (1986a: 537).

The Commune was the kind of society that Marx had in mind as a context for democratic governance. He hoped that it would create an egalitarian or democratized set of productive relations as a context for the exercise of equal citizenship and the ending of class domination:

> The Commune was therefore to serve as a lever for uprooting the economical foundations upon which rests the existence of classes, and therefore of class-rule. With labour emancipated, every man becomes a workingman, and productive labour ceases to be a class attribute. (Marx, 1986b: 334–5)

Hence, the communards, although not Marxists, exemplified democracy as a kind of society for Marx. Citizenship was not merely formal, as he had critiqued in 'On the Jewish Question' (1975d), but rather rested on an equal social foundation. While the Commune met a tragic end based on the cooperation of international armies to destroy it, it remained the model for equal citizenship in Marx's thought. Another significant practical context in which Marx advocated for the importance of democratic principles was the IWA. It was also a decentralized organization, which Marx insisted should be a place where different theoretical perspectives could thrive – although he would be put to the test on this point of pluralism. Most significantly, there would be no political litmus test for membership; the workingmen of each country were to decide the form and programme of their own movement (Marx and Engels, 1976: 505, 518–19; Ashcraft, 1984: 652). He famously rejected the development of parties and leaders separate from or not representing the labour movement itself, a position inherently critical of Lenin's later theory of the vanguard party (Marx and Engels, 1976: 497–8).

It was also in the IWA that Marx advocated universal male suffrage through his participation and work with Ernest Jones in the Reform League in London. This was some of Marx's most important political work accomplished during the agitations leading up to the Reform Bill of 1867. In the end he was disappointed with Reform League politics and the subsequent Liberal–Labour coalition because of their compromise in accepting the household suffrage. In short, Marx's advocacy for universal suffrage was unwavering (McLellan, 1973a: 345, 354; Nimtz Jr, 2000: 236). He further consistently supported republican political principles as well as civil liberties such as freedom of speech (McLellan, 1973b: 40; Springborg, 1984: 538).

While his *Critique of the Gotha Programme* (Marx, 1989) is sometimes taken as Marx arguing against democracy, his position is precisely the same as the one that he took in 'On the Jewish Question' in 1843 – that political democracy by itself is insufficient. He again insisted that political theory could not stand on its own if it investigated only the form of the state – as did liberal political theory (Ashcraft, 1984: 652–4). In the essay, he argued that while many of the demands for political rights had been achieved for (male) workers in the context of 1875, they were not meaningful to democratic agency without addressing the daily lives of workers. This also required democratization of economic structure, and he noted that rights were presupposed.

Marx concluded that liberal political theory, even as a good theory of the democratic state, could not solve the sociological effects of its own practices: economic exploitation, class inequality and domination, and ultimately an undermining of its own goals of the agency of equal citizens. This had two results. First, Marx abandoned liberal political theory for democratic reasons. Second, his critique shows democratic theory must have a social component. While liberal political theory advocates a state with *necessary* democratic rights, it errs in assuming that civil society is irrelevant to democratic agency or freedom and self-development or equal and effective citizenship (Ashcraft, 1984: 656–7; Graham, 1986: 184–6; Lockwood, 1999).

Disposable time

The condition for advancing civic expansion and inclusion is a challenge to the ecological dominance of capital accumulation in bourgeois society. The measure of wealth will no longer be labour time, but disposable time. Marx analyses this in *The Grundrisse*, which shows that in capitalist development 'real wealth is the developed productive power of all individuals. *The measure of wealth is then not any longer, in any way, labor time, but rather disposable time*' (Marx, 1973a [1857]: 708; emphasis added). Capitalism thus contains a 'moving contradiction' (Marx, 1973a [1857]: 708) that leads it to reduce labour time to a minimum even while postulating labour time as the measure and source of wealth (Howard, 2002: 283). And at that point individuals recognize that the free time they now have available to them in the new capitalism is not their own but that which comes to them as members of the collective social workforce (Howard, 2002: 15–16).

Marcello Musto notes that Marx did not entirely disagree that man was a *zoon politikon*, a social animal, but he insisted that he was 'an animal which can individuate itself only in the midst of society' (Marx, 1973b [1857]: 84; see Musto, 2008: 6). Thus, as civil society had arisen only with the modern world, the free wage labourer of the capitalist epoch had appeared only after a long historical process:

> The leaving behind of the ambiguity of the German *Bürger* enabled Marx to focus on the specific structures and mechanisms of modern bourgeois society: anonymous rule of exchange-value over use-value, of profits over human labor, commodification and reification of social relations, alienating structures of competition and exploitation, disastrous distortions of human forces of production, etc. (Rehmann, 1999: 11)

Antonio Gramsci

This account merits further development. Gramsci often regarded civil society as an integral part of the state and distinguished this usage from its Catholic interpretation, for which civil society is political society or the state, as compared with the society of the family and the Church (Gramsci, 1995: 75; 1975, Q6, §24: 703, cited by Texier 2009: 769). In his view, civil society, far from being inimical to the state, is, in fact, its most resilient constitutive element, even though the most immediately visible aspect of the state is political society, with which the state is all too often mistakenly identified. He was also convinced that the intricate, organic relationships between civil society and political society enable certain strata of society not only to gain dominance within the state but also, and more importantly, to maintain it, perpetuating the subalternity of other strata (Buttigieg, 1995: 4). Joseph Buttigieg, who fully translated the first eight *Prison Notebooks* into English, shows how Gramsci had already argued in the pre-*Prison* writings that 'the rules of the game were established by the dominant class and are themselves an integral part of what needs to be transformed before the fundamental principles of freedom and justice can be extended to the point of eliminating all forms of subalternity' (1995: 10).

Furthermore, Gramsci would go on to argue, the very fact that there exists a coercive apparatus to ensure compliance with the rules of the game itself indicates the non-universal character of the liberal or bourgeois state, notwithstanding its appeals to universal principles (Buttigieg, 1995: 10). Of course, for this state to become stable, the dominant class or classes must accept that the government apparatus cannot always assert their corporate interests narrowly and directly. It must maintain the fiction that the government of the state transcends class distinctions and can only do so if concessions are made to address the most pressing needs of disadvantaged groups and to accommodate some of their aspirations. Those excluded in this kind of state are allowed to aspire for power, but the prevailing *forma mentis* will induce them to pursue their goals in ways that do not threaten the basic order. In short, they will not aim to overthrow the state and establish a new kind of state, but instead will compete for a greater share of influence and power according to the established rules of the game (cf Buttigieg, 1995: 13).

It follows that revolutionary activity, for Gramsci, consists in a painstaking process of disseminating and instilling an alternative *forma mentis* by means of cultural preparation (that is, intellectual development and education) on a mass scale, characterized by critical and theoretical elaboration, and thoroughgoing organization (Buttigieg, 1995: 14). Gramsci's pre-*Prison* and *Prison* writings were intended to challenge 'the material organization meant to preserve, defend, and develop the theoretical or ideological "front"' (Buttigieg, 1995: 26, citing *Notebook 3*, §49).

> Civil society, in other words, far from being a threat to political society in a liberal democracy, reinforces it – this is the fundamental meaning of hegemony. It does not

follow, of course, that radical change is totally out of the question; what Gramsci makes clear, though, is that in a liberal democracy, one should refrain from facile rhetoric about direct attacks against the State and concentrate instead on the difficult and immensely complicated tasks that a 'war of position' within civil society entails. One such important task, as he points out in the same note, consists in "a reconnaissance of the terrain and an identification of the trench and fortress represented by the components of civil society"; in other words, one must arrive at a thorough knowledge of the intricate, wide-ranging, and capillary operations of the prevailing hegemony before devising strategies for supplanting it. (Buttigieg, 2005: 41)

Concluding remarks

This chapter has been concerned with the contributions of Marx and Gramsci to the appreciation of the role of civil society in liberal bourgeois democracies in the 19th and early 20th centuries. Marx was interested in the influence of the Hegelian concept of the state as the embodiment of the universal interest that synthesized this interest from the role of the market organized by corporate guilds and the civil society as embodied in the family. He argued that the state could not avoid being trapped in the tangle of private interests, and that only civil society could become a site for pursuing the public interest under the guidance of a political party that represented social forces that had nothing to lose but their chains. This claim was refined in his critique of the bourgeois state form and its institutional separation from the market economy and civil society, and he eventually saw the abolition of the economic–political separation as the key to a democratic future inspired by the experience of the Paris Commune.

Gramsci wrote during a period when popular forces had entered political life as important social forces (from the 1870s onwards) and needed to operate on the terrain of a state that comprised 'political society + civil society'. In contrast to the East, where the state was everything and civil society was weak and gelatinous, the West from the 1870s saw a state strengthened by its links with civil society. This altered the political strategies for a radical revolutionary movement, which required a long-term war of position to win popular hegemony plus a war of manoeuvre to destabilize the coercive power of the dominant classes. He cautioned his readers in the *Prison Notebooks* that this required a careful account of the structural bases of bourgeois power in the economy and the institutions of the state in its inclusive sense and how these were open to challenge in particular conjunctures.

While Marx had more fundamental insights in the nature of bourgeois class domination in the capitalist economy, Gramsci offered more insight into the modalities of the exercise of bourgeois hegemony in the modern era with its scope for civil mobilization. This makes him more relevant to the problems of political mobilization in liberal democracies and to the question of civic stratification and civic repair. In this sense, his work is more relevant to the modalities of the exercise of state power and civil society than Marx:

> On the one hand, there are more or less well defined "classes" identified through economic position, employment relations, life chances and "demographic" density; on the other there are more or less well defined categories of "citizens" identified through their different capacities to exercise various rights, their social categorization by the rights themselves and by their motivation to extend and enlarge them. Whether these two perspectives on the relationship between class formation and social integration are in competition or complementary is debatable. Class analysis does not claim to be able to explain socio-political class formation by reference simply to class position; and among the necessary additional factors that have to be taken into account the institutionalization and practice of citizenship may be thought to be the leading candidate. (Lockwood, 1999: 547)

Locating civil society in Foucault

As highlighted in Chapters 1–4 and elsewhere, there is no broad agreement on the concept of civil society. Its scope ranges from Enlightenment thinking to the critical perspectives put forward by Marx, Gramsci, Foucault and critical theorists. This chapter focuses on Foucault's view of civil society not as a historical given but as a mode of governance associated with changes in governmentality. In this regard, I distinguish Foucault's approach from the work of Anglo-Foucauldians, who refused to consider the state as the centre of control by political agents or classes in the exercise of power, legitimate or otherwise. Instead, they focused on the programmes and rationalities of government that work across multiple alliances between different actors – including those of the public sector, communities and community organizations, businesses and firms, and citizens themselves – and that enjoin these agents to take on certain forms of self-government and responsibility (Dean and Villadsen, 2016: 2). It is ironic, perhaps, that Foucault's Anglo-Foucauldian inheritors should end up favouring civil society politics over a state-based one, not least because Foucault himself was not only state-phobic but also suspicious of political action based on civil society (Dean and Villadsen, 2016: 3).

Foucault beyond Anglo-Foucauldianism

Building on Foucault's work, neo-Foucauldian scholars in the UK, Australia, Canada and the US contributed to what they called the 'Foucault effect'. Identified by Graham Burchell, Colin Gordon and Peter Miller (1991), the 'Anglo-Foucauldian' school is associated with scholars from these four countries. Peter Miller and Nikolas Rose, two of its key figures, write that it comprises 'an informal thought community that seeks to craft some tools through which to understand how our present had been assembled' (Miller and Rose, 2008: 8). Anglo-Foucauldians do not aim to be Foucault scholars but selectively[1] apply his initial insights on governmentality to new areas. They draw on *Discipline and Punish* (1977 [1975]) and the lecture on government from his 1977–78 course at the Collège de France, which appeared in English in 1979 (Foucault, 1979a; see also Foucault, 1991). This shared anglophone appreciation is reflected in the rise of a distinctive academic field: governmentality studies. The coherence of this field in the anglophone world rests on its narrow understanding of governmentality and resulting neglect of its place in Foucault's intellectual and political reflections. Indeed, it claims that: '[t]he analytical language structured by the philosophical opposition of state and civil society is unable to comprehend contemporary transformations in modes of exercise of political power' (Rose and Miller, 1992: 173).

Foucault's analyses of disciplinary power and governmentality marked just one step in an evolving intellectual project. Yet Anglo-Foucauldians tend to interpret them as a definitive statement of his opposition to macro theorization and relatedly, to any concern with how micro powers were assembled into bigger programmes and projects (cf Kempa and Singh, 2008: 340). Yet Foucault himself noted:

> I have not studied and do not want to study the development of real governmental practice by determining the particular situations it deals with, the problems raised, the tactics chosen, the instruments employed, forged, or remodelled, and so forth. I wanted to study the art of governing, that is to say, the reasoned way of governing best and, at the same time, reflection on the best possible way of governing. That is to say, I have tried to grasp the level of reflection in the practice of government and on the practice of government. [...] to grasp the way in which this practice that consists in governing was conceptualized both within and outside government, and anyway as close as possible to governmental practice. [...] In short, we could call this the study of the rationalization of government practice in the exercise of political sovereignty. (Foucault, 2008: 2).

This comment from a lecture delivered in 1978 suggests that Foucault was unwittingly distancing himself in advance from governmentality studies, especially as he also linked the emergence of governmentality or governmental practices to the macroscopic organization of the state and reflection on the government of government. He also argued for a combination of micro and macro analyses, presenting his later work on liberalism as a *scaling up* of his previous micro analytics of power to macro-level questions about the state and political economy (2008: 186; and see below). For good or ill, the Anglo-Foucauldian approach took shape in the early 1990s when many of Foucault's later texts on governmentality were unavailable in English, encouraging its early adherents to adopt a more micro focus in their development of

Foucauldian insights than might seem justified in the light of a broader understanding of his work in this area (Jessop, 2010b).

Thus Foucault's theoretical interests shifted from the microphysics of disciplinary society and its anatomo-politics of the body to the more general strategic codification of a plurality of discourses, practices, technologies of power and institutional ensembles around a specific governmental rationality concerned with the social body (bio-power) in a consolidated capitalist society. This opened a space for Foucauldian analyses of sovereignty, territorial statehood and state power and for less well substantiated claims about their articulation to the logic of capital accumulation.[2] As Mark Kelly (2009) notes:

> The concept of government appears in Foucault's thought as an attempt to deal with what his earlier analysis of power relations had deliberately bracketed, namely state power, as well as the other kinds of power which can be called governmental.[...] Having removed the state's status as the central concern of political thought in his earlier work, Foucault now moves towards understanding the state in the specific role that it actually does have in networks of power. (Kelly, 2009: 61, 61–2)

The scope for integrating the study of sovereignty, statehood and state power is reinforced when we recall Foucault's announcement that, if he could alter the title and theme of his 1977–78 course, he would no longer refer to '*security, territory, population*' but to the 'history of governmentality'. He would concentrate on 'government, population, political economy', which 'form a solid series that has certainly not been dismantled even today' (2007: 108). Thus sovereignty–territory–security moved to the margins of Foucault's theoretical concerns even though he acknowledged their continued importance into the 20th century. It is replaced by interest in: (1) government as a relatively new and certainly more important mode of exercising power than sovereignty, discipline, and so on; (2) population as the specific object of governmental practices (in contrast to the body as the anatomo-political object of disciplinary power);[3] and (3) political economy as the overarching object of inquiry and reference point for 'veridiction' that frames governmental rationality in the transition from the *administrative state* in the 15th and 16th centuries towards the self-limiting *governmentalized state* in the 18th century and beyond.

Foucault then proposed that, although the state has been overvalued as a cold monster and/or as a unified, singular and rigorously functional entity, it should nonetheless remain an important object of study. It should be approached as a 'composite reality' and 'mythicized abstraction' that has survived into the present because it has been governmentalized. He then elaborated this claim:

> ... it is likely that if the state is what it is today, it is precisely thanks to this governmentality that is at the same time both external and internal to the state, since it is the tactics of government that allow the continual definition of what should or should not fall within the state's domain, what is public and what private, what is and what is not within the state's competence, and so on. So, if you like, the survival and limits of the state should be understood on the basis of the general tactics of governmentality. (Foucault, 2007: 109; cf Mitchell, 1991: 78)

Foucault's interest here and in related work is different from that imputed to him by Anglo-Foucauldian scholars. He insisted in his earlier work, such as the first volume of the *History of Sexuality* (1979b [1981]), and in the three courses that directly or indirectly address the governmentalization of state power ('*Society Must be Defended*', 2003; *Security, Territory, Population*, 2007; and *The Birth of Biopolitics*, 2008) as well as in his so-called 'lecture on governmentality' (1991), not only that the state apparatus had a continuing importance as part of the general economy of power, but also that its overall form, its specific organization and its activities were shaped by the distinctive combination and the relative primacy of different forms of exercising power within and beyond the state. This approach influences the overall approach to governance and metagovernance in the current work.

In this regard, Foucault argued that the intelligibility of a given social phenomenon does not depend on the search for a cause but on the study of 'the constitution or composition of effects'. We should ask '[h]ow are overall, cumulative effects composed? [...] How is the state effect constituted on the basis of a thousand diverse processes?' (Foucault, 2007: 239; cf also 247–8, 287; 2003: 45). In short, Foucault was concerned with the 'state effect'. He wanted to explain how the state can act as if it were unified, as if it had a head even though it is headless (Dean, 1994: 156; cf Kerr, 1999; cf Jessop, 2010b: 62).

Foucault on civil society

The analysis of civil society must be located here, too. Indeed, for Foucault, civil society is populated by economic subjects, and he argued that '*homo oeconomicus* and civil society belong to the same ensemble of the technology of liberal governmentality' (Foucault, 2008: 296). He also stressed that the economic subject 'inhabits the dense, full, and complex reality of civil society' (2008, 296). This places civil society within a broader story about the 'governmentalization' of the state. He located the problem of how to govern civil society as one version of the emerging problem of government through self-government and thus linked it to liberal and Enlightenment thought. However, given the reemergence of *civil society* as a key term in the lexicon of contemporary governance, it needed to be explored more fully as, in Foucault's terms, 'something which forms part of modern governmental technology' (Foucault, 2008: 297).

In contrast to Marx and Gramsci, then, for political administration to be effective requires that the working class is reexamined not as a class but as a collection of atomized individuals. As objects of administration, individuals have to be recognized as subjects of right. Unsurprisingly, then, political administration developed alongside the expansion of citizenship and the extension of the franchise (Neocleous, 1996: 127). If we consider citizenship only through rights, we focus attention on the legal side of citizens' rights and obscure the importance of administration (Neocleous, 1996: 129). This also emerges in David Lockwood's critique of civic stratification, which pays particular attention to civic deficits rooted in ineffective administration and the need to engage in civic expansion and civic repair (Lockwood, 1999).

As Mark Neocleous (1996) remarks in this context:

> One can only understand the development of state power in Britain after 1832 through an understanding of the network of administrative apparatuses which serve to police civil society, subsume class struggle and mediate contradiction. The constant threat that civil society will be torn apart by its internal antagonisms requires that the state administer these antagonisms, to the point of constituting the organizations and subjects of struggle as part of the very action of the state itself. (Neocleous, 1996: 164–5)

Foucault's scalar perspective

In the 1977–78 lecture course, Foucault argued that the investigation of liberalism required movement beyond the microphysics of power to more macro analyses. He explains this shift in relation to his earlier concern with power relations as follows:

> What I wanted to do – and this was what was at stake in the analysis – was to see the extent to which we could accept that the analysis of micro-powers, or of procedures of governmentality, is not confined by definition to a precise domain determined by a sector of the scale, but should be considered simply as a point of view, a method of decipherment which may be valid for the whole scale, whatever its size. In other words, the analysis of micro-powers is not a question of scale, and it is not a question of sector, it is a question of a point of view. (Foucault, 2008: 186)[4]

So, the study of governmentality and the art of government need not be confined to the microphysics of power nor need the theorist privilege microphysics. Foucault's initial interest in micro powers reflected his concern with anatomo-politics and did not exclude alternative entry points into other topics (cf Gordon, 2001: xxv). Foucault's approach is *scalable* and can be applied to the state, statecraft, state-civil society or state–economy relations just as fruitfully as to 'the conduct of conduct' (Foucault, 2003: 138) at the level of interpersonal interactions, organizations or individual institutions. Thus, *The Birth of Biopolitics* is mainly concerned with macro-institutional issues and questions of government rather than specific governmental practices. Foucault traced the development of state projects and the general economic agendas of government over four centuries, noting how the problematic of government shifted during this period, and posed different problems at each turn regarding the limits of state power as well as about the rationales and mechanisms of such (self-)limitation. For example, Foucault notes that, whereas political economy leads to non-intervention in the economy but strong legal intervention in the field of *Ordnungspolitik*, totalitarianism subordinates the state to the governmentality of the party (Foucault, 2008: 106–17). Commenting on this perspectival shift, Michel Senellart (2008) argues that:

> … the shift from "power" to "government" carried out in the 1978 lectures does not result from the methodological

framework being called into question, but from its extension to a new object, the state, which did not have a place in the analysis of the disciplines. (Senellart, 2008: 382)

In contrast to the warm embrace by Anglo-Foucauldians of a decentred account of the state, Foucault proclaimed 'the problem of *bringing under state control, of "statification" (étatization)* is at the heart of the questions I have tried to address' (Foucault, 2008: 77; emphasis added). This translated into concern with the statification of government and the governmentalization of the state (Foucault, 2007: 109). He initially argued that the study of power should begin from below, in the heterogeneous and dispersed microphysics of power, explore specific forms of its exercise in different institutional sites, and then move on to consider how, if at all, these were linked to produce broader and more persistent societal configurations. One should study power where it is exercised over individuals rather than legitimated at the centre; explore the actual practices of subjugation rather than the intentions that guide attempts at domination; and recognize that power circulates through networks rather than being applied at particular points (Foucault, 1979b [1981]: 92–102; 2003: 27–34). This points to the importance of civil society as a strategic terrain of social mobilization. However, after this initial move, Foucault argued that, while starting at the bottom with the micro diversity of power relations across a multiplicity of dispersed sites, three further interrelated issues required attention.

First, whilst he did once celebrate the infinite dispersion of scattered resistances and micro revolts, he later conceded the need for resistances to be readjusted, reinforced and transformed by global strategies of transformation. Foucault noted that resistances needed coordination just as the dominant class organized its strategies to secure its political preponderance in diverse power relations (Foucault, 1979b [1981]: 96; cf 1980: 143, 159, 195, 203; 1979c: 60).

Second, Foucault suggests that the overall unity of a system of domination must be explained in terms of the strategic codification and institutional integration of power relations. This process is both intentional and non-subjective. It is intentional because no power is exercised without a series of aims and objectives, which are often highly explicit at the limited level of their inscription in local sites of power (Foucault, 1979b [1981]: 94). He refers here to declared programmes for reorganizing institutions, rearranging spaces and regulating behaviours (1980: 9). But it is also non-subjective because the overall outcome of the clash of micro powers cannot be understood as resulting from the choice or decision of an individual, group or class subject (cf Foucault, 1979b [1981]: 94–5). Things never work out as planned because:

> … there are different strategies which are mutually opposed, composed, and superposed so as to produce permanent and solid effects which can perfectly well be understood in terms of their rationality, even though they don't conform to the initial programming; this is what gives the resulting apparatus (*dispositif*) its solidity and suppleness. (Foucault, 1980: 10)

Or, as Foucault expressed it elsewhere: 'the logic is perfectly clear, the aims decipherable, and yet it is often the case that no one is there to have invented them, and few can be said to have formulated them' (1979b [1981]: 95).

And third, Foucault will suggest that power can be exercised at different scales and that the question of whether one focuses on micro powers or the organization of the state as a whole is a question of perspective. Thus, *The Birth of Biopolitics* applied the same nominalist analytics to the succession of forms of state and forms of the limitation or self-limitation of state power. This course explored the import of political economy and the emergence of the notion of *homo economicus* as an active *entrepreneurial* subject rather than as the bearer of exchange relations (2008: 225–94 passim).

There is some evidence to support claims of an anti-statist, anti-institutional and pro-social movement orientation in Foucault's work and political activism. In respect to the latter, Foucault suggested that he wished to stand beside the oppressed instead of representing or protecting them. He indicated the desire to make room for marginalized groups' self-formulated critiques rather than take on the role of spokesperson for them. In an interview published in 1977, for instance, he famously rejected the idea of the 'universal intellectual' who claimed to speak on behalf of others and charted the emergence of 'specific intellectuals' who speak on the basis of their own localized expertise and knowledge (Foucault, 2000: 126–8).

Foucault on civil society as a mode of governance

Foucault regarded civil society as an entirely constructed entity or kind of imaginary domain internal to liberal governmentality and a key site of 'veridiction' (Dean and Villadsen, 2016: 121). Government seeks a limit that is not completely penetrable by sovereign or disciplinary power. This limit is society, which has a complex and independent reality with its own laws and mechanisms of disturbance (Foucault, 1989 [1983]: 261). In this regard, 'civil society emerges, in Foucault's words, as a "transactional reality" that allows for balancing or integrating two divergent images of the governed subject – the juridical subject and the economic subject (2008: 296)' (Dean and Villadsen, 2016: 122).

Thinking about civil society ('which is very quickly called society' [Foucault 2008: 296]) comes about, then, as a correlate of an art and technology of government. It is conceptually different from the juridical discourse of sovereignty and from the transparent and effective relation of will between governors and governed realized in the *Polizeiwissenschaften* or police sciences, mercantilism and *Raison d'État*. Civil society has 'its own history, its own forces and struggles, its own groups and hierarchies, and its own voice' (Dean and Villadsen, 2016: 124).

> It is a third term that places sovereignty and economic governance, and their respective subjects, as relative moments within a specific and concrete milieu. It is not a natural domain that lies outside the state but a new way of organizing the art of government of the state and is a source of inherently progressive resistance against the state. (Dean and Villadsen, 2016: 124)

As such, it becomes not a substantial social domain but the key imaginary object *internal* to liberal governmental rationality.

As Mitchell Dean and Kaspar Villadsen show, Foucault displaced the concept of civil society in four ways. First, he denaturalized the concept by showing that it does not exist as a concrete reality and did not reduce it to an illusion or an ideological outcome. But it does exist as a reference point for certain practices that invoke it and organize themselves in relation to it. Second, civil society emerged as a 'transactional reality' that serves to balance or arbitrate the 'transaction' between two forms of knowledge of the subject – as a legal subject and as the subject of interest. It allows the integration into the administrative rationality of political rule of another figure: the culturally embedded subject about which the sovereign can never achieve exhaustive knowledge. Third, it is a transactional reality that exists 'at the interface ... of governors and governed' (Foucault, 2008: 297). It represents an 'interplay of relations of power and everything which constantly eludes them' (2008: 297). Civil society thus opens government to the governed in a more flexible and mobile fashion. Fourth, and finally, civil society has an open-ended, multivalent and almost virtual character. It is not founded on an original contract but on the specific practices, constraints and capacities existing at the interface between governors and governed. Civil society can be mobilized by very different political forces, which invoke divergent images of it (Dean and Villadsen, 2016: 125–6).

> By this route we can investigate how particular 'communities' emerge in strategies for crime prevention, urban renewal, health promotion, the integration of immigrants, and other domains. On the one hand, these communities are shaped through forms of expertise and multiple relations of government and power, as much as through the demands and aspirations of grassroots movements. On the other hand, insofar as they are systematically construed as a new locus of politics beyond and often opposed to the state, they fail to escape the classical position taken by the proponents of civil society. (Dean and Villadsen, 2016: 170)

Foucault on civil society as governmentality

Foucault focuses on the importance of governmentality and subjectivity in politics and the way the subject constitutes itself in the knowledge/power nexus. He formulates the term governmentality, which means 'governmental rationality', to explore the regularities of everyday existence that structure subjectivity and subject formation (subjectivization). This process is mediated by the construction of discourses and practices that form the governing rationalities, technologies and procedures in modern societies. These rationalities structure the 'conduct of conduct' and rule at a distance where the technologies of the self provide the key to understanding how power and subjectivity work through everyday life.

Deploying his insights on governmentality, he does not see civil society as a historical given that exists to oppose the state and its institutions (Foucault, 2008).

> In concrete terms, urgent biopolitical problems of securing hygiene, regulating trade, and controlling disease fundamentally superseded the legal framework of sovereign command. Foucault suggested, then, that civil society emerged as a solution to the 17th- and 18th-

146

century problem of how to govern individuals conceived as both juridical subjects and as living, economic-cultural agents. Commenting on Ferguson, Foucault said that a new 'reference plane' was required, which could not only reconcile these two figures, but also regard them as inserted in a complex reality (2007: 295). (Villadsen, 2016: 12)

In this context, Foucault said:

> I think we should be very prudent regarding the degree of reality we accord to this civil society. It is not an historical-natural given which functions in some way as both the foundation of and source of opposition to the state or the political institutions. Civil society is not a primary and immediate reality. (2008: 297; cited in Villadsen, 2016: 10)

Instead, civil society can be understood as an ensemble of modes of governance associated with changes in governmentality. For him, civil society is one site with multiple locations where society's governmental techniques hit the ground and can be combined with other forms of power (for example, panoptic and/or pastoral ones). Civil society governs through forms of self-techniques on the micro-political scale. These are mediated via a range of socially innovative forms of governance that are spearheaded by networks of private, civil society (for example, unions and non-governmental organizations [NGOs]) and state actors. The discourses of citizenship and stakeholders are deployed in these governance arrangements and practices. They organize horizontally in rule making, setting and implementing at different sites (for example, economic, social, environmental and infrastructural) and scales (for example, global, multinational, national, urban and local) with the potential for inclusion and empowerment, but there are also processes at work that point to great governmental control.

More specifically, these modes of civil society governance depict a new form of governmentality that 'conducts the conduct' (Foucault, 1982; Lemke, 2019) through particular governing rationalities (for example, stakeholders, empowerment, resilience, entrepreneurship and solidarity). Barbara Cruikshank, in her book *Will to Empower*, sees civil society empowerment and participation programmes as forms of control and power rather than something liberating. She sees these technologies of citizenship, however well intentioned, as modes of constituting and regulating citizens, that is, strategies for governing the very subjects whose problems they seek to redress – the powerless, the apathetic or those at risk (Cruikshank, 1999: 2).

Governmental rationalities of stakeholder and resilience

Participants in these modes of networked and non-exclusive governance are interpreted as stakeholders engaging in forms of decision-making based on 'stakes' they hold with particular issues. The 'stakeholder' and 'dialogue' languages, which moved round these governance circuits, were selected and deployed as objects that are pertinent to governmental calculations. These calculations produce a whole new pedagogy of 'stakeholder engagement' that governs and/ or disciplines them. New governing tools such as benchmarking, standards, methodologies, software, audit reports, matrices and manuals coexist with practices that include dialogues, consultation, discussion panels, focus groups, interviews, feedback, information gathering, data mapping/exchange, and so on. These constellations of power configurations are diverse with some more intrusive than others in the governance of stakeholder-engagement life. In some stakeholder schemes in which the private-corporate plays a more dominant role, there are examples of the use of 'stakeholder mapping' and 'stakeholder analysis' in identifying and prioritizing stakeholders into categories for diverse engagement and panoptic control.

The World Bank, for example, suggests that:

> A stakeholder is any entity with a declared or conceivable interest or stake in a policy concern. The range of stakeholders relevant to consider for analysis varies according to the complexity of reform area targeted and the type of reform proposed and, where the stakeholders are not organized, the incentive to include them. Stakeholders can be of any form, size and capacity. They can be individuals, organizations, or unorganized groups.... Four major attributes are important for Stakeholder Analysis: the stakeholders' position on the reform issue, the level of influence (power) they hold, the level of interest they have in the specific reform, and the group/coalition to which they belong or can reasonably be associated with. These attributes are identified through various data collection methods, including interviews with country experts knowledgeable about stakeholders or with the actual stakeholders directly. (World Bank, 2015)

This World Bank narrative sees stakeholders as both objects and subjects of policy governance with diverse political and social attributes that can influence the policy outcomes. They become time-sensitive targets for data collection, profiling and monitoring. Data generating and organizing tools such as Darzin software, charts, weightings, matrixes and continuums are deployed to construct stakeholder profiles. Based on this data, they are mapped on a continuum indicating support for the reform on a scale of 0 to 100 from low (far left) to high (far right). Their varying degrees of support are marked on the line with a value indicating their reform preference. This also provides a quick visual of the 'lay of the land', illuminating clusters of groups that support, oppose or are indifferent to reform (World Bank, 2015).

This form of engagement rule may facilitate participation but it is also overlaid by 'panoptic-style' systems of disciplinary tools and practices that are designed to: (1) map and contain stakeholder resistance towards policy reforms; (2) visibilize the micropolitical economy of a policy area; (3) build stakeholder coalition and support; and (4) produce value for the private and policy agencies (Sum, 2018).

There are also more communicative modes that organize more through technologies of the self and freedom. There are cogovernance projects that seek to enhance the subjectivities of empowerment, self-help, resilience and the solidarity of stakeholders and citizens. These ways of governing them at a distance operate via techniques of freedom and ethical individualization that structure these fields of their action. Individual autonomy is subjectified and managed by inciting and inviting stakeholders to self-responsibilize and self-oblige to improve policies and governing goals. Focusing on one of the current governing goals on resilience, these discourses are deployed in times of natural disasters, terrorist challenges and economic shocks by governments, NGOs and international organizations. It becomes linked to the ability to withstand shock through the capacity to 'cope' and to 'bounce back'.

In this regard, humans are then reframed as coping agents who are innovative, enterprising and risk-taking. This discourse and its practices thus shift from the need to deal with these systemic insecurities and danger to the neoliberal belief in the necessity of risk as a private good (Joseph, 2016). It justifies a certain approach to governance that is adaptive and can cope. In this regard, resilience becomes a tool of governance that operates at a distance by shaping expectations and measuring compliance with a set of norms. It subjectifies the governed to self-responsibilize themselves for self-coping and self-help. In case of not adapting, self-responsibilization attributes fault to the individual players and diverts criticisms away from the institutions. It shifts responsibility away from the system to populations in civil society and closes the former from criticisms.

Citizenship, self-responsibilization and self-emancipation

From the above comments on self-responsibilization, we can see the closing nature of micro techniques of governance in the everyday life of civil society. Its free but closing nature enables us to ask two questions. First, how can a self-responsibilized process of individualization have enough resources to present a serious challenge to a form of micro power that operates precisely through the management of individual autonomy (McNay, 1999)? What are the forms of counter-conduct that seek to resist and not to be governed so much? What is the space for self-emancipation and the care for the self in the making of civil society and citizenship? The possibility of forms of subjectivity with a less closed character may pave the way for self-emancipation that is discussed in Foucault's work on care of the self. Foucault sees in pre-Augustus antiquity, and even in further reading of the Roman and Hellenistic Neo-Stoics, a richness of the understanding of the self and care for the self. It is this care of the self that establishes someone as a citizen with political rights to self-government that Foucault finds most interesting. This focus is on the self as an ethico-political self who engages in political self-creation to undermine prescriptive moral and political models by fostering a dynamic and critical self-relationship. Such self-emancipation involves the creation and governmentalization of self as an autonomous form of being and doing. It requires a continuous practice of introspection that allows for a continuous introduction of oneself to new activities, ideas and challenges in one's internal and external life. Care of the self becomes a focal point for individual freedom, positive relationships with others and, potentially, ethical and self-emancipatory participation in civil activities. It is important to note that Foucault's idea of 'ethics of the care of the self' is not offering an account of oppositional political agency or a blueprint for political action; it merely outlines a set of ethical predispositions that provide preconditions for emancipatory practice.

Complementing this ethico-attitudinal focus, Foucault also discussed counter-conduct and the problem of resistance. In counter-conductive struggles, the resistance is not a single chief enemy, but plural governing assemblages to escape the 'involute' rationalities and techniques of conduct (Odysseos et al, 2016). This counter-conduct might exceed direct political opposition but may go on in apolitical settings in civil society where it could be difficult to draw clear distinctions between power and resistance, governance and cogovernance, discipline and liberation, responsibilization and irresponsibilization, as well as self-responsibilization and self-emancipation (Odysseos, 2016). The coexistence of this array of (counter-)conducting practices illustrates that they are never complete and there are unintended consequences of both conducting and counter-conducting in the governing of civil society.

Concluding remarks

In approaching Foucault's work in these terms, we can escape the dichotomy of micro and macro power, the antinomy of an analytics of micro powers and a theory of sovereignty, and the problematic relation between micro diversity and macro necessity in power relations (cf Jessop, 1990b; Kerr, 1999: 176). This is something that Foucault himself indicated was both possible in principle (because micro powers have no ontological primacy) and necessary in practice (to understand the successive but subsequently overlapping arts of government in the exercise of state power beyond the state) (2007: 15, 109; 2008: 186, 313; cf 2003: 36–9, 173, 242, 250). Foucault's insistence on the complexity, diversity and relative autonomy of local, everyday relations of power overturns neither Marxist accounts of the state nor liberal theories of popular sovereignty; it only exposes them as limited and inadequate (Deacon, 2002). The challenge is to show how they might, in some circumstances, in some contexts and for some periods of time, be linked. The idea of government as strategic codification and institutional integration of power relations provides a bridge between micro diversity and macro necessity and, as Foucault argues, a focus on micro powers is determined by one's choice of scale but involves analytical insights that can be applied across all scales. It is a perspective, not a reality delimited to one scale (Foucault, 2008: 186; cf 1977 [1975]: 222; 2003: 28–31). Foucault still argued for the dispersion of powers, insisted that the state, for all its omnipotence, does not occupy the whole field of power relations, and claimed that the state can only operate on the basis of other, already existing, power relations. Indeed, 'power relations have been progressively governmentalized, that is to say, elaborated, rationalized, and centralized in the form of, or under the auspices of, state institutions' (Foucault, 2008: 345).

The difference between the Foucauldian and Anglo-Foucauldian approaches to the state and governmentality can be explained in part in terms of Foucault's distinction between 'power relations understood as strategic games between liberties [strategic games that result in the fact that some people try to determine the conduct of others] and the states of domination, which are what we ordinarily call "power"' (1997 [1984]: 299). He added that:

> ... between the two, between games of power and states of domination, you have technologies of government.... The analysis of these techniques is necessary because it is very often through such techniques that states of domination are established and maintained. There are three levels to my analysis of power: strategic relations, techniques of government, and states of domination. (Foucault, 1997 [1984]: 299)

PART III

Governance failure and metagovernance

8

The multispatial governance of social and economic policy

There has been much talk of civil society in the past 30–40 years or so. This occurred not only during the crisis of state socialism in the Soviet bloc and the initial construction of post-socialist societies, but also in the heartlands of advanced capitalism. But does this mean that 'civil society' has become a really existing unified, extra-discursive phenomenon? Does it mean that there are major shifts in the residual space that has been conventionally described as 'civil society' and that these have important implications for economic, political and social struggles? Or does it mean only that major changes have occurred in the 'self-understanding' and 'self-description' of society and that these are reflected in the renewed discourse of 'civil society? My view, based on the theoretical arguments above and on current accounts of these changes, is that there is still no unified 'civil society'. This is reflected in the interest in civic stratification, civic deficits and civic repair in the current period of the WISERD research centre. This Lockwoodian interest is concerned with the interdependence of capitalist relations and citizenship or status relations and hence in the role of civil society in liberal bourgeois democracy. It identifies the endemic contradiction between citizenship and capital that has so far been managed by the fine-tuning of social rights (Lockwood, 1999: 535).

Economics and politics

Lockwood's approach to civic stratification is grounded in the Marshallian approach to citizenship rights and deficits (Marshall, 1950). But there have been significant changes in the relations between what one might, following Habermas, call the system world and the lifeworld, and these have major implications for the roles of state and politics (Habermas, 1984, 1987, 1989). Moreover, in Luhmannian terms, these changes can be described in terms of the increased functional differentiation of modern societies (thereby producing a paradoxical combination of greater operational autonomy for individual functional subsystems or institutional orders and greater social, material and temporal interdependence among them) and in terms of the greater significance of identities as a means to reduce the increased complexity of the system world, and to provide a basis for self-description and self-reflexion about the impact of these changes on values and interests. Reinforcing these arguments are the complexities produced in the global–local dynamics of time-space distantiation (the stretching of social relations out in space and the increased capacity to bind social relations over longer periods of past, present and future) and of time-space compression (the increased capacity to connect distant points in space and/or to make more distinctions, decisions, responses, and so on, within a given time period).

Much of the literature (and much political discourse) presupposes a separation between the economy and politics, the market and the state. From a critical political economy viewpoint, this is misleading – not because this separation is absent but because it is part of a bigger picture. It depends on the variable lines of demarcation between the economy and politics and their structural and strategic significance. Structurally, this separation is the condition for trade in free markets and the rational organization of production and finance as well as the existence of a constitutional state based on the rule of law. This interdependence between market and state is one reason why Milton Friedman (1962) (among other advocates of capitalism) described himself as a liberal rather than an anarchist. Strategically, differential accumulation depends on the use of economic *and extra-economic* resources to create the conditions of profitable accumulation and/ or to socialize losses, the forms and extent of separation between the profit-oriented, market-mediated aspect of accumulation and its crucial extra-economic supports in, *inter alia*, the legal and political system and, notwithstanding this variable institutional separation, by the continued reciprocal interdependence of 'market' and 'state' as complementary moments in the reproduction of the capital relation.

In this sense, the state is never absent from the process of capital accumulation, whether in stability or crisis – even laissez-faire is a form of state intervention because it implicitly supports the outcome of market forces (cf Gramsci, 1971: 162; 1975, Q13, §18). The state not only provides general external conditions of production, allocates money, credit and resources to different economic activities, and helps to frame and steer production, distribution and trade; it is also involved in organizing and reorganizing class alliances among dominant class fractions and disorganizing subordinate classes and forces, whether through divide-and-rule tactics or through articulating a national-popular interest that transcends particular class interests (Gramsci, 1971: 177–85; Poulantzas, 1978).

The nature of the *polity* is shaped by the 'lines of difference' drawn between the state and its 'constitutive outside', whether this comprises an unmarked residuum external to the political sphere (for example, state vs society, public vs private) or one or more marked spheres with their own institutional order, operational logics, subjects and practices (for example, the religious, economic, legal, educational or scientific fields). This is more productive analytically than the notion of 'political society + civil society'. Moreover, politicization, which, in this context, could usefully be designated *politization*, extends the frontiers of the polity (penetrating or colonizing the non-political sphere(s) and subordinating it/them to political factors, interests, values and forces). In turn, *depolitization* rolls these frontiers back, and *repolitization* reintegrates depoliticized spheres into the political (Jessop, 2014). These potentially alternating processes can occur for various reasons, be promoted by quite different forces and affect the balance of forces in diverse way. Their overall significance for politicization broadly considered nonetheless depends on how they are connected to changes in politics and policy.

Civil society has played a key role in political reflections, imaginaries and political practice since then, informing political strategies and political contestation. For practitioners, civil society is attractive for several reasons:

- It gives a fashionable, new legitimacy to old practices – thus, 'civil society' has acquired positive connotations such as 'middle way', 'consultation', 'negotiation', 'subsidiarity', 'reflexivity', 'dialogue', and the like.
- It provides a solution, however partial, temporary and provisional, to the crisis of state planning in the mixed economy and the more recent disillusion with excessively disembedded neoliberal market forces. This is now reflected in growing interest in modes of institutional design and economic regulation that might obviate the need for state control while still guiding the market. Political theorists now suggest that governance is an important means to overcome the division between rulers and ruled in representative regimes and to secure the input and commitment of an increasingly wide range of stakeholders in policy formulation and implementation. In this sense, governance also has normative significance. It indicates a revaluation of different modes of coordination, not just in terms of their economic efficiency or their effectiveness in collective goal attainment, but also in terms of their associated values.
- Above all, it offers a solution to problems of coordination in and across the private and public spheres in the face of growing complexity.

Political theorists now suggest that governance is an important means to overcome the division between rulers and ruled in representative regimes and to secure the input and commitment of an increasingly wide range of stakeholders in policy formulation and implementation. In this sense, governance also has normative significance. It has gained a key role as flanking and supporting measures.

Nonetheless, despite the good press for civil society, it is important to recognize that all modes of coordination – including the solidarity of civil society – are prey to dilemmas, contradictions, paradoxes and failures. These obviously differ. Market failure is said to occur when markets fail to allocate scarce resources efficiently in and through the pursuit of monetized private interest, and state failure is seen as a failure to secure substantive collective goals based on political divination of the public interest. There was once a tendency to assume that market failure could be corrected either by extending the logic of the market or by compensatory state action, and that state failure could be corrected either by 'more market, less state' or through improved juridico-political institutional design, knowledge or political practice. More recently, governance has been seen as an effective response to market and state failure. Unfortunately, growing fascination with civil society should not lead us to overlook the risks involved in substituting it for markets or hierarchies and the resulting likelihood of governance failure. It is not just markets and imperative coordination that fail; civil society as a mode of governance at the intersection of networks and solidarity is also prone to failure.

I illustrate these arguments from four pieces of work in this and the next chapter. In this chapter, I introduce my recent work on global social policy and my critique of the literature on 'good governance' to solve the problems of local economic development. Chapter 9 then presents my study of economic governance arrangements in Dartford and Greater Manchester, and concludes with my comparison of corporatism and the negotiated economy and social economy models. Chapter 10 introduces competitiveness as a mode of governance and its failures.

Global social policy

Global social policy (GSP) might be expected to address the problems of 'world society' or at least, to take world society as its 'ultimate horizon' for defining problems and proposing policy and governance solutions. However, 'world society' and 'global civil society' are just two among many competing ways to characterize society and are far from being well-established realities, let alone realities that dominate other scales of societal or social organization. World society is sometimes said to have superseded national societies as the framework of social organization and to have a decentred, functionally differentiated character rather than comprising a unified social order based on shared values, shared identity or single source of authority. But this account ignores the continued importance of segmented forms of societal organization, especially national territorial states, as well as the recalibration of centre–periphery relations (on these different forms of societalization, see Luhmann, 1997). A further challenge in dealing with world society is the very real prospect that one functional system is so dominant that it imprints the operation of other functional systems and civil society. While the profit-oriented, market-mediated logic of the modern economic system is often mentioned in this context, other cases that have been explored are juridification, politicization, militarization and sacralization.

The importance of functional differentiation on a global scale might imply that there are at least as many separate policy fields as there are functional systems and subsystems. This is reflected in part in the 'family' of agencies in the UN system and Deacon's idea of 'global ministries' that address different fields of economic and social policy (Deacon, with Hulse and Stubbs, 1997). Plausible examples are UNESCO for education and science, the International Court of Justice (ICJ) for law, the International Labour Office (ILO) for labour policy, the International Monetary Fund (IMF) for finance, the UN Committee on Trade and Development for trade, the World Bank Group for development finance, and the World Health Organization (WHO) for health (compare, in part, Kaasch and Stubbs, 2014). Other agencies deal with problems that crosscut functional systems or address issues rooted in 'civil society', such as the Department of Economic and Social Affairs (DESA), the United Nations Children's Fund (UNICEF) and the United Nations High Commissioner for Refugees (UNHCR). However, given that different functional systems have their own codes, programmes and operational logics, which are potentially inconsistent or even contradictory, it is difficult to coordinate them from outside and above through a world state or other single centre of global governance that stands at the apex of world society. Instead, global social governance is inherently pluralistic and involves different modes of governance and metagovernance that pose challenges of coordination across different social fields, sites and scales.

In addition, the copresence of centre–periphery relations and segmentation alongside functional differentiation is reflected in, for example, hegemonic states and client states, core regions and excluded regions, and the survival of territorial states in the world political system. These have their own effects on the forms, organization and dynamics of global social governance. For example, hegemonic states may seek to organize global governance based on a specific hegemonic project that claims to serve a general interest (as well as its own longer-term, particular interests) and is backed up by force, fraud and corruption. Likewise, the survival of formally sovereign territorial states underpins an *international* order, namely, one based on the interaction among economic, political and sociocultural entities that are identified with and/or operate within clear national boundaries.

I now consider global social policy (GSP). This can be defined initially in two ways: (1) the heterogeneous set of analytical object(s) of social policy at a global scale constructed by social scientists and/or (2) the governmental object(s) identified at this scale by policy-makers and practitioners. The latter alternative is more important here. A first step in this regard is to identify the social imaginaries or policy paradigms that frame 'social problems' as objects or targets of social governance. A second step is to examine the discursive, structural, technological and agential selectivities through which some imaginaries, paradigms, construals of social policies and policy proposals come to be translated into policies or governance. A third step, of course, is to examine how these four types of selectivity lead to the retention of some policy approaches and modes of governance. While policy effectiveness may influence retention, one should not ignore the difference made by hegemonic or dominant social imaginaries, subhegemonic imaginaries (which complement hegemonic or dominant imaginaries) and counter-hegemonic imaginaries and the shifting balance of forces. There is a so-called performative effect to hegemonic or dominant imaginaries and path-shaping aspects to governance regimes.

The productive fuzziness of GSP has enabled the emergence of a new transdisciplinary field of inquiry, but this also makes it hard to produce a coherent theoretical framework. I now unpack the three elements of GSP (albeit not in their order of appearance in this phrase), and then consider GSP as a whole.

Social

First, what distinguishes the social from its unmarked ('non-social') environment or from its marked (technological, economic, legal, political, familial ...) others? Exploring a similar question, Max Weber

(1949) distinguished: the economy proper, the economically relevant and the economically conditioned. Likewise, we can distinguish the social, the socially relevant and the socially conditioned. First, as an 'unmarked' or indistinct sphere, the social comprises the environment of a marked sphere, such as technology (and society), the economy (and society), law (and society), politics (and society), family (and society), and so on. As a marked sphere, it has positively identified rather than residual characteristics. In general, then, the social comprises a specific set of social relations (for example, civil society, social reproduction) with other social relations being consigned to an undifferentiated social environment. In the social policy field, for example, it has been defined to include: (1) the reproduction of the labour force: from day to day, over the life course and across generations; and/or (2) the biopolitical reproduction of the 'population' echoing Foucault. The latter is measured in terms of features such as 'variable levels of health, birth and death rates, age, sex, dependency ratios, and so on – as an object with a distinct rationality and intrinsic dynamics that can be made the target of a specific kind of direct intervention' (Thompson, 2012: 42). Regarding the other two analytical distinctions, the 'socially relevant' comprises those actors, factors and mechanisms that condition the delivery and success of social policy, and the 'socially conditioned' refers to the wider effects of social policy beyond the immediate site of social policy. A thorough analysis of GSP should address all three aspects and their linkages.

Global

One could link 'global' and 'social' by noting that today's ultimate horizon of sense- and meaning-making and social communication is world society (Luhmann, 1982b, 1997). Positing an 'ultimate horizon' does not entail that a consolidated 'world society' or 'global civil society' already exists and is, moreover, superordinate to other scales of organization. Integration in real time on a world scale is quite uneven across functional systems and, even where it is quite advanced (for example, the world market), the global is not necessarily the primary scale of organization or coordination. Scalar hierarchies can be tangled.

Despite the growing weight of the global as an arena and horizon of action, there is no world state or other unified global governance apparatus that has replaced the national territorial state as the primary scale of organization in the postwar political order. Indeed, economically and politically, there is intense competition among economic and political spaces to become the new anchorage point around which the remaining scale levels (however many, however identified) can be organized to produce structured coherence. Efforts to create a world state or true global governance cannot be confined to the global level alone and would have to be realized through complex forms of coordination across multiple sites and scales. Thus, it is unlikely that a global superpower or world state could effectively govern world society, let alone that this could be achieved at the global scale alone. This is improbable because of the inherent complexities of the global order and, more importantly, the limited capacity of any given societal subsystem to steer the operations of others. Even more modest attempts to establish global governance could not be confined to the global level alone and would have to be realized through complex forms of coordination across multiple sites and scales. This creates space for interscalar articulation and rescaling and enables new strategies and tactics based on uneven abilities to jump scale(s). It also implies that global social policy regimes or global social governance would not be *universal*, that is, even if a global policy were to be implemented by global agencies, they would have an uneven impact in particular sites.

Postponing the question of policy, to what might 'global' refer? Possible referents include:

- *A global aetiology:* the actual or construed causes and causal mechanisms of the 'social problems' that GSP addresses are generated at the global level by the complexities of an emerging world society and/or manifest themselves primarily or significantly at this level. Note that a global aetiology can refer to real causes and causal mechanisms identified by disinterested observers and/or to those proposed by participants in global social policy formation and implementation based on other considerations, including entry-points, standpoints and ideal and material interests.
- *Global politics and governance:* GSP is required because of the multiscalar, multispatial, multitemporal, multi-agential nature of global social relations. These complexities require coordination of problem definition, policy formulation and policy implementation at a global level, even if this takes account of problems and policies proposed elsewhere, and even if subsequent policy implementation is decentralized. In part this will be reflected in the adoption of instruments and disciplinary and policy technologies that are global in scope. Here, too, it is important to distinguish a 'scientific' (disinterested) analysis of coordination problems from diagnoses that are proposed (or contested) by interested participants in the social policy process.

- *Global spatial policy:* to resolve social policy problems requires some kind of spatial reorganization that rearticulates the TPSN spatial aspects of social policy formation and its governance from the local to the global scale. This is shaped by various spatial imaginaries, narratives and/or discourses that inform the spatial demarcation of the generative mechanisms (aetiology) of social problems from the potentially indefinite web of social relations in a changing global–regional–national–local nexus as a focus of intervention.

- *Global agents and agencies:* at stake here is whether the agents of global social policy are themselves organized at a global level (for example, global or international agencies and institutions) or become global by virtue of contributing to the definition of global social problems, participating in deliberation over global social policy issues, coordinating global social policy and governance regimes or being otherwise involved in global social governance in global arenas. These possibilities cover a wide range of actors and pose crucial questions about how an agent or agency acquires global significance apart from being part of the official 'family' of established world, international or transnational agencies, organizations or movements with global reach. Such agencies could comprise international governmental and non-governmental organizations, regional and other groupings of countries with global horizons of action, mainstream media with potential global reach, lobby groups and influential individuals. As Alexandra Kaasch (2015) notes, the procedures employed in establishing, reproducing and legitimating mandates for individuals, groups and organizations to participate in global social policy regimes and global social governance are quite varied. They can involve bottom-up support based on grassroots mobilization and/or sponsorship of significant organizations and movements in 'civil society' as well as official nomination or unofficial sponsorship by states or other authoritative bodies (such as the UN). Given the importance of the shifting balance of forces and the need for reflexive agents to calculate the broader repercussions of their actions in a complicated strategic field, even movements without a mandate or entitlement to participate in global social governance can nonetheless exercise power 'at a distance' to the extent that their likely reactions enter the calculations of those agents, agencies and social forces that are present in GSP forums, regimes and governance arrangements. This creates a field of tension between the need for operational autonomy and moral legitimacy, on the one hand, and, on the other hand, state sponsorship or tolerance to the extent that GSP and global social governance is conducted in the shadow of state authority.

Policy

Governance includes polity, politics and policy. Although policy conventionally comes at the end of this trinity, the three interact, with none providing the primary site of governance initiatives or acting as the 'prime mover' of governance practices. Governance is not instituted to govern pre-existing objects of governance. Rather, governance practices (mediated by institutions) attempt to delimit, unify, stabilize and reproduce their objects of governance and create willing governance subjects as the precondition as well as the effect of governing them. In other words, the objects, subjects (agents) and mechanisms of governance are co-constitutive and mutually transforming as well as sites of conflict and contradiction.

Governing global social policy

It follows that the governance of GSP has a range of possible meanings. These provide a grid for ordering, interpreting and evaluating the growing body of work addressed to this topic. Table 8.1 indicates the polyvalence of GSP by identifying three possible (sometimes compatible) meanings for each term in this compound noun. It also suggests the problems involved in locating and distinguishing the referent of each term. It reveals some conceptual complications in establishing the analytical and empirical scope of the global, social and governance. And it indicates some theoretical issues that arise from efforts to delimit the scope and utility of GSP.

These remarks indicate a need to look at three closely related issues about social policy: changing definitions of individual and social problems and their connections, the changing institutions charged with solving these interlinked problems, and the agents and practices that deliver the solutions thereto. A key issue here is whether GSP is driven by existing spatial divisions of authority (notably, territorial states in a world of states) and their associated political cycles or rhythms (for example, electoral cycles, regime shifts) or by the more complex TPSN aetiology of actually existing social problems. Administrative convenience often seems to matter more, and this can lead to the failure of social policy because they are too state-centred and ignore transversal and/or wider factors and repercussions of social problems and their treatment. The rise of 'global social policy' is one way to address such issues but is fragmented, in turn, by the plurality of problems, imaginaries, agencies, sites of possible intervention, and so on.

Table 8.1: Disambiguating global social governance

	Polyvalence	Levels	Conceptual complications	Theoretical issues
Global	Virtual horizon? Emerging reality? Established fact?	Is global a distinct scale with its own logic, or one among many scales or levels?	Multilevel? Multiscalar? Multispatial? Is the 'global' a dominant, nodal, or marginal scale (or does this vary)?	Global agencies Intergovernmental Supranational Transnational International ...?
Social	Directly social? Socially relevant? Socially conditioned?	Is 'social' a marked field, that is, a positively defined sphere? Is it the unmarked 'other' of another positive sphere? Or is it an aggregate of several marked spheres?	If 'marked', then social policy and/or governance focus on 'social' as a sphere with its own specificities, logics, dynamic? Does it include social (policy) effects of other policies or other processes? Does it include policies that integrate social dimension into policy formation as relevant consideration, for example, poverty as an obstacle to environmental policy?	Global social policy as a socially constructed policy paradigm with performative effects Global social policy as a (chaotic) socially constructed research area? Is it a *Kampfbegriff* (concept for discursive struggles) to limit primacy of security and economic issues?
Governance	Polity? Politics? Policy?	Social governance Social politics Social policy	Polity as state(s) or other mode of governance (including civil society) Politics as multiple actors, agencies and links to other political agendas Policy regimes, design, implementation	Problems of multispatial metagovernance Which mode of social governance is primary? What are the flanking, supporting mechanisms?

Source: Licensed from Table 2.1 in Jessop (2015)

The global scale is a horizon of action and an emerging social reality rather than an already constituted, fully integrated global social system. Even the world market is subject to frictions, resistance, uneven development and struggles over how best (even if this is desirable) it can be completed. There is still no coherent, smoothly functioning global governance system, let alone a world state. Indeed, global governance regimes and global civil society are uneven in extent and the density of their connections and linkages, and they are also skewed toward the Global North. And global solidarity has the intermittent character of mass movements, with fluctuating engagement based on sympathy and repulsion, and has only limited degrees of institutionalization.

As an incoherent ensemble of contested and competing governance arrangements with different kinds of discursive, structural, technological and agential selectivities, global social governance is characterized by a 'struggle for the right to shape policy and for the content of that policy' (Deacon, 2007: 143). As Kaasch (2015) notes:

> ... in the face of multiple agencies and fields of global social governance, and complex process patterns characterizing them – it might be better to speak of a number of global social "governances" rather than "a" global social governance. Each of the scenes of governance is characterized by different histories, different degrees of development, different actor constellations and inter-actor relationships, and different meanings and impacts. This would extend the broad empirical picture of global social governance (comprising prescriptions on different social policy fields as well as diverse forms of global social redistribution, regulation, and rights), by adding dimensions of varying process patterns dependent on place, time, context, and actor constellation. (Kaasch, 2015: 246)

The 'institutional attractors' of GSP governance are intergovernmental coordination, reflexive self-organization and an occasional appeal to horizontal and vertical solidarities. These are mediated through a complex interweaving of interpersonal networks (that crosscut any specific governance arrangements), interorganizational (or interagency) negotiation around mobilization of independently controlled but synergetically interdependent material and symbolic resources for the purposes of positive policy coordination, and recognition of intersystemic linkages and interdependencies that may require participation of representatives (individual or collective) from different functional systems in the specification of urgent social problems, policy formulation and policy implementation. This is reflected in growing concern with various forms of political coordination that not only span the conventional public–private divide but also involve 'tangled hierarchies', parallel power networks or other forms of complex interdependence across different tiers of government and/or different functional domains.

In general, the greater the material, social and spatio-temporal complexity of the problems to be addressed, the greater the number and range of interests that must be coordinated (assuming goodwill) if they are to be resolved satisfactorily. This imperative contra-indicates top-down command as well as the post-hoc mutual adaptation of the invisible hand, and points instead to the importance of heterarchic policy coordination based on networking, negotiation, noise reduction in deliberation through developed shared imaginaries and policy paradigms, and various kinds of partnership. Attention has turned to the networks and negotiated consent because they are allegedly better able to integrate the phenomenon of complexity more explicitly, reflexively, and, it is hoped, effectively than reliance on markets or command. Nonetheless, all forms of governance are failure-prone, albeit for different reasons, in different ways and with different effects. This prompts efforts to overcome governance failure, either through reforms within each mode, or through efforts to alter their relative weight. Self-reflexive organization also fails. Reasons for this include the inadequate definition of the object(s) of governance relative to the complexity of the real world, the general turbulence of the environment, the time required for continuing dialogue, competing governance projects for the same object of governance and the dilemmas involved in particular forms of governance.

'Good governance': The case of cities

Having considered the governance of global social policy from a multispatial perspective, I now turn to the scalar dynamics of economic and social governance of cities. Good governance principles for good, self-reflexive self-organization are generic but need to be modified for specific objects of governance. This stipulation reflects both the general argument that modes of governance are co-constitutive of objects of governance and the material fact that the specificity of different objects of governance must be reflected in a different set of practices with at least the minimal requisite variety needed to match the complexities of that object. For the sake of illustration, therefore, we will take an example of work on good governance to show how these ideas might apply. This is the case of the World Report on *Urban Future 21* (see Hall and Pfeiffer, 2000). This is just one illustration of how failure is both recognized and then resolved through a reorientation of governance mechanisms – from the mixed economy and/or statism towards appropriate forms of self-organization that are nonetheless market-friendly. Good governance is a response to state and market failure and attempts to avoid their respective modes of failure by developing a 'third way'.

Urban Future 21 is a specially prepared report that was written by a distinguished 14-member 'World Commission' moderated by Sir Peter Hall, the renowned professor of urban planning, and serviced by Ulrich Pfeiffer, a professional urban planning consultant, for URBAN 21. URBAN 21 was a prestigious international conference held in Berlin in June 2000, sponsored by the German government, with additional support from the governments of Brazil, South Africa and Singapore. The world commissioners who prepared the report were drawn from 'the great and the good' and have been involved in a range of public, parastatal, professional and private activities. Allowing for some overlap in experience and positions, they included: academic policy entrepreneurs, mayors, an ambassador, a vice president and ex–vice president of the World Bank, a senior civil servant, architects, jurists, ministers, senior UN officials, former parliamentary deputies and leaders of national and international NGOs. Sponsors of the conference symposia included international producer service firms, a major software house, a construction firm and a major German regional bank. While no single report should be taken as wholly representative of thinking on urban governance, let alone good governance, this one does provide some useful insights into the naturalization of neoliberalism and its implications for sustainable cities in an era of the globalizing, knowledge-driven economy. It has since been published in book form, cited as Hall and Pfeiffer (2000).[1]

Background to the report

The report is a response to crises in cities around the world and advocates a new set of economic, political and sociocultural policies for them, linked to the idea of good governance. In line with the more general shift from concern with the conditions for national economic growth in the period of postwar economic expansion, the report identifies cities as the main engines of economic growth, as key centres of economic, political and social innovation, and as key actors in promoting and consolidating international competitiveness. Moreover, with the transition to a post-industrial era, the rise of the knowledge-driven economy and the increasing importance of the information society with its requirements for lifelong learning, cities are seen as being even more important drivers for innovation and competitiveness than before.

Second, in line with the familiar neoliberal critique, welfare states are seen as costly, overburdened, inefficient, unable to eliminate poverty, overly oriented to cash entitlements rather than empowerment, and so on. The report argues that, where it already exists, the welfare state should be dismantled in favour of policies that emphasize moving people from welfare into work, that link social and labour market policy, and that provide incentives to learn and/or prepare for a new job. Likewise, where they have not yet developed, welfare states should be firmly discouraged. Instead, arrangements should be instituted to encourage family, neighbourhood, informal or market-based and market-sustaining solutions to the problems of social reproduction. States should not try to provide monopoly services but should contract them out or at least introduce internal competition. In hypergrowth cities, for example, this translates into a call to revalorize the informal economy and/or the social economy and neighbourhood support mechanisms as a means of tackling social exclusion. In more dynamic or mature cities, the report recommends other projects to produce 'active and productive citizens' who will not burden the state or demand entitlements without accepting corresponding responsibilities. Thus, education and informal self-help are the key to survival and sustainability, and, in principle, education should be made available to all. Cities should develop their stock of indigenous 'human capital' and their local labour markets in order to promote local wellbeing as well as international competitiveness.

Third, the report clearly recognizes the emerging crisis of the national scale of economic, political and social organization, the increased importance of the global level (especially in the form of a still emerging 'single global urban network' that crosscuts national borders) and the resurgence of local and regional levels. Its response is to promote the principles of subsidiarity and solidarity. Problems should be resolved at the lowest level possible, but with capacity-building and financial support from the national administration. This requires integrated action between various levels of government, with an appropriate allocation of responsibilities and resources. Unsurprisingly, the report envisages a key role for cities in managing the interface between the local economy and global flows, between the potentially conflicting demands of local sustainability and local wellbeing and those of international competitiveness, and between the challenges of social exclusion and global polarization and the continuing demands for liberalization, deregulation, privatization, and so on.

Fourth, there is a strong emphasis on partnership and networks rather than top-down national government. Thus, in addition to subsidiarity and solidarity across different scales of economic, political and social organization, the report also calls for partnership between the public and private sectors and between government and civil society. Public–private partnerships should nonetheless work *with* the grain of market forces, not against it. In addition, partnerships should involve not only actors from the private economic sector but also NGOs, religious groups, community action groups or networks among individuals. Promoting partnerships requires a retreat of the state (especially at national level) so that it can do well what it alone can do. Nonetheless, the latter tasks do include steering partnerships and moderating their mutual relations in the interests of 'the maximum welfare of all the people'. This is reflected in the report's call for 'good governance, seen as an integrated effort on the part of local government, civil society and the private sector' (Hall and Pfeiffer, 2000: 164).

Neoliberal dimensions of the report

While calling for modernization, reform and good governance in an apparently neutral way, the report actually serves to endorse neoliberalism implicitly in how it describes recent economic and political changes, ascribes responsibility for them and prescribes solutions for the problems they create. In this sense, it is a deeply ideological document and contributes to the 'New World Order' by sharing in a 'new *word* order' (Luke, 1994: 613–15). Ideology is most effective when ideological elements are invisible, operating as the background assumptions that lead the text producer to 'textualize' the world in a particular way and that lead interpreters to interpret the text in a particular way (Fairclough, 1989: 85).

Indeed, alongside its diagnosis of the various failures of previous modes of economic growth and urban governance in different types of city, said in each case to justify neoliberalism, the report recognizes that neoliberalism has its own limits and also generates major social tensions. Its authors accept the perceived need to re-embed neoliberalism in society, to make it more acceptable socially and politically, and to ensure that it is environmentally sustainable. Here, Karl Polanyi lives! Yet they make as few concessions as possible to forces that oppose the programme, protagonists, and driving forces of neoliberalism. Hence, the report also identifies and advocates different sets of strategies to support and complement the neoliberal project in different regions and/or types of cities. Its proposals for the informal, weakly regulated and vulnerable hypergrowth cities of the developing world combine neoliberalism with a strong emphasis on mobilizing popular energies, the informal or social economy and communitarian values. In these cities, then, it ascribes a key role to neocommunitarianism in sustaining neoliberalism. In contrast, no such dilution is recommended for the mature but declining cities of the Atlantic Fordist regions: they must take their neoliberal medicine. A different prescription again is offered for East Asia's dynamic cities. This comprises a mix of neoliberalism with public–private partnerships to improve the infrastructure and policy environment for international as well as local capital. Here the developmental state is allowed to remain proactive, provided that it is rescaled and becomes more open to world market forces. In no case is there a challenge to the wisdom of the 'accumulated knowledge and experience' noted by the report that market forces provide the best means to satisfy human wants and desires and that, provided they are steered in the right direction through good governance, they can also solve the most pressing problems facing humankind in the new century.

The report also illustrates another key feature of neoliberalism. The latter's success depends on promoting new ways of representing the world, new discourses, new subjectivities that establish the legitimacy of the market economy, the disciplinary state and enterprise culture. The language of the report shares in this tendency to naturalize the global neoliberal project, most notably in its concern with renewing and consolidating neoliberal principles at the urban scale. Thus, the many changes associated with this project are variously represented in the report as natural, spontaneous, inevitable, technological and demographic. It takes technological change and globalization as given, depersonalizes them, fetishizes market forces and fails to mention the economic, political and social forces that drive these processes.

Moreover, the same processes that cause the problems identified in the report will also solve them: technological change will provide solutions to emerging problems, democratization will occur, population growth will decline, economic growth will continue, the informal sector will expand to deal with social problems. The report does not indicate that technological change and globalization are deeply politicized processes and objects of struggles within the dominant classes, within states and within civil society. Instead, it presumes an equality of position in relation to these changes: *they* are objective and inevitable, *we* must adapt to them. Thus, whereas globalization, technological change and competition are depersonalized, human agency enters in through the need for survival and sustainability. It is, above all, local communities, women and workers who must adapt to these impersonal forces. They must be flexible, empower themselves, take control of their pensions by self-funding them, undertake lifelong learning, put democratic pressure on urban administrations to support their informal initiatives, and so on. Likewise, cities can become competitive, take control of their economic destinies, develop their local markets, especially the localized labour markets, their local infrastructure and their stock of housing, develop good governance and become attractive places for working and living. Moreover, on the rare occasions where blame is attributed for economic and social problems, it tends to be localized. Thus, urban poverty results not so much from capitalism as from ineffective local administration – which a judicious combination of mobilization from below and capacity-building from above can correct.

Economic analysis and social agents

The report (Hall and Pfeiffer, 2000) contains no analysis of capitalism and its agents. The dynamic of the knowledge-driven economy is described in objective, factual terms. The report contains only one reference to 'the present economic system' (undefined), and this admits that it is massively suboptimal and inefficient – but does not pause to ask why. The only economic actors it identifies are local urban networks of small-scale producers and services, small firms, private companies and (clearly benign) 'world-class companies'. The only capital identified is human capital. The only social actors are people around the world with shared or common aspirations; the weak, the old and the young; the rich and the poor; women; families; informal neighbourhood support networks; and members of civil society. The only political actors mentioned are urban leaders, citizens and city administrations. There is no reference at all to the economic, political or ideological roles of multinational companies, transnational banks, strategic alliances among giant companies, the military-industrial complex, an emerging transnational class, the World Economic Forum or the overall dynamic of capitalism. There is no reference to popular movements, new social movements, grassroots struggles, trade unions or even political parties – good governance is, apparently, above party politics. Also unmentioned are the crucial roles of the IMF, the World Bank, the Organization for Economic Co-operation and Development (OECD), the World Trade Organization (WTO) and other international economic agencies, and the efforts of the US and its allies to promote globalization or redesign political and social institutions to underwrite and complement neoliberalism. Presumably, these must be left to operate above the national level (at which ultimate responsibility for social justice and redistribution is apparently to be located) and to define (technocratically) the framework within which cities pursue sustainable development. Pollution and environmental destruction appear to be facts of nature rather than products of specific sets of social relations. The empowerment of women appears to be a key mechanism of social transformation, but patriarchy figures nowhere as a mechanism of domination or oppression – and neither states nor firms, neither political nor business leaders, seem to have vested interests in sustaining it.

In short, here is a text that simulates egalitarianism (that of a 'we', a collectivity of individuals, families and communities all equally confronted with objective, inevitable changes and challenges) and lacks any explicit reference to power and authority, exploitation and domination. It is no surprise, then, that these challenges can be met in ways that will reconcile international competitiveness with local autonomy, economic growth with sustainability, market forces with quality of life, the needs of the highly skilled with the economic development of the entire city. This harmonization of contradictions and antagonisms is to be achieved at the urban level through a rallying of the good and the great, the movers and shakers, the rich and the poor, shanty dwellers and property capital, men and women, to the banner of 'good governance'. And that they will so rally is, it appears, assured through the same 'accumulated knowledge and experience' that has recognized the virtues of multidimensional sustainable development. Adequate forms of urban governance are thus central to securing the neoliberal project as it is pursued in different forms and to different degrees in different local, regional, national and transnational contexts.

Concluding remarks

I have considered the meaning of GSP and the 'good governance' of cities in relation to world society as a horizon of social communication and action. This connects to the social constructivist theoretical paradigm, with its emphasis on the construal of social problems as occurring prior to the pursuit of social policy and having a performative role in constituting the social field. Likewise, it provides a link to Foucauldian studies of truth regimes and governmental technologies. However, from a CPE perspective, it is essential to explore the structural, discursive, technological and agential factors that select some construals for policy action and that lead to some policies being consolidated rather than being rejected. A third theme was multiscalar agency, noting that GSP is construed and pursued at many scales and that good governance is likewise multiscalar. In developing this argument, however, multiscalar has been reinterpreted in terms of multispatial metagovernance (MSMG) and agents should therefore be related not only to a scalar division of labour but also to their territorial, place-based, and network-mediated forms and modes of agency. Fourth, comments on governance failure, metagovernance, metagovernance failure and collibration were combined with more focused arguments about the governmental technologies that have been deployed in the framing, formulation and implementation of social policy. This theme is taken further in Chapter 9.

The dynamics of economic and social partnerships and governance failure

I now turn to the scalar dynamics of economic and social governance through two further case studies. I address the failure of local economic governance in two local English regions in the 1990s that pursued different projects – Dartford in the North West Kent region and Greater Manchester. I conclude this chapter with the long-term historical dynamics of corporatism and its contemporary evolution.

Two regional case studies

This section briefly illustrates some of the above themes by considering two cases from my two regional research sites, the Thames Gateway and the North West. The first concerns an interorganizational partnership centred in Dartford in North West Kent in the UK and concerned with a particular property-led development project; the second concerns networks mobilized around the Manchester Olympic bids as a larger place-marketing exercise for Manchester and the North West. Both cases can be interpreted as instances of governance failure as well as governance success.

Kent Thames-side Agency and London Science Park at Dartford

When the research team conducted interviews in Dartford at the beginning of research on the Thames Gateway region in 1993–96, we were confidently informed by various politicians, local government officers and spokespeople for Dartford Chamber of Commerce that one of the town's big successes was to have secured planning permission for the London Science Park at Dartford (hereafter LSP). (For the background to the expansion of the Thames Gateway region, see DCLG, 2006.) At the conclusion of our research in 1996, the Science Park project had been scaled down and was still far from being fully established (see Dartford Borough Council, 1999):

A district comprising the London Science Park at Dartford, the University of Greenwich and Littlebrook Lakes Business Park. This is being promoted by Dartford Borough Council, The University of Greenwich, the Wellcome Foundation and South Thames Regional Health Authority. This mixed use proposal has been described as the first in a new generation of science parks, one which does not act as an isolated "park", but that is integrated with nearby Dartford town centre. It includes a research and development centre, higher education facilities and student residences, a forum for business innovation as a catalyst for new scientific and manufacturing collaboration, plus a range of housing, shops and restaurants, all well served by public transport. (Thomas and Cousins, 1996: 286)

In 2005, the University of Greenwich wound up the dormant company, London Science Park Limited, and allowed the trademark registration for 'London Science Park at Dartford' to lapse at the end of its current registration period. Exploring why illustrates many of the constraints on local governance.

The first set of constraints has to do with the dynamic of capitalism that was far beyond the control of the local authority and its partners. Three major obstacles (among many) to the LSP's timely establishment can be noted: the uneven development of the South East economy, the problems of property-led development under a neoliberal regime and the conflicting temporal and spatial horizons of action of different public and private sector partners. The Thames Gateway initiative (initially flagged as the East Thames Corridor) was intended to redress the overheating of the South East economy (especially to the west of London) and to exploit the opening towards Europe by promoting growth in the east; this would have the additional advantage of exploiting brownfield and derelict land along the Thames and thus relieve pressure on the green belt. But the problems of industrial and urban decay affecting the East Thames region were not removed simply through declaration of the Thames Gateway initiative (especially given the emphasis on private enterprise more than public funding), and continued to disfavour investment in the region for high-tech projects. Moreover, as the property-led development approach needs continued economic expansion to justify investment, the collapse of Chancellor of the Exchequer Nigel Lawson's boom in the late 1980s and the resulting overhang of property investments in the City and South East proved a further disincentive. This, in turn, produced conflicting expectations about the various time horizons and priorities for profitable development of the proposed LSP site between private and public sector partners – compounded by the greater spatial scope of action for the two partners whose activities extended well beyond the local to the regional, national and international scales. This was reflected in conflicts around three issues: the most appropriate uses, the ideal sequencing and the proper distribution of profits from bringing different parcels of land in different ownership into development. A merger between the two pharmaceutical companies, Glaxo and Wellcome, also altered the interests of a key partner in the LSP project.

The second set of constraints has to do with the insertion of the LSP project into the wider set of local government and governance arrangements. Of significance here was the turbulent political environment for the partners in the Kent Thames-side agency concerned with the LSP. The rationale for the partnership was the pooled interdependence of Dartford Borough Council (a major local landholder and planning authority wishing to upgrade the town's image and economic prospects), the Wellcome Foundation (a leading international pharmaceutical company and major local employer, that later merged with Glaxo in 1995 and later became Glaxo-Smith-Kline), the local health authority (with a redundant hospital site and plans for expansion), Blue Circle Industries (a major landowner and property developer by virtue of its disused chalk pits in North West Kent) and the University of Greenwich (interested in developing a new campus, including student accommodation, and boosting research links with industry by locating at the LSP site). Three sources of uncertainty and turbulence (among others) that affected the project were: (1) central government-induced changes in the status, powers and ownership rights of the health authority (in turn, a regional health authority, a district authority and NHS trust) and hence in its interests in the project; (2) politically motivated delays in government commitments to infrastructure projects and spending essential to the overall growth dynamic of the subregion, notably around the Channel Tunnel Rail Link, the international rail terminal and road links; and (3) changes in central government policy on HE and training that affected the interests of the University of Greenwich regarding campus accommodation and research strategy.

Paradoxically, the partnership itself appears to have worked well. A clear recognition of pooled interdependence provided a continuing framework for negotiation around the need to balance conflicting property interests and the overall economic, political and social benefits of cooperation; a flexible framework that avoided a once-and-for-all decision on the appropriate legal form and membership of the partnership encouraged a balance between openness and closure and between governability and flexibility; and the insertion of the LSP into a broader and largely consensual local and regional accumulation strategy developed by the borough council permitted balance between economic efficiency and political accountability. As delays in complementary economic projects (a major regional shopping centre, an international rail terminal, the high-speed Channel Tunnel Rail Link) were overcome and the Thames Gateway role as the bridge between London and Europe became a reality, the prospects for a scaled-down version of the LSP feeding into a more general pattern of synergetic growth looked better than they did at the end of our research. This can be seen in the subsequent development of The Bridge scheme at the site in 2016–17 (see www.thebridgedartford. co.uk/).

The Manchester Olympic bid

The Manchester Olympic bid for 1996 illustrates the paradox of a successful failure, a project that could be successfully marketed despite failing in key respects (Bovaird, 1994).[1] If one regards them as place-marketing exercises linked to property-led development, they helped market Manchester, mobilized important grants for urban regeneration and secured widespread recognition and support at home and abroad. Indeed, if one accepts that the actual staging of the Games could prove costly, the eventual failure to secure them could even be considered a success (contrast the Olympic experiences of Montréal and Barcelona or Sheffield and the World Student Games). The presentational politics of the bidding process required a united front among local partners and this, combined with the broadly positive-sum nature of the Olympics-legitimated but state-aided and property-led development project, provided the context in which the various dilemmas of partnership were managed in the short term.

From a governance viewpoint, three points need making. First, Manchester's Olympic strategy illustrates the complementarity and interdependence among different scales of economic and political action. Local governance is not confined to the local level. The bid strategy and outcome involved a complex interplay between (1) local economic and political capacities and priorities, (2) national and international systems of rule setting (especially those of the Department of the Environment and the International Olympic Committee), and (3) European and central government political and economic strategies.

Second, the broad-based grant-coalition that fronted the Olympic bids was firmly rooted not only in material interdependences but also in established informal interpersonal networking among business leaders, political figures and other local elites. This was the basis of trust for interorganizational negotiations and the formation of a broad-based hegemonic project for the region. Although Sir Bob Scott (whose role as leader of the Olympic bid was famously described as 'a man and his secretary sitting in an office and masquerading as an institution') achieved a high profile in the bid process as the public (and acceptable) face of private capital, a key metagovernance role was also performed by the local authorities under the leadership of Manchester City Council. This is clear not only in promotional activities but also in various project management activities.

And third, the Olympic bid provided a positive-sum game for developing a broadly consensual local accumulation strategy and hegemonic project. They provided the basis for levering European and central government funding, secured property-led regeneration, enhanced the image of Manchester (with some skilfully contrived confusion between Manchester City Council and Greater Manchester), promised benefits to the North West more generally and attracted considerable local popular support. With the second failure to win the Olympics nomination, much of this unity and support was dissipated. A pattern of fragmentation and duplication of partnerships reasserted itself. This illustrates the role of strategy and vision as well as structures in maintaining local governance (for further details on the Manchester Olympics case study, see Cochrane et al, 1996; Jessop et al, 1999).

At first sight, the Olympic bid process underlined claims that British urban politics are becoming more like those in the US: pro-growth, dominated by business, departing from the British party political norm, and, despite the continued concentration of power at central government level, tending towards relative disintegration at local governance level. Manchester's Olympic bid was locally judged to be less about sport than about economic growth and, in the context of a declining regional economy, regeneration. The bid was initiated, and run, by people from the private sector, although there was strong moral and material support from both local institutions of governance (the local authority, the local urban development corporations) and later, national government. Support for the bid was not politicized and attracted all-party support. In a very short period, the Olympic bid acquired almost hegemonic status: it was regarded as self-evident that winning the Olympics would be good for Manchester, a truth proclaimed by companies supporting the bidding process. As growth machine theory would predict, there was heavy representation from local construction companies, regional utilities, the only bank with local headquarters and the local media. Likewise, there was strong support from those institutions that Logan and Molotch (1987: 75) view as 'auxiliary players': the universities, organized labour (inasmuch as the regional Trades Union Congress [TUC] supported it), and corporate capitalists. The Olympic bid also saw the City Council's senior officers and political leaders take part in transforming the modus operandi of local economic development. The new approach would be based on elite networking, opportunism and a more entrepreneurial approach on the part of officers and the whole organization.

Yet, Manchester politics, particularly those played out in the Olympic bid, also show that, however great the superficial convergence of state structures, growth machine theory is far from an adequate explanatory framework. The bid actually demonstrates the limitations of local strategic capacity. This conclusion would still hold even if the Olympic bid had been successful: success would have depended just as much on playing the game according to the rules and on a playing field shaped by extra-local forces. Both sets of partners – public and private – had only limited control over the development process. At its most benign, this might result in a mutually beneficial local pooling of resources and influence, but it could just as often ensure that both parties' goals are undermined. This possibility could occur through subordination to the (geographic) centre or through constraints rooted in the wider – global – rules by which the place-marketing game is being played. Obsessive concern with how power and control are being redistributed locally can mask the full extent to which the locus of power has already shifted away from all local actors, whether in business or local government. Despite this, in the new language of partnership, it must be presented as a process of local negotiation.

> 'It's very difficult, in some of the partnerships that we have, to say that the control is absolutely here [with the City Council]. You can say, if it comes to some of the schemes, that the control is with the Council, ... you can say that control is with central government, ... you can say it's with the people who are actually running the bid ... [In reality] they're partnerships where people have vetoes.' (Councillor, Manchester City Council)

Few in the city were inclined (or indeed, sufficiently knowledgeable) to question this informally regulated system of local checks and balances as long as there was still some prospect of winning the Olympic Games nomination. Eyes were firmly fixed on the big picture – the possibility of winning the Games and the need to maintain a unified voice during the bidding period. It was deemed counterproductive and even treacherous to question the politics or finances of the bidding process during a time of maximum global exposure. Any bid for the Olympics must, above all, be about 'feel-good politics' (see Hill, 1992). Thus, the bidding process exerted a kind of local hegemonic discipline on urban political actors: it was taken as axiomatic in Manchester that the city's ability to 'deliver' the Games depended on the continued strength of its new 'partnership'.

Despite the emergence of what looked like a more vibrant localized politics, Manchester's Olympic project was heavily dependent on the decisions of national political actors. Manchester's 'new money' was, of course, anything but, since it was top-sliced from urban spending programmes (Dalby, 1993), and Manchester achieved the unique position of having its own expenditure line in the Department of the Environment's published spending plans (DoE, 1993). Thus Manchester's Olympic bid must be seen as part of a wider reorganization in the funding and delivery of urban aid, as part of what Stewart (1994) sees as a competitively (and centrally) orchestrated 'new localism [based on the] decentralization of administration as opposed to the devolution of power and influence' (1994: 143). Despite this state-sponsored rush to form partnerships, local business coalitions are still very fragile. In fact, they often rupture when confronted with divisive issues or challenges of political priority setting (Peck and Tickell, 1994, 1995).

In short, while there were superficial similarities between urban governance in the US and urban regimes emerging in the UK, this convergence is due neither to the actions of autonomous political elites nor to the dominance of local property interests. Instead, they have arisen from changing structural constraints, the redefinition of strategic contexts, changed modes of political rationality on the part of the British central state and the European Commission, and the gradual adaptation of local states to these constraints as they seek to manage the repercussions of uneven development in ways that sustain local political legitimacy. I would particularly highlight the following factors:

- the crisis of Britain's flawed Fordism and of its associated Keynesian welfare national state, which has prompted demands for supranational crisis management and also generated space for regional and local resurgence;

- the discursive constitution of new policy paradigms that emphasize flexibility and entrepreneurialism as appropriate responses to the rigidities of a crisis-prone Fordism and the increased significance of structural competitiveness in international, inter-regional, and indeed, intraregional competition;
- the tendential hollowing out of the national state – a process that, in the UK at least, is nonetheless regulated by the national state through enhanced central control over the legitimate forms and objectives of local authority economic intervention as well as through vigorous promotion of the shift from local government to quite specific forms of local governance;
- the parallel promotion by the European Commission of local and regional partnerships – motivated, however, by a desire to weaken national states and secure support for a 'Europe of the regions';
- the search by local authorities themselves for some autonomous political space in which to continue to deliver goods and services to local communities and secure re-election in a period of after-Fordist crisis;
- the emergence of new forms of 'political capitalism', that is, the search for new opportunities for profit through support for specific political projects (including politically administered recommodification) and wholly or partly state-financed economic undertakings.

Corporatism and its periodization

Corporatism is a word with many meanings, reflecting the long history of the institutions and practices to which it refers, and the range of economic, political and social interests that it mobilizes and affects, whether positively or negatively (for a literature survey, see Cardoso and Mendonça, 2012). For present purposes, it comprises a continuous, integrated system of representation, policy formation and policy implementation that is organized in terms of the function in the division of labour, broadly understood, of those involved in such arrangements. Other features, however important in practice, are contingent. They include the ideological justification, the political legitimation, the specific functional bases and the precise organizational forms of corporatist representation, the levels and sites where corporatist structures operate, the actual scope, purposes and mode of policy-making, the particular forms of implementation, and the place (if any) of corporatism in the overall state system (Jessop, 2007c: 503). Changing corporatist institutions and practices, and their variable importance in economic performance, political stability and social cohesion, exclude valid transhistorical definition or easy generalization from specific cases.

Disregarding earlier guild arrangements and the system of estates (*Ständestaat*) that preceded the modern state, corporatism in modern Europe and societies elsewhere influenced by European ideas and/or colonization has seen four main phases. The significance of each phase varies across different territories, places, scales and social networks. In addition, later phases partly overlay earlier ones and thereby transform their forms and functions (for further discussion, see Jessop, 2007c).

Periods in corporatist development

Corporatism first arose in the modern era as a politico-ideological critique of liberal capitalism. This reflected oppositional movements among feudal and traditional petty *bourgeois* classes (such as artisans and yeoman farmers), Catholic and/or other religious groups and some intellectual circles. They criticized the rampant individualism, social disorder and open class conflict produced by the transition to capitalism and its subsequent laissez-faire operation, and they demanded the restoration of social order through cooperation among professional and vocational associations. Inspired, in part, by medieval guilds and estate representation, and oriented to a universalistic, harmonistic state and society, this organic corporativism was both reactionary and utopian. It could not halt the rise of a 19th-century liberal capitalism that was mediated through anarchic market forces or of a mass democracy based on individual suffrage. But it remains as a minor current in the corporatist intellectual tradition, and is often reinvoked in periods of economic crisis.

The second phase coincided with the rise of monopoly capitalism and growing competition among capitalist economies and was linked with notions such as 'organized capitalism'. The dominant corporatist projects did not oppose capitalism, which was now consolidated and displaying imperialistic tendencies, but aimed to avoid proletarian revolution and/or domination by foreign capital. They called for new forms of interest organization and/or societal regulation to defuse social unrest, and for new institutional means and strategies to enhance national competitiveness or compensate for its relative weakness. This sort of corporatism was typically promoted by firms and business associations. In addition, during periods of acute political crisis, prolonged war or immediate postwar reconstruction, it was also promoted by the state. In doing so, it acted as a sovereign power to defend its own authority and social cohesion more generally, and/or as an intermediary of corporatist interests in the business community. How far labour movements were involved alongside business and the state depended on the reformist economic and political orientation of organized labour, the importance of skilled labour and productivity in the prevailing mode of growth, and the balance of economic and political forces.

The crisis-ridden period between the two World Wars reinforced the corporatist tendencies of this second phase, leading to two kinds of outcome in Europe and the American hemisphere. Some corporatist structures and strategies were imposed from above by fascist or authoritarian regimes to address acute economic, political and ideological crises. Others emerged from below (often with state sponsorship) to assist economic or political crisis management in more liberal democratic regimes. These patterns were so common by the early 1930s that one Romanian economic and political theorist, Mihaïl Manoïlescu, with mercantilist and fascist proclivities, predicted (indeed, recommended) that the 'twentieth century will be the century of corporatism just as the nineteenth century was the century of liberalism' (Manoïlescu, 1934). He had earlier suggested that corporatism, whether in pure form or as a subordinate element in hybrid regimes, could help (semi-)peripheral economies to catch up with more advanced industrial economies, and could also enhance representation and legitimation for more developed social formations (Manoïlescu, 1929). Nonetheless, these societal and statist corporatist tendencies were not all-powerful or ubiquitous. Sometimes, they were a subordinate but functional part of the economic and political order. And, in cases such as fascist and authoritarian regimes, corporatist projects often proved little more than an ideological cloak for other practices and institutions.

The third wave emerged in attempts at economic crisis management in liberal democratic regimes in the 1960s and 1970s. It was usually tripartite, involving business, organized labour and the state. Successful cases helped to stabilize societies oriented to economic growth and mass consumption by underpinning existing macro-economic measures with incomes, labour market and industrial policies. Corporatism was intended to supplement and reinforce these policies by legitimating new forms of state intervention that went beyond traditional methods of parliamentary and bureaucratic rule and by securing more effective representation for producer interests than was feasible through generalized pluralism or catch-all electoral parties. This 'neocorporatist' wave tended to be partial, intermittent and ad hoc. It enjoyed a limited revival in the 1990s in the guise of 'social pacts' designed to underpin active labour market policies, progressive competitiveness strategies, 'flexicurity' and similar forms of crisis-induced selective corporatism.

Phase four emerged in the 1980s and is still expanding. It involves a wider range of functional interests, including local authorities, scientific communities, professional associations, NGOs and social movements, and it extends beyond reactive economic and political crisis management to include proactive strategies for competitiveness and activities in other issue areas that are politically sensitive as well as complex. This phase is less often discussed under the rubric of corporatism, in part because of the negative association of this term with 'over-mighty' unions and the crises of the 1970s. It is more often analysed in terms such as public–private partnerships, stakeholding, networking, interorganizational collaboration, regulated self-regulation, generalized political exchange, productive solidarity, productivity coalitions, learning regions, the social economy, participatory governance, associational democracy, and so on. These diverse forms can be linked via the notions of governance and metagovernance.

This fourth phase partly reprises the second, with its twin emphases on tackling a 'democratic deficit' in political institutions and mobilizing the relevant private, public, third sector and civil society 'stakeholders' to develop more effective economic and social policies in an increasingly complex world. Moreover, just as advocates of tripartism tried to distance it from the discredited period of authoritarian corporatism, advocates of the current phase emphasize its differences from phase three by calling for wider participation in corporatist arrangements, and referring to 'new governance', social or territorial pacts, the networked economy, and so on. The 'open method of coordination' (OMC) in Europe exemplifies this new phase, linked, as it is, to concerns about competitiveness, the 'democratic deficit', social cohesion and the complexity of policy-making and policy implementation in a global era (Zeitlin and Pochet, 2005).

As this brief periodization indicates, corporatism, albeit in varied guises, tends to recur in modern societies. This reflects four features of capitalist formations: (1) the growing socialization of the forces of production, despite continued private ownership of the means of production; (2) the dilemmas posed by the shared interest of producer classes and groups in maximizing total revenues and the conflict over their allocation; (3) the need for operationally and organizationally distinct but functionally interdependent forces to consult about the economic impact of state policies and the political repercussions of private economic decision-making; and (4) the challenge of reconciling particular interests in civil society. Each feature creates incentives to adopt one or another kind of functional representation to address the problems that it generates for economic policy and political stability. It is sometimes posited that corporatist and governance arrangements insert a neutral third terrain between market and state, where such social problems can be resolved impartially. In fact, they add another site, with its own representational asymmetries and policy biases, where the conflicts, contradictions and dilemmas inherent in capitalism and other features of modern society are contested. Yet, corporatism cannot eliminate these sources of tension. Thus, the same features of economic, political and civil society that generate corporatist tendencies also limit their effectiveness and survival capacities. The resulting instabilities help to explain the recurrent rise, fall and return of corporatism (Jessop, 1990b). Its most recent incarnation is 'governance'.

Corporatism and modes of governance

Governance is a polysemic notion in need of disambiguation. It has both broad and narrow referents. In broad terms, it is common to distinguish three or four main modes of coordination of complex, reciprocal interdependence: exchange, command, network, and sometimes, solidarity. These correspond to: *ex post* coordination through exchange (for example, the anarchy of the market); *ex ante* coordination through imperative coordination (for example, the hierarchy of the firm, organization or state); reflexive self-organization (for example, the heterarchy of networked negotiation to secure the consensual coordination of a complex social relations); and solidarity based on unconditional commitment to others (for example, loyalty inside small communities or within imagined communities during crises). Each type has its own modes of calculation and logics of action, but also has distinctive forms of failure (Kooiman, 1993a; Jessop, 2002b; Meuleman, 2008). In each case, successful governance requires complementary activities and operations by other actors, which depend, in turn, on complementary activities and operations performed elsewhere in a social system. This is the basis for hybrid forms, the search for complementarities among modes of governance and the practices and institutions of metagovernance.

Heterarchic governance tends to fail due to the general problem of 'governability', that is, the question of whether a specific socially and discursively constituted object of governance could ever be manageable given the complexity and turbulence of the material, social and spatio-temporal conditions in which it is embedded. This is a basic feature of any attempt to 'problematize' selectively and resolve challenges in the natural and/or social world. As Foucault noted, this requires appropriate discourses, the development of corresponding technologies of government, governance, or governmentality, appropriate subjects able to govern, be governed, or govern themselves, and a *dispositif*, apparatus or institutional ensemble with the requisite variety of resources, capacities and powers to manage the problem as it has been defined (Foucault, 1977 [1975], 2007, 2008). Governance failure is also related to specific 'governability' issues rooted in specific objects and agents of governance, specific modes of coordination of reciprocal interdependence and problems of unacknowledged conditions of action and unanticipated consequences. This is especially troublesome where the objects of governance are liable to change and/or their environment is turbulent, making strategic learning difficult (Dierkes et al, 2001; see also Haas and Haas, 1995; Eder, 1999). As elaborated below, the dominance of capital accumulation as a principle of societalization is a major source of such ungovernability thanks to the inherent contradictions and antagonisms in the capital relation and their generalization through world market integration. However, just as love of money is not the source of all evil, capital does not generate all governance problems! Other societalization principles produce other sets of problems.

Modern systems theory and societalization

Niklas Luhmann, the well-known postwar German systems theorist, distinguished three modes of societalization: segmentation, centre–periphery relations and functional differentiation. Although he tended to present them as successive stages in societal organization, they are not mutually exclusive, and can be combined in different ways. Regarding the third (and allegedly final) mode of societalization, Luhmann argued that each functional system had its own specific operating codes and programmes that served to define its unique and enduring role in world society. To take just four examples, the modern economy is a self-perpetuating system of payments; the modern legal system is a self-contained and self-modifying system of legally binding legal decisions; the science system is a self-perpetuating system of scientific communications coded in terms of true/false; and the political system produces collectively binding decisions that generate further political decisions. That said, he also stressed that a system's operational autonomy is limited by its embedding in a complex environment and by its material dependence on the performance of other systems that have their own codes and programmes. This holds for each and every system, creating inordinately complex reciprocal interdependence. From this, Luhmann concludes that modern societies are so highly differentiated and polycentric that no single system, central decision-making body or ruling class could ever coordinate their diverse interactions, organizations and institutions, and ensure their harmonious cooperation towards a common end.

Despite such complex reciprocal interdependence, Luhmann argued that each functional system can maintain its operational autonomy in so far as it has its own operating codes, has sufficient time to implement them, faces competing demands so that it can choose which demands to process, and has the general legitimacy or societal trust needed to operate without having constantly to justify its specific activities on each occasion. Without these four conditions, a functional system can lose its operational autonomy. In this respect, although Luhmann insisted on the *formal equivalence* and *non-substitutability* of functional systems, it is clear that some systems can be more or less *substantively dominant* in the still emerging world society and therefore have more power to shape its overall development than other systems. Even Luhmann conceded that the economy, law and political system (especially the state) are more tightly coupled than other systems and tend to have more influence in the evolution of world society than other systems. He added that this is reflected in how a dominant system shapes how the codes and programmes of other systems are implemented (see Luhmann, 1988, 2005). This poses an interesting question regarding the conditions and modalities in which a given functional system might weaken the operational autonomy of other systems.

In this regard, if we accept, for the moment, that modern societies are functionally differentiated, there are likely to be competing societalization principles, processes and projects associated with efforts to extend the code and programme of one system at the expense of others. Rival principles could include economization, juridification, politicization, militarization, sacralization, medicalization, scientization, aestheticization and ethicalization. It is also possible for identities and values anchored in civil society (or the lifeworld, rather than system world) to become the basis of societalization. Examples might include ethnicity or 'race' (apartheid), gender (patriarchy), generation (gerontocracy) or nationality (nation-statehood). This argument is developed below in relation to the logic of profit-oriented, market-mediated economic action as the primary basis of capital accumulation, organization of a social formation under the dominance of profit-oriented, market-mediated differential accumulation as the axial principle of social organization involves far more than market exchange and continuing accumulation. These can also occur in theocracies, national security states, new nations, revolutionary situations or state socialist societies. In addition to capitalist commodity production for the market, the development and consolidation of capitalist (or *bourgeois*) societalization requires the relative subordination of an entire social order to the changing imperatives and logic of capital accumulation. Four factors contribute to this: economic determination, economic domination, *bourgeois* hegemony, and ecological dominance. Each factor has many aspects, involves several causal mechanisms and has its own contingent conditions of existence (see Jessop, 2002b).

Ecological dominance exists to the extent that one system in a self-organizing ecology of self-organizing systems imprints its developmental logic on other systems' operations more than any of these can impose their respective logics on that system. In short, even if all functional systems are equal, some may be more equal than others. As the term implies, ecological dominance involves an *ecological relation* where one system becomes dominant in a complex, coevolving situation; it does not involve a one-sided *relation of domination* in which one system unilaterally imposes its logic or will on others (Morin, 1980: 44). This capacity is mediated in and through the operational logics of other systems and the communicative rationalities of the lifeworld. The concept can also be fruitfully applied, as the field of organizational ecology indicates, to interorganizational relations. There is no 'last instance' in relations of ecological dominance – they are always differential (rather than applying equally across all systems), have conjunctural as well as structural aspects, and are contingent.

Further remarks on ecological dominance

This section presents seven analytically distinct, but empirically interrelated, aspects of the social world that affect a system's potential to become ecologically dominant. They can be grouped into internal, transversal and external mechanisms. For the sake of brevity, the features are described in general terms only in Table 9.1, and the following discussion shows their specific relevance to the profit-oriented, market-mediated economic regime based on the rule of capital, with its distinctive, self-valorizing logic. I argue that capital accumulation tends to have just those properties that favour its ecological dominance over other types of social relations.

- First, as the capitalist economy becomes disembedded from other systems and the world market becomes more integrated, the treadmill of competition for above-average rates of profit becomes

Table 9.1: Factors relevant to ecological dominance in the relations among functional systems

Internal	• Scope for self-transformation because internal competition matters more in its development than external adaptive pressures
	• Internal structural and operational complexity and the scope for spontaneous self-adaptation faced with perturbation or disruption
	• Capacity to engage in time-space distantiation and/or compression to exploit more opportunities for self-reproduction
Transversal	• Capacity to displace internal contradictions and dilemmas onto other systems, into the environment, or defer them into the future
	• Capacity to redesign other systems and shape their evolution via context-steering and/or constitutional (re-)design
External	• Extent to which other actors accept that the ecologically dominant system's operations are central to societal reproduction and orient their own actions to support or preserve support this system
	• Extent to which a given system is the biggest source of external adaptive pressure on other systems and/or is more important than their respective internal pressures for system development

Source: Licensed and adapted from Jessop (2010a: 178)

an ever more powerful driving force in accumulation. Pressures originating in other systems are simply opportunities for capital to seek profits and/or avoid losses, and are thereby translated into another source of internal competition. Finance capital controls the most liquid, abstract and generalized resource, and is therefore better equipped to respond to opportunities for profit and external perturbations, especially with the development of derivatives and other means of globally commensurating risks and assets (cf Bryan and Rafferty, 2006).

• Second, the capitalist economy is internally complex and flexible thanks to the decentralized, anarchic nature of market forces and the dual role of price formation as a flexible mechanism for allocating capital and other resources and as a stimulus to adaptive learning and self-reflection. Capital is better able to tolerate disturbances in its environment because of its greater internal complexity (multiplicity and heterogeneity of elements), the looser coupling among these elements and its capacity for self-monitoring (Baraldi et al, 1998: 151). This is facilitated where there is a complex, self-organizing ecology of organizations, institutions and apparatuses that specialize in different tasks and/or have different spatio-temporal horizons of action that provide more scope for the logic of differential accumulation to continue even as individual capitalist enterprises succumb to the effects of shock and competition.

- Third, capital has developed strong capacities to extend its operations in time and space and/or to compress them in these regards. These capacities facilitate the real-time integration of the world market and make it easier for capital to maintain its self-expansionary logic in the face of perturbations. They are related to the anarchic, formal, procedural rationality of the market, its reliance on the symbolic medium of money to facilitate economic transactions despite disjunctions in time and place, its highly developed abstract and technical codes (with well-developed mechanisms of capitalist accounting and monetary returns as its easily calculable formal maximand), and the requisite variety of its internal operations. This increases capital's 'resonance capacity' to react to internal and external conditions (Luhmann, 1988: 44–50).

- Fourth, through its comparative advantage in organizing STFs, capital develops its chances of avoiding the structural constraints of other systems and the attempts of actors within these systems to control capital accumulation. This increases its 'indifference' to the environment (cf Lohmann, 1991; cf Luhmann, 1988). This holds especially for the only economic *sub*system that has become more or less fully integrated on a global scale: international finance (Luhmann, 1996). Of course, finance (let alone the economy more generally) cannot escape its overall dependence on the performance of other functional systems or evade the crisis tendencies associated with its own internal contradictions and dilemmas. But efforts to escape particular constraints and attempts at control occur through its own internal operations in time (discounting, insurance, risk management, futures, derivatives, hedge funds, and so on) or space (capital flight, relocation, outsourcing abroad, claims to extra-territoriality, and so forth), the integration of exchange value or revenue considerations into the calculations and operations of non-economic organizations central to capital accumulation or simple personal corruption.

- Fifth, compared to natural evolution, social evolution may involve reflexive self-organization and efforts to redesign the environment. This may extend to efforts to shape the coevolution of organizations, systems, and eventually, world society, and to change the mode of social evolution (for example, through extending market relations into ever more spheres of social life). Where different organizations and systems seek to adapt to and/or to change their environment, 'the logic of evolutionary progress is toward ecosystems that sustain only the dominant, environment-controlling species, and its symbionts and parasites' (Bateson, 1972: 451). This poses the question of the relative capacity of different organizations and systems to change their environment rather than adapt to it and the general limits of societal steering.

• Sixth, the primacy of accumulation over other principles of societalization (for example, national security, 'racial' supremacy, religious fundamentalism, social solidarity) exists to the extent that the self-descriptions and social values of profit-oriented, market-mediated accumulation are articulated, represented and accepted in everyday language, the mass media and public sphere, and are central to struggles for political action. It therefore represents the singular identity of (world) society. And accumulation is represented as the illusory interest of an entire population (cf Marx and Engels, 1975; Gramsci, 1975). Where hegemony is secured, economic considerations will become decisive in how other functional systems interpret their codes and programmes, for example, in choosing scientific research topics, deciding what is newsworthy, calculating the 'quality of life years' in the medical system, and so on. It also influences the decision premises of organizations, including weighing the relative priority accorded to economic interests when they seek to limit negative externalities on other systems and 'civil society' that arise from their own operations. Parallel power networks are a key mechanism of system and social integration when negative as well as positive coordination are at stake (Poulantzas, 1978; Baecker, 2001, 2006).

• Seventh, the ecologically dominant system is the main source of external adaptive pressure on other systems. In general, any increase in the complexity of one functional system tends to increase the complexity of the environment of other systems, and forces them to increase their own internal complexity in order to maintain their capacity for autopoiesis (Baraldi et al, 1998: 96). For reasons stated above in relation to the first factor, the world market is currently the most internally complex functional system in a still emerging world society and hence, the biggest source of adaptive pressure on other systems. An alternative criterion, proposed by Wagner (2006), is that the ecologically dominant system is the one that causes more problems for other systems when it fails than other systems cause for this system when they fail. Moreover, where the internationalization of the state and the development of international governance arrangements are most advanced, we can observe a strong penetration of capitalist economic imaginaries and interests. This uneven integration of world society enhances the capacity of the profit-oriented, market-mediated economy to colonize other functional systems and the lifeworld through their acceptance of the logic of commodification and the adoption of net revenues as the major secondary criterion in choosing among preferred options in terms of their respective primary codes (see the preceding discussion of factor six).

This does not exclude reciprocal influence from other systems as their operations and dynamic disturb, irritate or disrupt the circuit of capital and thereby influence, in turn, its profit-oriented, market-mediated evolution. Nor does it exclude a short-term shift towards the primacy of another functional system and its operational logic in the face of emergencies for which that system is better suited, and solving it is critical for the reproduction of all systems, including the economy. For example, during major wars or preparations for them in a peacetime war economy, states may try to plan or guide the economy in the light of military-political priorities. After such states of emergency end, path-dependent traces may remain. Continuing the example, this might include a strong military-industrial complex. Even here, however, as a state of exception is dismantled, the logic of the ecologically dominant system is likely to reassert itself, reordering priorities in its favour within these path-dependent legacies. In this case, military expenditure would be driven by capitalist interests and oriented to profitability rather than by military logic established through 'the audit of war'.

I suggested that, in the current stage of world society, which involves the increasing integration of the world market in the shadow of neoliberalism, these factors tend to give the profit-oriented, market-mediated economic order just those properties that enable it to cause more problems for other systems than they can cause for it. The same factors also influence the internal organization, operations and dynamics of the world market. This situation conditions the viability of both societal and state corporatism. Thus, a backward-looking corporativism (phase one), organized capitalism (phase two), and tripartite neocorporatism (phase three) encountered, in turn, barriers to survival. These arose from, respectively, the irreversibility of modernity (phase one), the growing importance of the space of flows in industrial economies relative to the imperialist logic of territorial conquest (evident both in the heyday of imperialism and its prolongation into the interwar period in phase two), and the internationalization of advanced capitalist economies after 1945, especially through the expansion and deepening of transnational commodity chains and through the global organization of financial flows (phase three). This last trend not only intensified the crisis of postwar Fordism and its tripartite mode of regulation, but also prompted calls for 'more market, less state', be it through neoliberal regime shifts or more piecemeal neoliberal adaptation. As the limits of liberalized, deregulated market forces as a governance mechanism were encountered once more, neocorporatism was partially revived in the form of selective national growth and stability pacts, and, more significantly, there was a growing momentum in the development of heterarchic governance (phase four).

Concluding remarks

In short, markets, states, network governance and solidarity all fail. This is not surprising. Failure is a central feature of all social relations: 'governance is necessarily incomplete and as a necessary consequence must always fail' (Malpas and Wickham, 1995: 40). Indeed, given the growing structural complexity and opacity of the social world, failure is the most likely outcome of most attempts to govern it in terms of multiple objectives over extended spatial and temporal horizons, whatever coordination mechanism is adopted. This emphasis on the improbability of success serves to counter the rhetoric of partnership that leads commentators to highlight achievements rather than failures and, where they recognize failure, to see it as exceptional and corrigible regarding their preferred mode of coordination even as they see coordination failure elsewhere as inevitable. This polarization is reflected both in the succession of governments and in policy cycles within governments in which different modes of policy-making succeed each other as the difficulties of each become more evident. Postwar British politics offers plenty of evidence of this through the increasingly hectic oscillation among liberal, dirigiste and corporatist modes of economic intervention (witness the successive U-turns in the Heath government of 1970–74 and the Wilson–Callaghan governments of 1974–79).

For reasons that I have explored in more detail elsewhere (see, for example, Jessop, 1997, 1998), I suggest that public–private partnership in its various forms is especially appropriate for securing economic, social and community development in the current period despite its inevitable tendencies towards governance failure. This suggests the need to put such governance arrangements at the core of the coordination repertoire with diverse flanking and supportive measures from other modes of coordination. But there must also be greater commitment to a participatory politics based on stakeholding and to sustainable economic and community development.

10

Competitiveness vs civil society as modes of governance

Extending competition is often proposed as a simple solution to complex problems,[1] yet competition is itself too complex a process to permit simple definition and implementation, and too complex for use as a mode of governance with predictable consequences. However, it has been a key element in New Public Management and, despite disappointing results, remains a major theme in reform proposals. Underpinning the nature and effects of actually existing competition are the competition landscape and the uneven distribution of resources and abilities to compete, whether or not these are fully activated in any given conjuncture. This poses questions of 'competitiveness' – which has again become an important object of state action. Yet this is another conceptually ambiguous, politically controversial and ideologically charged topic. As Robert Reich remarked, unfairly, the idea of national competitiveness moved from obscurity to meaninglessness without any intervening period of coherence (Reich, 1991, cited in Reinert, 1995). Although competitiveness is neglected in neoclassical economics, it does figure in heterodox economics and has also been mobilized to inform economic, political and societal strategies. There are many ways to define and measure it, and past and current economic, legal, political and policy debates indicate the many issues at stake. The two terms are also articulated in different ways in the ideas and practices of the competition state and competition law, and they are also deployed in efforts to promote competition as an ideal (and idealized) mechanism of governance within and far beyond the 'economy'.

My argument proceeds in seven steps. It first considers how competition might become a principle of economic organization and relatedly, how it may become part of state projects and practices. Second, it comments on the discursive and material dimensions of competition, considering it as a social construct and a social constraint. Third, it examines the rather idealized representations of competition in the broader doxa of liberalism and neoliberalism considered in terms of a rough threefold distinction among economic, political and ideological imaginaries, and the limits to the reproduction of these doxa in terms of the complexities of capitalist social relations. Fourth, it explores the complexities of competition in the actually existing world and their role in differential accumulation. Fifth, it considers efforts to steer competition through, inter alia, the competition law and the competition state. Sixth, it relates competition to other modes of governance and identifies limits to its role in this regard and introduces 'metagovernance' as a response to these limits. Finally, it comments on the fetishization of competition as a means to subsume society under the dominance of profit-oriented, market-mediated accumulation.

Competition and societalization

To discuss the conditions in which competition might become a principle of societal organization presupposes that there are fields of social relations that are not yet (or no longer) oriented to economic activities and/or that are not yet organized along market (or quasi-market) principles of one kind or another. We can interpret economization in terms of market extension – with the full integration of the world market as its ultimate horizon of realization. There are six possible steps in this regard, and each involves a different mode of competition. Distinguishing these steps helps explain the uncertain meaning and scope of competition in the economic field:

1. An *exchange economy* develops when want-satisfying material means are distributed, reallocated or circulated through exchange, whether through barter, a separate medium of exchange or debt relations. Exchange replaces other principles of economic organization: householding, reciprocity among similarly organized economic units and redistribution through an allocative centre linked to a political regime (Polanyi, 1957). This step does not require that exchange becomes central to social organization. Indeed, historically, markets existed on the borders of more significant households, redistributive communities and reciprocity-based networks (cf Weber, 1927 [1923]; Polanyi, 1957; Marx, 1996 [1883]).

2. A *commercial economy* develops when commodification and monetization become basic features of economic organization. This occurs insofar as material provisioning acquires the form of commodity production and/or economic agents seek to derive monetary revenues from material provisioning or immaterial activities that were previously outside monetary exchange. This need not be a competitive society, however; monopolies, limits on

competition, principles of fair exchange or just price, and so on, could limit the degree and forms of competition.

3. A rational *market economy* is the site of free trade in commodities, the rational organization of production based on formal book-keeping principles, and trade in money and credit with a view to maximizing gains (Weber, 1927 [1923], 1978 [1922]). The rational organization of production could also be subordinate to non-competitive principles (for example, monastic production). Weber also identified three internally heterogeneous forms of 'political capitalism' in which gain is sought in ways that contradict a rational market economy, namely, through force and domination, unusual deals with political authority or funding political adventures and enterprises.

4. A *capitalist economy* develops when the commodity form is generalized to the four main *fictitious commodities*: land, labour power, money, and knowledge (cf Marx, 1996 [1883]; Polanyi, 2001 [1944]; Jessop, 2007a). This could result from a quantity–quality shift in which the continuing extension and consolidation of the three preceding developments interact to produce a distinctive mode of production. This affects many areas of social life. In particular, capitalism is distinguished from other modes of production through the extension of property rights, contracts and markets to include labour power. This leads to distinct tendential laws (in a descriptive-sociological, not normative-legal, sense) of competition that are the external expression of the immanent nature of the self-valorization and expanded reproduction of the capital relation (Marx, 1996 [1883]: 178).

5. A *competitive financialized economy* develops when the organization and dynamic of capitalism are subordinated to the circuits of capitalist credit money. This process intensifies competition by: (a) enhancing the equalization of profit rates as finance capital *qua* functioning capital is reallocated among competing profit-generating investments; and (b) enhancing the equalization of interest rates as finance capital *qua* property, that is, fictitious capital, is reallocated among alternative asset classes (for example, government bonds, derivatives, gold or fine art). This marks a further step in the economization of all social relations.

6. A fully fledged *finance-dominated capitalist economy* is based on a strategy of ever-increasing *market completion* and ever-more rarefied forms of fictitious capital (reflected in, inter alia, the explosive growth of derivatives), and leverage is used in a competitive search for super-profits. This reinforces the dominance of finance capital

qua property rather than functioning capital, and works both to universalize competition for gain and to generalize and intensify the inherent contradictions of capital accumulation.

The ambiguity of exchange and competition as principles of economic organization also has implications for their role as a mode of governance in reorganizing the polity, politics and policy. This can be seen in different forms of neoliberalism, which emphasizes the virtues of liberalization and deregulation in the market economy, and promotes the fictitious commodification of land, labour power, money and knowledge through their subsumption under market logic. It also aims to extend the principles of market rationality by organizing internal markets in the state and/or adopting market proxies and rank-ordered benchmarks to simulate market competition. This is one of the core principles of New Public Management. The principle of competition can also be extended to calls to privatize state activities (that is, transfer them into a commercial, market or capitalist economy) where these are not deemed to belong to the essential core functions reserved for the sovereign state. A powerful mechanism in this regard is the commitment of the EU to reform the public service around the distinction between services of general economic interest and social services of general interest. A possible future extension of market principles and competition, whether through privatization or competitive tendering by capitalist enterprise to provide publicly funded services, was one goal of the proposed Trans-Pacific Partnership (TPP) and Transatlantic Trade and Investment Partnership (TTIP), which are being strongly promoted by neoliberal governments, led by the US before the rise to power of President Trump and his commitment to 'making America great again', as well as by associated think-tanks and lobbies, and transnational commercial and financial capital.

A further step in enhancing competition would come from financialization. This is already inherent in the modern state's dependence for revenue on taxes on the private sector and/or on loans backed by its monopolies of taxation and coercion. Both means of finance limit the state's activities through threats of tax resistance, avoidance or evasion and/or through the threat of a bondholders' strike as public or sovereign debt increases. More recent examples of financialization include sovereign wealth funds, hedge fund speculation in public and sovereign debt, the entry of private equity into erstwhile public sector activities and the securitization of portfolios of privatized activities (for example, of income flows from the Private Finance

Initiative [PFI] in the UK). These could also be seen as examples of market completion, which, as noted, subordinates all social activities to the logic of profit-oriented, market-mediated competition.

Competition as a social construct and constraint

The preceding section indicates that there is nothing natural about exchange or competition as principles of economic organization and nothing automatic (or, one might add, irreversible) about the progression from an exchange economy to one subordinated to a fully fledged finance-dominated accumulation regime. Likewise, there is no general need to complete the world market and extend competition and competitive principles into an increasing range of social relations. There is no 'natural' or 'spontaneous' implementation of market mechanisms. Each of the six steps identified above is linked to different economic imaginaries that include ideas about competition, competitiveness, economic calculation and the appropriate scope of markets, money, capitalist credit money and the role of financial capital. With each step much effort is required on the part of interested social forces to extend market principles and consolidate them in the face of resistance, frictions, conflicts and crisis tendencies. The nature of market forces varies with the nature of markets (for example, perfect vs monopoly competition, free trade vs protectionism). Different dispositions of resources, different sets of economic agents and different market rules will produce different market outcomes. This highlights the importance of institutional design and suggests that market forces are not a fact of nature but depend on specific social relations. This supports the sociological commonplace that markets must be socially constructed via a set of agreed-on or imposed rules of the game. If specific markets seem to be self-equilibrating mechanisms, this results from adherence to sophisticated regulations concerning the quality of goods exchanged, the inner organization of transactions, the legal penalty for non-compliance, and so on. Without such surveillance mechanisms, private sector opportunism and corporate self-interest would severely distort the alleged smooth adjustment process of supply and demand (see Boyer, 1996).

An important barrier to the extension of competition and market completion is found in the character of land, money, labour power and knowledge as *fictitious* commodities (cf Jessop, 2007c). This claim can be linked to the first four steps discussed above, which were presented here analytically rather than in strict chronological terms. Step one begins when a product (a good or service) is offered for exchange. This may involve no more than a surplus beyond the immediate needs of their producers, can originate in many kinds of production relations and may not involve money as a unit of account, medium of exchange or means of deferred payment. In a commercial economy, commodities are produced for sale and exchanged for money. Merchant capital could have a key role in organizing commerce across space and time. Step three is associated with the development of *capitalist commodity* production, that is, the production of commodities in a labour process subject to capitalist competition to reduce socially necessary labour and turnover times. This works most efficiently where the commodity form is generalized to land, labour power, money and knowledge. These are *fictitious commodities*, that is, they have the form of a commodity (can be bought and sold) but are not produced *in order* to be sold. They do not originate in a profit-oriented labour process subject to competitive pressures of market forces to rationalize production and circulation.

To assume that these four categories are simple and/or capitalist commodities obscures the conditions under which they enter the market economy, get transformed therein and contribute thereby to the production of goods and services for sale. Taking each in turn, land as a fictitious commodity comprises land that has been enclosed and appropriated and then sold or rented in a private commercial transaction with its price reflecting its productive potential and/or market demand; labour power is the capacity to perform useful labour, a capacity reproduced outside the market economy and entering the labour market in return for a wage; money is a marketable store of value and medium of exchange, with competing commodity monies (for example, gold, silver), fiduciary monies (tokens, paper money, bank credits, fiat money) or tradable currencies (for example, dollars, euros, yen); and knowledge as intellectual commons becomes a fictitious commodity when it is transformed into intellectual property, appropriates surplus in the form of royalties and other intellectual property revenue streams, and is treated as an asset class to be securitized and otherwise traded. Markets in fictitious commodities have to be created and institutionalized. Each of these resources could also be redistributed in other ways, for example, territorial conquest, enslavement, requisition or confiscation, direct or indirect reciprocity, and so on (cf Jessop, 2007c).

'The market' can be interpreted as a simplifying self-description of the economy, enabling actors to orient their economic strategies without having to fully comprehend the economy in all its complexity in real time. Understandings of competition and competitiveness are discursively shaped by specific frames, categories, strategies – original, mimetic or imposed – that simplify what would otherwise be too complex to observe, calculate, manage, regulate or govern. Different framings of competition and competitiveness involve forms of action with an uneven impact on positioning of firms, sectors, regions, nations and continents, as well as on the balance of economic and political forces in and beyond the state system itself. But 'the market' is also the actual form of movement of a complex material substratum of economic interactions that are more or less embedded in a wider nexus of social relations. The three processes of marketization, capitalization and financialization are increasingly important vectors in this form of movement. They contribute to the equalization of profit rates and interest rates, the concentration and centralization of capital, generalize 'best practice' (which is often bad practice) through the treadmill of competition, reinforce the logic of differential accumulation based on a political economy of time realized in space, and drive the completion of the world market. Social agents (or indeed, observers) cannot fully comprehend the market in this sense and, *a fortiori*, cannot regulate the market.

Competition, liberalism and neoliberalism

An idealized account of competition became a key element in the promotion of liberalism, and has become even more important in the ideological justification of neoliberalism. But the different forms of *economic* competition noted above are only one moment of liberalism and neoliberalism as principles of *societal* organization. There are also political and ideological moments, and their weight varies within and across liberal and neoliberal regimes.

Economically, liberalism endorses the expansion of the market economy, that is, spreading the commodity form to all factors of production (including labour power as well as land, money and knowledge) and extending formally free, monetized exchange to as many social practices as possible. *Politically*, it holds that collective decision-making should involve a constitutional state with limited substantive powers of economic and social intervention, and a commitment to maximizing the formal freedom of actors in the economy and the substantive freedom of legally recognized subjects in the public sphere. Competition for votes should be confined within the limits of the rule of law to prevent the tyranny of the majority. *Ideologically*, it claims that economic, political and social relations are best organized through the formally free[2] choices of formally free and rational actors who seek to advance their material or ideal interests in an institutional framework that, by accident or design, maximizes the scope for formally free choice. These three principles can lead to conflict over the relative scope of anarchic market relations, collective decision-making and spontaneous self-organization as well as the formal and substantive freedoms available to economic, legal and civil subjects. Consequently, the relative weight of economic, political and civic liberalism within the matrix of liberal principles depends on the changing balance of forces within an institutionalized (but changeable) compromise. This means that the role of competition also changes its meaning across these fields, and, if it is the most important principle of organization of a liberal capitalist world, it is one that is internally heterogeneous and even incoherent.

The recurrence of liberalism is related to its nature as a more or less 'spontaneous philosophy' within capitalist societies. Of course, there is nothing 'spontaneous' about 'spontaneous philosophies'. They do not emerge *ex nihilo* from an ideational act of will, but are grounded in (and help to reproduce) specific practices and institutions; they can also become objects of more explicit reflexion and articulation into more elaborate economic, political and social imaginaries (cf Gramsci, 1971: 323–4, 420–1, on the 'spontaneous philosophy' of common sense; and Althusser, 1990, on the spontaneous philosophy of scientists as reflected in unconscious assumptions about their scientific practices). Much effort is required to create the conditions for such commonsensical, almost self-evident, economic, political and social imaginaries. These conditions are linked to four specific features of bourgeois society.

The first feature is the institution of private property, that is, the juridical fiction of 'private' ownership and control of the factors of production (including fictitious commodities). Here 'rule Freedom, Equality, Property and Bentham, because both buyer and seller of a commodity, say of labour-power, are constrained only by their own free will' (Marx, 1996 [1883]: 186). They feel entitled to use or alienate their property without regard to how this might affect the operation of the *market economy* and cohesion of a *market society*. Second, 'free choice' seems to rule in consumption as those with sufficient money choose what to buy and how to dispose of their purchases. Third, the institutional separation and operational autonomies of the market economy and state make the latter's interventions appear as external intrusions into the activities of otherwise free economic agents. If pushed beyond some minimum nightwatchman role, these also appear as fetters on free markets and/or political oppression of private economic agents. Fourth, the institutional separation of civil society and the state encourages the belief that, once rules for social order are agreed, the state intrudes into the formally free choices of particular members of civil society.

Opposition to liberalism may also emerge 'spontaneously' on the basis of four other features of capitalist social formations that are closely related to the former set. First, the growing *socialization of the forces of production* despite continued *private ownership of the means of production* suggests the need for *ex ante* planning or deliberate self-organization among producer groups to limit market anarchy. Second, there are the strategic dilemmas posed by the *shared interests of producers* (including wage earners) in maximizing total revenues through cooperation and their *divided and potentially conflictual interests* over how to distribute these revenues. Various non-market governance mechanisms may help to balance cooperation and conflict here. Third, contradictions and conflicts are posed by the coexistence of *the institutional separation and mutual dependence* of the economic and state systems. This leads to different logics of economic and political action but also generates a need to consult on the economic impact of state policies and/or the political repercussions of private economic decision-making. Fourth, civil society involves a sphere of *particular interests* opposed to the state's supposed embodiment of *universal interests*. This indicates the need for institutional and discursive means to mediate the particular and universal by providing forums to articulate and contest a hegemonic – and necessarily selective – definition of the 'general interest'.

This suggests that there are limits to liberalism as a 'spontaneous philosophy' that are grounded in those same social relations that generate its seeming self-evidence. Polanyi identified these in his critique of 19th-century liberalism and the resistance that developed as social groups mobilized against its one-sided treatment of land, labour power and money as fictitious commodities. The eventual compromise solution was a *market economy* embedded in and sustained by a *market society* (Polanyi, 2001: 60). This compromise broke down in the 1920s and 1930s, however, leading to various reactions, including the New Deal, fascism and state socialism.

The limits to marketization without a market society are also seen in neoliberalism. This is a more complicated phenomenon and has taken many forms since the neoliberal project was first translated into government actions after Pinochet's *coup d'état* in Chile in 1973. The key neoliberal *economic* policies comprise: liberalization (making markets more competitive), deregulation (reducing state intervention in the market forces), privatization (bringing state-owned or state-funded activities into the private profit-oriented, market-mediated sector), the use of market proxies in the residual public sector, internationalization (to promote competition and the spread of best practice) and reductions in direct taxes (to enable consumers greater freedom to spend 'their' money and thereby enhance consumer sovereignty in a global market economy). There is wide variation in initial starting points for pursuing these policies, their sequencing, the manner in which they are implemented, and the political and social contexts in which they are implemented are quite varied. For example, the neoliberal economic policy set has been pursued by military dictatorships, post-Soviet and post-apartheid states, technocratic regimes imposed by the IMF, 'Third Way' governments, ruling social and/or Christian Democratic parties and openly neoliberal movements. Together with the differential location of economic and political spaces in the world market and changing conjunctures, this explains the different forms of neoliberalism and the variegated nature of neoliberalization seen as a process rather than a one-off accomplishment (see Jessop, 2010a; Peck, 2010).

The complexities of competition

This section turns from the less reflective, more simplified, 'spontaneous philosophy' of liberal and neoliberal 'common sense' about markets and competition. It focuses on the complexities of actually existing competition, regardless of how they have been conceived as the foundation of classical political economy (Smith, 1976 [1776]; Mill, 2004 [1848]) and subsequently vulgarized in neoclassical economies (for which the assumption of perfect competition rules out effective strategies to win long-term competitive advantages; see Hayek, 1948). Thus, it draws on various contributions of evolutionary and institutional economics as well as on some arguments from critical state theory and governance studies. There are two reasons for this. First, this heterogeneous body of work is more sensitive to the varieties and modalities of competition and competitiveness, and typically asks 'what must the world be like' for particular competitive dynamics to exist. This contrasts with the mathematized ideological modelling that currently dominates the neoclassical tradition. Second, given its double hermeneutic (Giddens, 1984 [1976]), social science reasoning draws on both common sense and actual practices to construe and explain the social world and in turn, influences common sense and practices. This is evident in the attempts to extend and complete the market through the redesign of policies, politics and polities.

Let me begin with the statement that it is through competition that the contingent necessities of differential accumulation of particular enterprises, clusters or sectors and differential growth of particular economic spaces are realized. As Marx's analysis of the metamorphosis of capital showed, capitalist competition is not simply for market share or for sales, but for profit earned on investment. As such it can clearly take many forms and it plays out in many ways as capital is reallocated in the search for profits across space-time within a still emerging world market. The latter changes not only through the anarchic effects of market-mediated competition (and the crises that this periodically produces), but also through competing hierarchical or heterarchic efforts to redesign its rules and institutional architecture and to govern the conduct of economic (and extra-economic) forces with stakes in the competitive game.

Profit-oriented, market-mediated competition in rational capitalism (Weber, 1978 [1922]) occurs in two main ways. Merchant capital continually compares purchase and sale prices for its merchandise because its profits derive from buying cheap and selling dear. This principle also shapes more refined forms of arbitrage (including the activities of interest-bearing capital) and can be generalized to regulatory and other kinds of institutional arbitrage too. In contrast, '[t]he industrial capitalist always has the world-market before him, compares, and must constantly compare, his own cost-prices with the market prices at home, and throughout the world' (Marx, 1998 [1894]: 335). For profit-producing[3] fractions of capital, this puts the organization of production at the heart of competition. There is also a vital role for the credit system and interest-bearing capital in promoting competition on the world market (see below).

Another important distinction is that between competition in the routine activities of firms in a stable competitive market oriented to price competition and competition in the disruptive, creatively destructive, effects of entrepreneurship in dynamic markets. This distinction is conventionally associated with Schumpeter (1962 [1934], 1975 [1943]), but was anticipated in Marx's critique of political economy. The Austrian rejected the notion of perfect competition both in reality and as an abstract reference point for analysing imperfect competition. He argued that entrepreneurship disrupts equilibrium through the 'creative destruction' of innovation, and that it is constantly altering the pace and direction of economic growth. Every mode of differential accumulation rests on a balance of competition and entrepreneurship. The former is hard to regulate without undermining innovation. Yet celebration of innovation can often serve as a legitimating cloak for predatory activities, such as in the recent examples of what one might call 'financial criminnovation' (see below).

Schumpeter identified five areas of innovation. These are: (1) the introduction of a new good or a new quality of a good; (2) the introduction of a new method of production or a new way of commercially handling a commodity; (3) the opening of new markets for one's own products; (4) securing a new source of supply of raw materials or half-finished goods; and (5) the reorganization of an industry, for example, the creation of a new cartel or monopoly position, or the breaking up of existing cartels or monopolies (Schumpeter, 1962 [1934]: 129–35). Successful competition in these areas allows, in the short term, monopoly profits. But in a well-functioning market, these higher profit levels will eventually be competed away as other firms adopt these innovations or seek to counter them with their own innovations (whether competitive or anti-competitive). Without directly following Schumpeter's arguments, the Austrian School of Economics, which also rejects the ideal of a perfect competition, is another theoretical paradigm that emphasizes the importance of dynamic competition as opposed to static, price and production cost competition.

These considerations grow more significant the more integrated the world market becomes in real time, as this tends to universalize competition. It continually rebases the modalities of competition, reinforces their treadmill effects, promotes the concentration and centralization of capital, facilitates the equalization of profit and interest rates and intensifies the contradictions of capital accumulation on a world scale. The recent ascendency of financial capital over productive capital, together with the enormous expansion of liquidity associated with derivatives and securitization, has further reinforced these tendencies. This development pressures other capitals to achieve rates of return obtained by financial capital (or expected by financial capital on the basis of maximizing shareholder value) and establishes a new form of commensuration that allows for further universalization and standardization of competition (cf Bryan and Rafferty, 2006).

The governance of competition

This section adds two further perspectives on competition. One concerns the regulation or governance of competition from the idealized viewpoint of its role as a public good. Assuming perfect competition is possible, there is a rational kernel to this approach, namely, the interest of capital in general, as opposed to particular capitals, in securing a level playing field. However, existing capitalism and its differential accumulation suggest that the effects of competition

206

policy merit at the very least a sceptical interrogation. The other perspective concerns the role of competition as a direct principle of governance, and implies a radical ideological critique of discourses about competition and competitiveness. This is because actually existing competition is so heterogeneous and complex a process that most, if not all, efforts to promote it as a mode of governance must rest on serious cognitive and normative simplification, if not on fetishism and ideological mystification.

Two useful entry points here are the competition state and competition law. Although 'competition' figures in both, its respective connotations illustrate the polyvalence of the concept and the complexities of its referent. Whereas competition (or anti-trust) law attempts to regulate *competition*, the competition state attempts to promote *competitiveness*. Competition law draws mainly on orthodox analyses of (perfect) competition and/or on institutional analyses of contestable markets (for example, in the law and economics movement). It prioritizes micro-economic competition and may be supplemented by efforts to remove or control tariff and non-tariff barriers to trade (extending into questions of new constitutionalism, and so on). In contrast, the competition state draws on 'the other canon', that is, heterodox analyses of competition that justify strategies and policies to promote competitiveness at various scales from micro through meso and macro to meta-competitiveness. Paradoxically, perhaps, many policies pursued by competition states (as in the field of industrial policy) might well be ruled illegal according to the principles of competition law.

Competition law

I examine this from three aspects. One is the complexities of its object. If these are neglected, regulatory failure is likely to be blamed on the design of competition law rather than the inherent ungovernability of its object. This poses interesting questions for competition law that are also reflected in the contrasting traditions of US anti trust law (now weakened by the growing influence of the Chicagoan 'law and economics' movement) and the Continental European tradition, which still owes something to Ordoliberalism despite the growing integration of the world market in the shadow of neoliberalism. For example, first, should competition law aim to govern competitive behaviour in dynamic markets or to secure the conditions for perfect competition? And how has the balance between these goals changed as competition and anti-trust law have changed over the years? A second aspect is the place of competition law as one among several means through which economic and political forces seek to design modes of regulation to promote the accumulation of some capitals at the expense of others. The third aspect concerns the problems of governing competition alongside boosting competitiveness in an increasingly integrated world market.

Traditionally, competition law seeks to regulate *micro-economic* competitiveness, that is, competition in the structure and behaviour of firms. This is often measured in terms of market share, profits and growth rates. An extensive managerial and industrial economics literature argues that 'firm-specific advantages' (factors that are unavailable in the short term to competing firms) are crucial to such competitiveness and indeed, underpin monopolistic competition. They might originate in factors of production (patent rights, know-how, R&D capacity) or marketing capacity (design, image, knowledge of likely demand, sales networks). They can also derive from extra-legal or illegal activities (for example, predatory pricing, political deals, mafia-like conduct). This is the primary site of the conflict between individual capitals' search for super-profits at the expense of other firms and the interest of capital in general in conditions that create an average profit rate, an average rate of interest, and so on.

Competition law tends to operate with a relatively static notion of competition centred on the formation of market prices. But, as an *actual* rather than *idealized* process, competition is inherently disequilibrating and, in Schumpeterian guise, creatively destructive. The latter matters especially in periods when a previously dominant productive technology and/or associated forms of finance and enterprise are displaced by another technology and its accompaniments (cf Perez, 2002). Such transitions tend to disrupt competition law, which lags behind changes in products, processes, marketing, sourcing and corporate organization. Whereas a particular system of competition law can weather relatively minor disruptions and crises, ruptural transitions between long waves of development tend to trigger a search for a new regulatory system. World market integration has its own effects. It is reflected in the growing transnationalization of competition law (Gerber, 2010) and the growth of new, state-centred structures of 'global competition law' (Dowdle, 2013). These include transnational networks among national competition agencies; treaties affecting state-level responsibilities for implementing competition policy; and interstate arrangements for transnational enforcement of national competition law.

Efforts to regulate competition are further complicated by the many bases for competitiveness considered as a set of real capacities/

powers. In this regard there is typically a specific hierarchy of forms of competition and competitive players and, as this alters, the dynamics of competition also change. Among relevant changes are: (1) the relative importance of different markets in setting the parameters of competition; (2) the relative super- and subordination of forms of competition; and (3) the types of firm associated with advantage in given fields of competition. Not all of the factors shaping these hierarchies can be regulated by competition law.

In addition to market relations, for example, competitive advantages are pursued to boost profits of enterprise within corporations. Such actions exemplify 'dynamic allocative efficiency', a form of competition that is hard to regulate through competition law (Graham and Smith, 2004).[4] Moreover, not only does competition occur between economic actors (for example, firms, strategic alliances, networks) but also between political entities representing specific spaces and places (for example, cities, regions, nations, triads). The expanding world market and plurality of states create further regulatory problems, regarding, for example, the role of international private law, how to handle conflicts of laws and the reach of extraterritoriality. Competition and competitiveness also depend on extra-economic as well as economic conditions, capacities and competencies. Thus, if competition is hard to regulate through law, how can it govern the factors making for 'competitiveness'? At best, regulators can identify a subset of interactions among profit-oriented economic agents, isolate them as an object of regulation or governance and seek to govern them through the development of appropriate rules, regulations, agencies, mechanisms and institutions (all steps being contested). But many sources of competitive and anti-competitive behaviour remain beyond the reach of competition law. This is one of the sources of market and regulatory failure.

The competition state

Definitions and discourses of competition and competitiveness date back centuries and have different implications for state action. Mercantilist notions from the 17th century tied to state policies to control trade and increase financial reserves can be contrasted with 1890s imperialism oriented to state enclosure of territory for military-political as well as geo-economic goals. With the transition to a more liberal postwar order (in the shadow of US hegemony), competition focused more on domestic growth and multinational foreign investment, leading to conflicts between techno-nationalism and techno-globalism (Ostry and Nelson, 1995). Likewise, with the rise of the current neoliberal transnational financial order and with the theoretical and policy interest in a globalizing knowledge-based economy, competition has refocused on innovation (including in finance and securitization) and on how best to link extra-economic factors to the 'demands' of economic competition.

Different framings of competition and competitiveness involve different forms of action with uneven impacts on the positioning of firms, sectors, regions, nations and continents, as well as on the balance of economic and political forces in and beyond the state system. Moreover, many leading firms and banks are transnational in operation, with complex internal divisions of labour and complex forms of embedding into global production chains and financial flows that may nonetheless be regarded as important for national or bloc competitiveness, especially where they have significant bases in a national state (contrast the US and EU). Once competitiveness is accepted as a real phenomenon that varies across scales of economic (and extra-economic) organization and affects capacities to compete in a world market characterized by a stratified terrain of competition, uneven development, centre–periphery relations, and so on, it can become the target of strategies and policies to enhance, neutralize or weaken competitive capacities.

This is reflected in the developmental state (oriented to catch-up competitiveness) and the more general form of the competition state. Broadly defined, the latter is a state that aims to secure growth within its borders and/or to secure competitive advantages for capitals based in its borders, even where they operate abroad, by promoting the economic and extra-economic conditions currently deemed vital for success in economic competition with economic actors and spaces located in other states. Paradoxically, offshore, more peripheral national economies also become an element in competition insofar as they can be sponsored (or tolerated) by states to secure competitive advantages for domestic or international capitals based in their own territories (such as via transnational supply chains) (Palan, 1998; Urry, 2014). As such the competition state prioritizes strategies to create, restructure or reinforce – as far as this is economically and politically feasible – the competitive advantages of its territory, population, built environment, social institutions and economic agents. The same idea is sometimes expressed in the notion of 'entrepreneurial state', which is more closely associated with Schumpeterian views on competitive advantage, promoting 'sunrise' technologies, industries and other cutting-edge innovations. This has been extended to support for financial innovation (including, tacitly, 'criminnovation') to secure competitive advantage – sometimes linked to a regulatory race to the bottom (which London won vis-à-vis New York). Just as there are different forms of competition, so, too, are there different forms of developmental, competition or entrepreneurial state (for the second, these include neoliberal, dirigiste and social democratic competition states; see Cerny, 1997; Jessop, 2002b).

Although developmental and competition states have been studied primarily at the national level, this is not justified by the historical and contemporary record. Since the 15th century, catch-up competitiveness has been pursued at different scales from the city through regions and provinces to national states and international or supranational blocs (imperial blocs, the capitalist and communist camps, the EU, and so on). In turn, these state strategies to develop 'laggard' economies have met resistance by more advanced states that seek to maintain their advantages by promoting free trade (Reinert, 2008). In short, although the 'developmental', 'competition' and 'entrepreneurial state' are new concepts, significant historical analogues have guided state policy at different scales for almost 600 years.

Unsurprisingly, a wide range of factors has been identified in different economic imaginaries, theoretical and policy paradigms and at different times as relevant to competitiveness. In the 1980s, for example, the OECD listed these factors:

> ... the size of domestic markets, the structure of domestic production, relationships between different sectors and industries ... the distribution and market power of supplier firms ... the characteristics and size distribution of buyers, and the efficiency of non-market relations between firms and production units.

Other factors included:

> ... no exaggerated conflict in the field of income distribution, price stability, flexibility, and the adaptability of all participants in the market ... a balanced economic structure based on small, medium-sized, and big companies ... the acceptance of new technology, favourable scientific and technological infrastructure and realistic requirements for risk containment and environmental protection. (OECD, 1986: 91–2; cf Esser et al, 1996; Campbell and Pedersen, 2007; Pedersen, 2011)

Because of the importance attached to structural, systemic, institutional or societal competitiveness, economic competition expands to become a virtual competition between social worlds. This increases pressures to valorize a wide range of institutions and social relations that were previously regarded as extra-economic. One consequence is that hard economic calculation increasingly rests on the mobilization of soft social resources that are both irreducible to the economic and resistant to such calculation. Recent examples include 'social capital', 'social trust', 'collective learning', 'institutional thickness', 'untraded interdependencies', 'local amenities', the knowledge base, the 'triple helix' of business–university–local state interactions, and even 'culture'. Such discourses are linked to rapid growth in (competing!) benchmarking exercises and in associated commercial services to construct league tables and recommend how to enhance or manipulate scores.

Although state strategies may target specific places, spaces and scales and even be directed against particular competitors, these efforts are always mediated through the operation and audit of the world market as a whole. This extends the importance of the three main forms of capitalist competition: reducing socially necessary labour time, socially necessary turnover time, and the naturally necessary (re)production times of nature (for example, plants, animals, raw materials), both as a source of wealth and, if commodified, a source of surplus value. It also extends the importance of extra-economic factors bearing on competitiveness and profitability: in addition to those illustrated above, we can add tax competition, regulatory arbitrage, offshoring, and so on. Moreover, following Weber's account of political capitalism, we could also include measures to promote competition through force and domination, unusual deals with political authority, lobbying for favourable, anti-competitive legislation, 'desupervision' and decriminalization (on the latter two, see Black, 2005, 2011).

Competition as a mode of governance

According to Polanyi, the 'economistic fallacy' describes all economies in terms of categories that are actually unique to the (capitalist) market economy and explains all economic activities in terms of maximizing behaviour. This fallacy is seen in the neoclassical theoretical tendency to strip commodities (and fictitious commodities) of their specific properties and assume that they can all be organized in the same way along competitive lines to produce efficient market outcomes (Alam, 2014). It is also seen in the liberal and neoliberal tendency to focus on the exchange-value rather than use-value aspects of commodities and fictitious commodities. For example, the wage is seen as a cost of production rather than source of demand and capital is seen as a sum of (credit) money for investment in any asset anywhere rather than as a stock of assets to be valorized in a particular time-space (for further examples, see Jessop, 2010a). This tends, in turn, to produce such powerful tensions and crisis tendencies in capitalist market economies that, as Polanyi (2001) observes, 'society' eventually fights back against their environmentally and socially destructive effects. Neglecting this set of problems is the basis for extending market and competitive principles into the operations of the state and civil society where they cannot be privatized.

Different principles of governance seem more or less well suited to different stages and forms of capitalism. These may have distinctive economic and political imaginaries and institutional attractors (or centres of gravity) around which regulatory or governance principles oscillate. This is reflected in successive generations of the comparative capitalism literature, from the German historical school to recent work on varieties of capitalism. A key issue here is whether changes in governance practices reflect economic and political imaginaries more than structural complementarities or result from their interaction in a dialectics of path shaping and path dependency. A recent test case for exploring this issue is the crisis of finance-dominated accumulation and the switch from the celebration of 'more market, less state' to quite exceptional and unprecedented forms of state intervention to restore the momentum of neoliberal reforms and to rescue failed finance-dominated accumulation regimes.

Exchange based on the anarchy of the market or quasi-market arrangements is one of the four principal modes of governance in complex societies. The others are command based on hierarchy; heterarchic networks and partnerships; and solidarity based on unconditional commitments. Hybrid forms also exist. Historically all four have coexisted, albeit with varying weight across different social fields and across space-time. Neoliberalism privileges the market and, above all, (capitalist) market competition as a principle of governance even more than liberalism. It advocates liberalization, deregulation and privatization, and introduces market proxies in those social areas, in the state, public sphere and 'civil society', where profit-oriented, market-mediated principles based on the commodity form, price form and money form are absent and, in addition, deemed inappropriate. This prompts the neoliberal search for functional equivalents to these principles and their associated forms.

Whereas the 1960s and 1970s saw the highpoint in advanced capitalism of the discourses and practices of planning and productivity, the 1980s marked a turn towards markets and flexibility. Driven by neoliberal regime shifts (with New Zealand being the most radical exemplar), increasing emphasis was placed on counteracting state failure by redrawing the boundaries between government and market and, for the residual public sector, engaging in 'administrative recommodification' (Offe, 1984). This was expressed in the development of market governance (where the state designs, creates, monitors and polices a market to fulfil a public purpose – for example, though the issue of vouchers to be spent in a competitive market) and the rise of 'New Public Management' and, in the US, a movement for 'reinventing government' (cf Osborne and Gaebler, 1992; Donahue and Nye, 2002; Peters, 2009).

Pollitt and Bouckaert (2011) identify a common trend in this regard in advanced capitalist economies. In broad terms, this posits that the public sector can be improved by importing business concepts, techniques and values. More specifically, it comprises a 'bundle of specific concepts and practices'. These include: (1) greater emphasis on 'performance', especially through the measurement of outputs; (2) a preference for lean, flat, small, specialized (disaggregated) organizational forms over large, multifunctional forms; (3) substitution of contracts for hierarchical relations as the main coordinating device; (4) a widespread injection of market-type mechanisms including competitive tendering, public sector league tables and performance-related pay; and (5) an emphasis on treating service users as 'customers' and on the application of generic quality improvement techniques such as Total Quality Management. These authors also note that this bundle of specific concepts and practices has two variants: a 'hard' form that relies on rational systems of control based on measurement, rewards and penalties to 'make managers manage'; and a 'soft' form to 'let managers manage' by enabling creative leadership, entrepreneurship and cultural change oriented to customer service.

In both cases, this approach tends to fail. As Offe noted over 45 years earlier, whereas capitalist enterprises have a clear formal maximand that is easily measured in monetary terms (profit maximization), governments have confused, often inconsistent and sometimes clearly contradictory substantive goals that are politically contested and hard to quantify, sometimes deliberately so (Offe, 1975a, b). In addition, the one-sided neoliberal focus on the exchange-value and value-added aspects of economic calculation leads to neglect of the substantive use-value aspects that are equally necessary to capital accumulation (see above). Attempts to address the use-value aspects of private, public and third sector goods and services have been made through developing multidimensional, substantive mission-oriented targets, performance prisms, 'balanced scorecards', and the like (cf Niven, 2010). In the private sector, these measures were often used as leading indicators of future financial performance (thereby reinforcing the logic of profit-oriented, market-mediated accumulation) (Pidd, 2012). In the public sector, they are constrained by budget cuts, demands for regular 'efficiency gains' and a shift towards enduring austerity and fiscal consolidation. This tends to undermine the balanced approach.

The highpoint of neoliberalism and New Public Management occurred in the early 1990s as neoliberal regime shifts were being consolidated and before the limits of 'more market, less state' become glaringly evident. This led to recognition that the formula of 'disaggregation + competition + incentivization' (Dunleavy et al, 2006) was leading to fragmented, incoherent outcomes conducted by too many arm's-length and unaccountable agencies in the private, public and third sectors that needed to be reconnected through 'joined-up government' or 'governance in the shadow of hierarchy' (Scharpf, 1994; Meuleman, 2008; Bouckaert et al, 2010; Pollitt and Bouckaert, 2011). In terms of administrative theory and practice, this prompted interest in 'metagovernance', that is, the governance of governance. Substantively, it stimulated interest in 'Third Way' efforts to create flanking and supporting mechanisms to soften the impact of neoliberalism and enhance its legitimacy while sustaining its transformative momentum.

Metagovernance and collibration

As evidence has mounted in the last two decades that each form of governance has its own forms of governance failure, attention has turned theoretically and practically from concern with specific forms of governance to efforts at metagovernance. This involves the judicious mixing of market, hierarchy, networks and solidarity to achieve the best possible outcomes from the viewpoint of those engaged in metagovernance (Dunsire, 1996; Jessop, 1998; Kooiman, 2003; Scott, 2006). Governments have a key role to play here, but even this kind of 'metagovernance' is fallible. The emerging system is a complex, multiscalar, hybrid and tangled system of metagovernance. Yet the very complexity of the interweaving of forms of governance and government on different scales means that the resulting system is more complex than any state, or political or social entity, can understand,

and its overall evolution lies beyond the control of a state or its society. This is evident, as indicated above, in the actions of the competition state and the limits of competition law. It also means that, compared to more traditional forms of state organization, based on constitutional law and public accountability, metagovernance, even when conducted in the shadow of hierarchy, is ineffably ungraspable and intransparent and as such, inherently unaccountable. A post-bureaucratic and post-democratic political system in which competition becomes the governing principle and market completion on a world scale is the ultimate goal is a dystopian future.

Concluding remarks

General Stanley McChrystal, commenting on an offensive to retake territory controlled by the Taliban in southern Afghanistan, declared, hubristically:

> We've got a government in a box, ready to roll in.[5]

For some 20 years we have been experiencing and witnessing the consequences of the naive neoliberal belief that 'we've got competition in a box, ready to roll out'. In both cases, these consequences can be described in terms of 'blowback' (Johnson, 2000). This chapter has addressed the effects of the fetishization of competition as a principle of societal organization and its role in subordinating society to the logic of profit-oriented, market-mediated accumulation. It began by noting the polyvalence of the 'market economy' (commercial economy, market economy, capitalist economy, financialized economy, finance-dominated economy) and the extent to which this could be exploited in efforts to legitimate neoliberal financialization and the drive towards a finance-dominated accumulation regime that extends markets and capitalist (and even financialized) market proxies into areas where they tend to be far more creatively destructive than destructively creative. Competition has a formal, procedural rationality suitable for supplying standardized goods and services (and even then, it is prone to unplanned disruption through Schumpeterian innovations), and is unsuited to the four categories of fictitious commodities and the supply of goods and services that advance human flourishing.

It was also argued that simple governance solutions to complex problems do not work and are especially inappropriate where there are multiple substantive goals that are hard to specify consistently, let alone measure in terms of a single metric. In this context, the rolling out of competition as a principle of regulation and governance has actually been just one in a repeated succession of attempts to overcome government and governance failure by turning to another mode of governance – which is also doomed to fail, albeit in its own distinctive ways. The growing unaccountability of capitalist market forces and their tendency to generalize and intensify the contradictions and crisis tendencies inherent in the capital relation make it imperative – but also increasingly hard – to reclaim some measure of democratic accountability in material provisioning and the care economy by limiting markets to areas where the invisible hand works well and restricting and regulating it where it produces substantively irrational results for humankind and the planet.

11

Conclusions

Civil society has been a basic concept (*Grundbegriff*) in political theory from the early modern period in Europe onwards, and has been approached from many philosophical, theoretical and normative perspectives. It is also a key reference point in political strategies and political contestation. More recently, it has become a policy paradigm in the sense that civil society, the third sector, public–private partnerships, solidarity and community (and cognate referents) are seen as important vectors for policy delivery, often in response to disquiet about market failure and state failure. In turn this is reflected in the integration of civil society in various guises into modes of governance. As this has occurred, attention has turned to the limits of civil society as a mode of governance and the attempts to improve it in this regard or to find ways to flank and support it, including new forms of self-responsibilization and subjectivation, new *dispositives* (apparatuses) and new discourses. This book has reviewed these different facets of 'civil society' to establish the linkages and disjunctions between them. It then focused on the policy paradigm, mode of governance and responses to governance failure aspects. Of special interest is the churning of attempts to mobilize civil society as an instrument of state power, the recurrent failures of participation and communitarianism, the attempts to explain this away and the new policy responses and modes of governance that follow from this.

There are also ethical questions about the duties and obligations of political actors, about the best forms of political life, community and state, about the best ways to reconcile the individual and the social, private interests and public ethics, egoism and altruism, individual passions and public reason, and so on. Thus, Seligman sees 'the core component of the classical theory of civil society as an ethical vision of social life' (1992: 10) – a vision that, 'if it does not overcome, at least harmonizes, the conflicting demands of individual interest and social good' (Seligman, 1992: x).

The limitations of this interpretation are shown in John Keane's history of how the conceptual distinction between state and civil society has developed through four overlapping ethico-political stages: (1) a sovereign, centralized constitutional state standing over its subjects versus a series of independent societies that can check the state's authoritarian potential; (2) a belief that a strengthened civil society can check the state in the interests of justice, equality and liberty; (3) a strong state needed to check the paralysis, conflict and anarchy of civil society; and (4) an emphasis on the pluralist self-organization of civil society as a means of resisting the encroachment or colonization of society by the state (Keane, 1988). To these four stages we could add (5) the pluralist self-responsibilization of civil society as a means to compensate for market and state failure. I have noted the scope for tension between the fourth and fifth phases, and how it provides one key to interpreting the conflict between self-responsibilization as a top-down strategy to offload governance problems and self-emancipation as a form of resistance and self-empowerment within wider society.

This chapter explores three different approaches to putting civil society in its place, and then considers the dynamics of governance as they are reflected in changes in civil society. This is related to Gramscian and/or Foucauldian notions that civil society is not only an integral part of the changing exercise of state power in modern societies, but also offers opportunities for resistance. This theme is explored by listing the postwar dynamic of civil society in advanced social formations and its modification through recent changes in the capitalist market economy, state forms and civil society and their impact on the identities and interests of civil society actors. Next, the analysis turns to the scope for resistance. Finally, the book ends with some reflections on the limits of the WISERD Civil Society programme when seen from this perspective.

Approaches to civil society

This section identifies three approaches to putting civil society in its place. The first uses the Enlightenment triangle of capitalist market economy, the state, and civil society to frame the analysis. The second identifies six ways of framing civil society without resort to the Enlightenment tradition. And the third adopts a social science and humanities perspective to identify different analytical questions about civil society.

Putting civil society in its place

One approach is to start with the Enlightenment triangle and locate the range of social practices that conform to its logic and those that lay outside it (see Figure 11.1). The interior space within the triangle shows the individualistic parameters within which the space is expected to operate. It depicts that the relation between capitalist markets and

Figure 11.1: The Enlightenment triangle

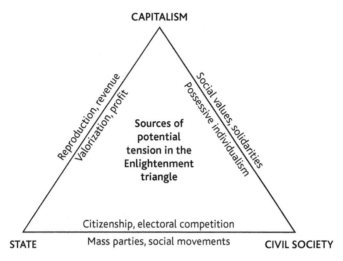

Source: Author's own

the state is motivated by profit-oriented, market-mediated valorization; the relation between capitalist market and civil society is understood as the sphere of possessive individualism (cf Macpherson, 1962); and state–civil society is shaped by citizenship rights and electoral competition. The three external planes of the triangle show the limits of these individualistic perspectives. They highlight the importance of social reproduction and revenue in mediating state–market relations, the role of social values and solidarities in shaping the relation between market and civil society, and the relevance of mass parties and social movements in guiding state–civil society relations.

This matrix can be used to locate the development of the 'Third Way' and its limitations. The 'Third Way' comprises:

- An economic and political imaginary that seeks to redefine the relation between capital and the state – it conforms neither to pure markets nor state planning but promotes public–private partnerships and social enterprise.
- A political and social imaginary that seeks to redefine the relation of state and civil society through practices of social inclusion, active citizenship and promoting stakeholding as opposed to shareholder value.
- An economic and social imaginary that seeks to redefine capital and civil society relations through enterprise culture, social capital, public–private partnerships, Big Society and social liberalism.

The Third Way failed as a project to redefine the Enlightenment triangle in the UK because its political advocates could not escape the ecological dominance of the internal logic of valorization and profit, possessive individualism, and citizenship rights and electoral competition. It emerged in neoliberal regimes as the failures of 'more market, less state' became evident and was offered as an alternative solution that avoided a simple return to 'more state, less market'. Its subsequent crises had the effect of pushing crisis management in directions that reinforced rather than challenged neoliberal logic because bourgeois hegemony was not challenged (see Jessop, 2007b). This can be contrasted with the Scandinavian experience that produced a different balance of forces more favourable to 'Third Way' strategies, in which pragmatic neoliberal policy adjustments were made to maintain the postwar social democratic compromise rather than to overthrow it in a principled neoliberal regime shift (cf Jessop, 2016).

Six approaches to civil society

Here we list six approaches to defining civil society, the first three of which are less useful than the second three. They comprise:

1. *A unified social sphere:* this is a Habermasian public space of communicative rationality, ideal speech acts and undistorted communication around public interest. Despite its unrealistic assumptions and neglect of much recent work on civil society, its treatment in these terms shows an ethico-political resurrection of the Enlightenment project and is consistent with normative critical theory.
2. *A residual category:* here society (and civil society) figures as the residual 'other' of any given primary object of analysis. It is what emerges when the focus is on 'economy and society', 'law and society', 'family and society', and so forth. In this analysis, society is simply what is left out of the primary focus. Its content varies with the primary analytical object and, in this sense, needs to be studied in relational terms.
3. *An essentially contested concept:*[1] this approach studies civil society as the locus of disagreements among social scientists and political theorists about its nature and importance. It is useful and necessary for the history of social science and humanities, but does not advance the study of actually existing civil society without links to one or more of the next three meanings.

4. *Open horizon of action:* in this perspective, civil society is an ensemble of social relations that is not directly integrated into specific functional or institutional orders but crosscuts them (for example, stage in life course, gender, nation, citizenship, human rights, orientation to the environment, and so forth). Here horizon denotes what can feasibly be achieved by specific actors in given spatio-temporal circumstances, and is therefore deeply conjunctural, varying across space and time and depending on the capacities and imaginaries of relevant actors.

5. *Potential site of resistance:* as Habermas and Gramsci, among others, highlighted, civil society can serve as a site of resistance to system or institutional logics and to the colonization of 'the lifeworld' through systemic processes such as commodification, juridification and statization. The scope for resistance depends on the respective institutional logics and, of course, on the identities and interests of those resisting.

6. *A space for hegemonic struggles:* this approach regards civil society as a space for hegemonic, subhegemonic and counter-hegemonic struggles. It comprises a heterogeneous, asymmetrical playing field in which it is easier to articulate and advance some projects than others. This is the view that emerges most clearly from a Gramscian approach to the modalities of state power in 'political society + civil society' as different social forces struggle to constitute political, intellectual and moral leadership, and to form social alliances that advance the relevant projects.

The strength of civil society analyses depends on the choice or combination of choices regarding the fourth to sixth approaches and which social forces are included in the study and what their goals are.

Disciplinary perspectives

A third way of putting civil society in its place is to examine diverse approaches to its study by considering different research foci and different disciplines. Thus, civil society has been studied in terms of its genealogy or historical formation, its semantics as a kind of political imaginary, an agent-centred institutional approach that prioritizes the orientation and practices of agents in situated contexts, an approach to governmentality that draws on Foucault and/or critical governance studies, a figurational analysis inspired by the work of Norbert Elias (2000), and a formal analysis of state forms and modalities of state power inspired by historical materialist form analysis (see Table 11.1).

Table 11.1: Approaches to civil society

Approach	Focus	Some key themes	Some disciplines
Historical formation	Genealogy of 'civil society' and its changing relation to 'state', 'family' and 'market'. Disembedding and re-embedding of civil society	Formation of bourgeois and proletarian public spheres. Self-organization vs top-down creation of civil society	Archaeology (agora, and so on), anthropology, history, communication studies, organization studies, sociology
Semantics, political discourse	'Civil society as idea', philosophies and theories of civil society, its complements, antagonists, and 'others'	Political and social imaginaries, relation to mass society and democracy, hegemonic visions, *Ideologiekritik*	Conceptual history, critical discourse analysis, cultural studies, political philosophy and theory
Agent-centred institutionalism	Intellectuals, print culture, civil society actors, associations, and supporting institutions	Social innovation and entrepreneurship, social bases, subaltern groups, power blocs, hegemony	Actor-network theory, innovation studies, sociology, historical institutionalism, cultural studies
Governmentality and/ or critical governance studies	Governance techniques: disciplinary techniques, normalization, governmentality, metagovernance, collibration	Microphysics of power, anatomo/ biopolitics, Big Society, third sector, strategic codification	Discourse analysis, dispositive analysis, public administration, policy studies
Figurational analysis	Process of civilization, 'state and civilization', 'state and society', social embeddedness	Civil society in context, historical cleavages, passive revolution, how 'society fights back'	Historical sociology, history, geography, political economy, cultural studies
Formal composition	Co-evolution of the state as 'political society + civil society' and their implications for relative autonomies of state and (civil) society	'Relative autonomy'. Differentiation and centralization. Democracy and dictatorship	Historical materialism, international relations, law, policy sciences, political science, state theory, social theory

Source: Jessop (2017)

Each approach can be associated with a mix of disciplines and methods with somewhat different analytical foci.

A Gramscian-Foucauldian synthesis

These three ways of putting civil society in its place raise the question of whether 'civil society' is an autonomous domain of social life with its own logic or comprises no more than heterogeneous sets of social relations that are not (yet) dominated by other institutional orders. The foregoing arguments exclude the former autonomous approach in favour of the heterogeneity of a pluralistic civil society with complex connections to other spheres of social life. In this sense, it serves as a site of practices with a potentially distinct field of operation that is motivated by identities and/or interests that lie outside and/or crosscut the relevant institutional orders by virtue of their relationship to the 'lifeworld' and experience of whole people or communities of feeling and interest. Taking civil society as an integral element of contested state formation is important here, and links to Gramsci's account of state power as comprising 'political society + civil society'. In this interpretation, civil society serves both as a site and horizon of action for strategies and tactics to secure the dominance of specific institutional orders and modes of societalization; it can also be a reservoir of antagonistic 'instincts' (rooted in other identities) and social resources for resisting such colonization.

This reading is also consistent with a Foucauldian approach to state power and practices, which regards the emergence of the modern state in relation to its internal relations with civil society:

> ... it is the tactics of government that allow the continual definition of what should or should not fall within the state's domain, what is public and what private, what is and what is not within the state's competence, and so on. So, if you like, the survival and limits of the state should be understood on the basis of the general tactics of governmentality. (Foucault, 2008: 109)

The scope for a synthesis of these interpretations depends on reading Foucault from a strategic-relational perspective that adopts Gramsci's analysis of the state in its inclusive sense and reading Gramsci from a governmentality perspective. In this sense, one could translate Gramsci's integral definition of the state as indicating state power as comprising 'government + governance' exercised in the shadow of hierarchy (cf Jessop, 2015: 176–9). The resulting synthesis would facilitate a strategic-relational analysis of civil society dynamics and practices of the kind related in this book.

The five main trends in civil society

This said, let us briefly comment on the five trends that are reshaping contemporary 'civil society' as a horizon of action that serves as a site for self-emancipation as well as self-responsibilization and political contests over societalization. 'Civil society' judged as a reality is changing under the impact of a complex dialectic of tribalism-cosmopolitanism, the rejection of egalitarianism and the rise of identity politics, and an increasing emphasis on (transnational) human rights as superior to national citizenship and/or national sovereignty.

First, just as a denationalization of statehood is occurring relative to the heyday of the national territorial state – which occurred from 1945–80 and indeed, even later in the case of post-Soviet states – we are witnessing the 'denationalization' of civil society. There is no one-to-one relationship between these processes because they follow their own partly independent logics and have different motives. Regarding civil society, there are at least three forms of reorganization: the trend towards cosmopolitanism, 'tribalism' (that is, the rediscovery or invention of primordial, affectual identities at the expense both of liberal individualism reflected in citizenship rights and of civic loyalty to an 'imagined' national community), and expansion of diverse social movements that operate across national boundaries.

Second, particularly in the 'West', where civil society as a horizon of action has had its firmest (albeit still fragile) roots, several major changes have affected the principles and practices of civil society considered as a (residual) social sphere. This occurred in part due to the crisis of the Keynesian welfare national state, in part due to the market-driven and/or state-sponsored commodification of 'civil society', and in part due to the rise of new forms of public–private governance arrangements.[2] This has produced a contingently necessary series of changes in the principles and practices of civil society considered as a social sphere in its articulation with political society. Among these I would mention the rejection of class-based egalitarianism (with its emphasis on redistributive politics) in favour of greater concern with empowerment in the sense of securing lifetime access to participation in different institutional orders for diverse actors. This is evidenced by ensuring security of employability in the economy, access to legal services, lifetime education in the 'learning society', subsidiarity in the political system, freedom of access to scientific assessment of risks, and so forth. It can also be seen in the growth of identity politics (with its emphasis on respect, authenticity and autonomy regarding different identities), and expansion of the so-called 'third' or voluntary sector (operating outside both the pure market and the bureaucratic state).

Third, although national citizenship rights are still important in many established national states, there is increasing emphasis on (transnational) human rights that can be invoked even where individuals are not citizens of a given state in which they reside and/or where the state resists attempts by civil society and external agencies to impose human rights. In part the development of human rights is related to the globalization of the legal system, the economy and the political system. But it also represents the development of a cosmopolitan 'public sphere' in which liberal principles can be extended beyond national boundaries and thereby challenge the bases of purely national citizenship and the rise (or reinvention) of liberal humanitarian intervention.

Fourth, the 'denationalization' of civil society prompts state policies to deal with the challenges to many of the traditional bases of national citizenship and mutual solidarity that arise from multiethnicity, multiculturalism and divided political loyalties. These three trends can be inherited from earlier stages of state formation or emerge from more recent regional or global shifts in population and/or from other economic, political and sociocultural transformations. This is where the issue of national identities and global civil society surfaces – whether in terms of their potential opposition or reconciliation. For example, growing individualism and the rise of identity politics potentially weakens national identity. A 'melting pot society' may also do so but, in states like the US, it could also reinforce identification with the *Staatsnation* and promote patriotism. Multiethnicity is potentially threatening to the *Volksnation* (an imagined community based on shared ethnic features). Multiculturalism could weaken the *Kulturnation* (an imagined community based on shared national culture). Cosmopolitanism and nested political loyalties may promote identification with infra- and supranational regimes (for example, with Wales or Scotland in the UK and/or with the EU). In addition, when tied to plural identities, cosmopolitanism may promote demands for a global civil society.

Fifth, the promotion of human rights by transnational social movements and parts of the legal profession can challenge the sovereignty of the nation-state and/or national state. This creates the possibility of cross-border identity politics and mobilization, and may promote the denationalization of civil society.

Countertrends and limitations

Having considered five recent trends in the reorganization of the national state and civil society, I now comment on some important countertrends and limitations.

First, the tendential denationalization of statehood is being countered by an increasing role for stronger national states in managing the transfer of old and new state capacities upwards, downwards and sideways. Not all states are equal in these respects. But individuals and organizations still expect that, however complex the real world may be and however global the world's functional systems may become, there should somewhere be a social power (typically the state) that is able to manage crises and secure social cohesion despite the tendencies towards uneven development that inevitably occur in a modern social formation. Paradoxically, the state is an interdependent part of a more complex system but is held responsible for that system's overall performance. This paradox is reinforced by the residual significance of the national state as a focus of political loyalties, especially regarding the continued expectation that the national state should be held accountable for securing social cohesion within its territorial boundaries. Indeed, it is the survival of national identities that has helped to block the development of a supranational state with powers equivalent to those of national states. This is reflected in Europe, for example, in efforts to develop a sense of European political identity and to promote the Europeanization of extra-economic institutional orders such as education, science, health and law. This is proving hard due both to the survival of national sentiments and to the more general trend to cosmopolitanism and globalization.

There are important asymmetries among national states in this regard with the US seeking, especially following the decomposition of the Soviet Union and the broadening of its claims to exercise 'extra-territorial' power, to pursue something close to what Noam Chomsky calls a 'single standard'. This is the principle that whatever is in the interests of the US as currently perceived should be pursued and that no state, international organization or set of foreign economic interests should be permitted to interfere with this (Chomsky, 2006; cf Blum, 2001). This is reflected in the extra-territorial powers and privileges claimed by the US. Whether this makes the US more effective internationally or intensifies the risks of 'blowback' is, of course, another matter (cf Johnson, 2000, 2004, 2006). Nor is the US alone in seeking to implement such a standard – it is simply better placed structurally to do so, even as China rises to become a powerful economic and politico-military power.

Second, while there is a steady shift from govern*ment* to govern*ance* in the polity and similar shifts from hierarchical authority to 'heterarchical' coordination in many other social fields, there is a countervailing shift from government to metagovernance. This often involves the role of states (especially, but not exclusively, national territorial states) in organizing the framework for self-organizing governance regimes. States' control of organized coercion and their constitutional claim to treat almost any activity as politically relevant tends to give them greater authority to engage in governmental, governance and metagovernance activities than any other organization within their territory. Hence social relations are typically organized and conducted 'in the shadow of (state) hierarchy'. Moreover, even when state managers try to reject responsibility for specific fields of action, social forces tend to hold the state responsible for the effects of withdrawal and to call for it to reengage in one form or another. The response may be renewed direct intervention by the state and/or modifications in attempts to modify the rules of the game and/or the balance of forces as the state seeks to organize self-government through its continuing role in metagovernance.

Third, given the increasing recognition of (transnational) human rights that can be invoked to govern international society, there can be two contradictory countertrends. One involves more nationalist, populist and authoritarian discourses and the other is a more neoliberal demand for 'more market, less state' in a more open global economy. The resulting paradox is reinforced by the residual significance of the national state as a focus of political loyalties, especially regarding, as noted above, the expectation that the national state is responsible for securing social cohesion within its territorial boundaries because it is allegedly better placed to do so. In this sense, the promotion of human rights by supranational agencies, transnational social movements and parts of the legal profession is still best seen as a secondary rather than dominant feature of political and social organization.

Fourth, regarding the emergence of national identities and global civil society, whether in terms of their potential opposition or reconciliation, while we can surmise that growing individualism weakens national identity, it can produce blowback effects that strengthen constitutional patriotism, reinforce ethnic identities or boost national identities. The rise of populism is one countertrend to the expansion of governance (Stoker, 2019).

Fifth, humanitarian intervention risks becoming another means of interstate conflict with the rationale, timing, extent and purposes of securing intervention being contested and the incidence of intervention being explained more in terms of reasons of state than universal principles. This is reflected in the politics of the reception of migrants, refugees and asylum-seekers that is part of the WISERD project.

Once more on why governance, why now?

The emergence of governance based on network and solidarity reduces the 'bounded rationality' problem that stems from imperfect information about markets or lack of clarity about how to attain a collective goal. In this sense, 'a problem shared is a problem halved'. It can provide access to knowledge and resources that an individual, household, single organization, and so on does not have and thereby provide the basis for cooperation. In addition, governance arrangements can lock partners into interdependent decisions over different time horizons to reduce the problem of opportunism. It inhibits the early exit of early winners when they want to cash their gains and it rewards early losers by providing long-term benefits from cooperation. It also develops solidarity by promoting organic linkages and reducing the risks associated with the specificity of individual partners' assets through pooling resources.

In this context, there are some favourable conditions for successful governance that were reviewed in preceding chapters. These are:

- The availability or creation of simplifying models and practices that are 'fit for purpose' as a basis for 'going on in the world'.
- Stabilizing key stakeholders' orientations, expectations and rules of mutual respect, which reduces opportunism and can build solidarity.
- Developing the capacity for dynamic interactive learning when confronted with problems, crisis, failures and resistance.
- Self-reflexive self-organization: monitor the progress and adequacy of organizational forms and modes of governance and change them when it appears appropriate through metagovernance and collibration.

If it's so smart, why does it fail?

Resort to heterarchic governance based on networks and solidarity is prone to fail, like other forms of governance based on exchange or command. There are eight factors relevant to the failure of these forms of civil society in this regard. They can be summarized as follows. First, there are general problems of maintaining dialogue and solidarity in civil society. Second, there are general costs in terms of the time required for dialogue through networks and solidarity. Third, these modes of governance can be disrupted by the turbulence of the governance environment, which makes past lessons seem irrelevant and discourages efforts to learn new lessons. Fourth, this relates to different definitions of the object of governance, which can lead to different strategies towards them that may not be compossible. Fifth, there can be competing projects for the same object of governance that cannot be reconciled through dialogue or managed by deferring or displacing likely failures. Sixth, even then, there are also limits to deferring or displacing likely failures. Seventh, some objects of governance have specific problems that make networks and solidarity more or less unsuited to successful governance. And eighth, an absence of reflection on the preceding problems can lead to failure. The strength of these conditions varies with the actors involved, some of whom are more capable of self-reflection than others.

This set of risks can inspire a contrarian approach to governance and metagovernance. Governance is often sold as an effective solution to new problems but, if markets and states fail, why should governance that is based on networks and solidarity work? Telling actual and potential partners that these modes of governance will work can backfire. This suggests it is better to explain the difficulties of governance and metagovernance and get governance partners to reflect on this risk and anticipate problems. This would involve noting the inherent limits of all forms of governance due to the inevitability of contradictions and dilemmas. This, in turn, invites concern with how to respond to governance failure. I have argued for romantic public irony in this regard. As explained in the Preface to this book, in contrast to the cynical and opportunists, ironists are sceptical and romantic. They act in 'good faith' and are prepared to admit to failure and bear its costs. One cannot choose to succeed completely and permanently in a complex world, but one can choose how to fail. This makes it imperative to choose wisely! Shared self-reflection enhances choice in this regard when combined with metagovernance practices and collibration.

Thus, while some theorists of governance rightly emphasize that governance takes place in the shadow of hierarchy, this does not always succeed. The shadow of hierarchy should be understood to produce better governance when it occurs in democratically accountable, socially inclusive arrangements organized around the problems of maintaining responsible metagovernance in contrast to relying on unilateral and top-down command. This places issues of constitutional design at the heart of debates on the future of governance and metagovernance. It also invites a massive expansion of civil society as a site of public action and horizon of action.

The prospects of achieving this cooperative framework have been challenged by the rise of populism. As Gerry Stoker notes, 'the governance paradigm and the rise of populism are responses to a degree to the same set of forces' (2019: 14). As he remarks:

> Populism poses a profound threat to the assumptions of the governance paradigm and its claim to identify new practices of governing fitted to the needs of the twenty-first century. Populist thinking rejects the understanding of how governing works that lies at the heart of the governance paradigm and the logic of populist thought is hostile towards two of the favoured instruments of the paradigm: the greater use of markets and networks on governing. (Stoker, 2019: 4–5)

He continues:

> The governing challenge from a populist perspective is not to build on interdependence but rather about how to deny it. The second assumption of governance – that looks to the reconstitution of actors and the building of new identities to express mutuality and solidarity – is … also plainly an anathema to many populists who see a political world as defined by regret or nostalgia about the loss of past identities. (Stoker, 2019: 10)

This is reflected in the way that populists challenge the third assumption that Stoker identifies in the governance literature, namely, that governing practice assumes that there is a large grouping of citizens committed to governing themselves: 'Governance valorizes citizens doing it for themselves as everyday makers, but the populist paradigm is rather about getting government to do the right thing by the people' (Stoker, 2019: 10).

From this, he concludes that:

> Governance procedures then need to be promoted as open to revision; backed by a recognition that they can develop faults – networks can become too closed and markets can become too controlled by a narrow set of interests. To be

open to revision is a better answer to claims of dissatisfaction with political processes than a dubious claim of having achieved smartness. Networks and markets as forms of governing need to be defended not as stable parts of the governing system but as constantly open to revision through sunset clauses, periodic reviews and stringent accountability. (Stoker, 2019: 15)

Stoker's analysis highlights the limits to governance procedures during turbulent times when new political subjects and issues emerge and are mobilized around populist projects. He identifies the need for careful institutional design to enable revision of governance arrangements when these are deemed to be failing. This was stressed in the preceding chapters in terms of the need for requisite variety, requisite reflexivity and requisite irony.

The future of civil society research

As Maurizio Lazzarato argued, civil society is not a first and immediate reality or something that does not exist but something that belongs to the modern technology of governmentality (Lazzarato, 2005: 2–3). Civil society can be understood as an ensemble of technologies of governance that can be mobilized by different social forces for different purposes. This is linked to a continuing search for forms of inclusion in the political process that go beyond the relationship of individual citizens to their respective sovereign states and for forms of participation that would enable various stakeholders to influence the operation of other systems too. As such, civil society is a rich and confused ensemble of multiple and contestable identities that can be mobilized for both pro- and anti-systemic purposes. Compounding this already ample complexity are recommendations that governance be used to guide interactions between systems and the lifeworld in response to issues such as ecological crisis, social exclusion and the risk society.

Just as the state cannot be a sustainable research object in its own terms but must be considered as a social relation, civil society cannot be theorized as an autonomous system with its own logic. Instead, it requires a reflexive, relational approach that sees this terrain in strategic-relational terms. Civil society is better seen as a loosely bounded arena of social contestation and contention that has asymmetrical effects in terms of the capacities of social forces to advance their identities, interests and objectives. Even in liberal bourgeois democracies with institutionalized citizen rights, there are processes of social exclusion as well as inclusion and patterns of civic deficits and civic gains. This is reflected in the range of objectives that can be pursued in ad hoc ways through civil society mobilization: to demand rights, to exercise them vis-à-vis states, markets and other actors in civil society, to achieve social emancipation or exercise self-responsibilization. Social forces are useful allies or harmful antagonists for agents whose primary identity is grounded in economic relations or political positions. This is what Gramsci argued in his analysis of the state in its inclusive sense, written from the viewpoint of a communist who was contesting the rise of fascism and observing European and US history and the Stalinist deformation of the Bolshevik revolution. He demonstrated the need to distinguish structural and conjunctural moments in analysing the current situation, and to judge the balance of forces in an organic way.

For Gramsci, one important task is to engage in 'a reconnaissance of the terrain and an identification of the trench and fortress represented by the components of civil society, etc' (Gramsci, 1971: 238; 1975, Q7, §16: 866). In short, one must obtain a thorough knowledge of the intricate, wide-ranging and capillary operations of the prevailing hegemony before devising strategies for supplanting it (cf Buttigieg, 2005: 41).

Foucault is also relevant here because he denied that civil society exists as an autonomous external reality, and regarded its development in governmental terms as part of internal technologies of governance:

> Whereas liberal and neoliberal thinkers conceive of civil society as an actual domain of forces outside of the state that constitute a necessary, limiting counterweight to the state, exerting control upon governments and bureaucracies, Foucault reversed this view. He re-positioned civil society as a restrictive principle internal to liberal governmental rationality. Instead of a palpable social domain, civil society emerged as an imaginary figure within modern liberal thought which served to rationalize – but not necessarily limit – governmental practices. (Villadsen, 2016: 22)

Such a theoretical exercise has not been not central to the WISERD Civil Society research programme because the researchers have tended to use 'civil society' as an organizing discursive framework for a transdisciplinary grant coalition tied to their past careers and current intentions, the availability of databases and a commitment to serving the interests of the Welsh government in promoting more efficiency and greater wellbeing. Less concerned with the overall structure of Welsh civil society, the first phase focused on smaller projects in rural areas and developed city regions and on the intersectional dimensions of civil society membership – generation, gender, language, faith, leisure activities, educational experience, migratory experience, and so on. The second phase is seeking to give a stronger thematic unity to civil society research by using Lockwood's ideas of civic stratification and civic repair, which organized the four main themes of the second stage research (see Chapter 5). This explains the attention that the WISERD research has given to individuals and households and to small-scale partnerships. It also questions the utility of the research for putting civil society in its broader place as an organizing concept.

Against this, it can be argued that the present book has been too concerned with abstract theorization in approaching civil society in more macro-social terms as an ensemble of social relations organized in terms of modes of governance and governmentality that may offer general explanations of governance failure but does not in itself advance efficiency, effectiveness, deliberative goal setting or solidarity. In contrast, the WISERD project has a clear policy-relevant agenda and cooperates with CSOs as well as government apparatuses and the business community in Wales and elsewhere, and its success in this regard was the basis of a second five-year funding round for the Civil Society programme. Its reflections on civic stratification, civic expansion and civic repair are eagerly awaited. They are not yet provided in the book on the foundational economy and civic repair published at the same time as this volume (Barbera and Jones, 2020).

Concluding remarks

To conclude, romantic public irony is the best means to optimize the governance of complexity because it recognizes the complexity of governance. It also subordinates the roles of market forces, top-down command (especially through the state), networks and solidarity (with its risk of localism and/or tribalism) to the overall requirements of participatory governance. Thus, while some theorists of governance rightly emphasize that governance takes place in the shadow of hierarchy, this should be understood in terms of a democratically accountable, socially inclusive hierarchy organized around the problematic of responsible metagovernance rather than unilateral and top-down command. For immediate practical action, one must work with existing institutions and actors. For the longer term, issues of institutional, agency and constitutional design should be at the heart of debates on the future of governance and metagovernance. This invites a massive expansion of civil society as a site of public action and as a horizon of action that encompasses contestation over political, intellectual and moral leadership. The institutional design of civil society in this respect depends on the shifting balance of forces and is not scale-specific – tied to particular territories, places, scales or networks. Nor can Wales be designated as the right scale because other sites of action are relevant to the organization of Welsh civil society. There is no single meta-governor of past, present or future design. Indeed, even if 'the logic is perfectly clear, the aims decipherable, … it is often the case that no one is there to have invented them, and few can be said to have formulated them' (Foucault, 1979b [1981]: 95).

Endnotes

Chapter 1

[1] Thus, alongside the emphasis on public–private partnerships and strategic alliances, we also find talk of network enterprises, network economies, global city networks, policy networks, the network state and the network society.

[2] In highlighting the explosive interest in theories of governance since the 1970s, it would be wrong to imply that these paradigms have no pre-history and no current competitors. After all, if governance is not to be reduced to the explicit adoption of a specific word, one must recognize that the (set of) concept(s) to which it refers could also be presented in other terms. Theories of governance have obvious precursors in institutional economics, work on statecraft and diplomacy, research on corporatist networks and policy communities, and interest in 'police' or welfare. And although the idea of 'governance' has now gained widespread currency in mainstream social sciences, it has by no means displaced other research on economic, political or social coordination. This might point us towards an interest in the social and/or political agendas that are driving forward the governance debate.

[3] 'Heterarchy' is a neologism introduced for forms of coordination that involve neither anarchy nor hierarchy.

[4] 'Police', 'policey' or *Polizei* concern the governance of conduct in ways that will enable those in charge of 'affairs of state' to produce an orderly 'state of affairs' in a state's territory. This is an issue much debated in early doctrines of statecraft and discussed more recently in Foucault's work on governmentality (1991).

[5] For an interesting self-criticism from a leading member of the Köln School of governance studies, admitting that students of governance have tended to assume that state managers are primarily motivated by the desire to solve problems for the common good, see Mayntz (2001).

[6] This is certainly the view taken by Benko and Lipietz (1994). Hollingsworth et al (1994) also suggest that governance excludes the state (which has a key role, nonetheless, in organizing governance and facilitating – or blocking – shifts in governance).

[7] *Steuerung* is the main German equivalent of 'governance', the latter being a term derived from the medieval Latin word, *gubernantia*. In turn, this is related to the Greek word for steering, piloting or guiding.

[8] This balance will vary in light of specific sectoral problems.

[9] This is especially clear in the concern with governance in Africa that has been prompted by the World Bank, among other international agencies: see World Bank (1991); Hyden (1992); Ghai (1993); Leftwich (1994).

[10] This is not to deny the claim that modes of governance in part constitute their own objects of governance. Not all constituted objects of governance are amenable to governance as defined in specific governance projects.

[11] Cf Atkinson and Coleman's remark that 'networks and communities are natural conceptual responses to both the limits of markets and hierarchical arrangements, to the enormous expansion in the types of societal actors involved in policy-making and to the dispersion of specialized political resources' (1992: 162). This

remark clearly links theoretical and practical problems and neatly illustrates the more general argument made in the text.

[12] This nice term was coined by Robert Delorme (1995) in criticizing alternative approaches to the political economy of complexity.

[13] Scharpf (1994) distinguishes between pooled and reciprocal interdependence. Whereas pooled interdependence requires only a one-off agreement on a common standard that individual actors then accept as the parameter within which to make their own independent choices among the options available to them individually, in the case of reciprocal interdependence, outcomes depend on the combined choices of all participants among their interdependent options (Scharpf, 1994: 36n).

[14] This typology is influenced by the Luhmannian distinction between three levels of social structure (interaction, organization and functional system or institutional order), and by a correlative distinction between different forms of social embeddedness (the social embeddedness of interpersonal relations, the institutional embeddedness of interorganizational relations and the societal embeddedness of intersystemic relations) (see Luhmann, 1982a).

Chapter 2

[1] Thus 'the reduction of complexity through the formation of ever more numerous, differentiated, and sophisticated systems [is] a phenomenon which necessarily generates ever new complexity, and thus feeds upon itself' (Poggi, 1979: xii).

[2] The term 'lifeworld' refers to domains of action in which consensual modes of action coordination predominate. It indicates the background resources, contexts and dimensions of social action that enable actors to cooperate on the basis of mutual understanding: shared cultural systems of meaning, institutional orders that stabilize patterns of action and personality structures acquired in family, church, neighbourhood and school (Habermas, 1984; Bohman and Rehg, 2017).

[3] For Stig Hjarvard, 'mediatization is to be considered a double-sided process of high modernity in which the media, on the one hand, emerge as an independent institution with a logic of its own to which other social institutions have to accommodate. On the other hand, media simultaneously become an integrated part of other institutions like politics, work, family and religion as more and more of these institutional activities are performed through both interactive and mass media. The logic of the media refers to the institutional and technological modus operandi of the media, including the ways in which media distribute material and symbolic resources and make use of formal and informal rules' (Hjarvard, 2008: 105).

[4] The scope for interaction among complex entities, the emergence of new entities and processes therefrom, the simplifications that are introduced by operating agents or systems to reduce complexity to manageable limits and the emergent effects of such simplifications all mean that complexity becomes self-potentiating (Rescher, 1998: 28).

[5] Asset specificity exists to the extent that assets have limited uses and are immobile.

[6] Autopoiesis is a condition of radical autonomy secured through self-organization. It emerges when a system defines its own boundaries relative to its environment, develops its own operational code, implements its own programmes, reproduces its own elements in a closed circuit and obeys its own laws of motion.

[7] Positive coordination involves multilateral exploration and concerted strategic action towards a joint goal (cf Scharpf, 1994: 38–9, 48).

8   In this way, they may generate *policy synergy*, that is, 'a process by which new insights or solutions are produced out of the differences between partners' (Hastings, 1996: 259).

9   For example, Campbell et al (1991), in their work on sectoral governance, note that 'sectors are socially constructed through self-organization and/or through public policy so they can be effectively administered' (1991: 9).

10 A good example comes from the speed and sequencing of reforms in and across different social domains in post-communist transition (cf Hausner et al, 1995).

11 State-socialist fusion of economic and political systems tends to lead to more authoritarian and repressive attempts at tension and crisis management operating on the symptoms rather than the causes of system failure.

12 Subsidiarity normally refers to the principle of devolving power to the lowest possible level in a hierarchical system compatible with effective solutions to defined problems; here I extend the idea, by analogy, to the principle that as few functional systems as possible but as many as necessary should be strategically involved in solving a problem.

13 Time-space distantiation can also anchor present action to the past through the 'politics of memory' and/or organizational techniques such as files, records and the like. See Giddens (1984 [1976]).

14 In this regard, de Certeau's view is dualist in so far as it mechanically opposes strategy and tactics; Gramsci develops a dialectical approach to war of position and war of manoeuvre whereby a counter-hegemonic war of position can prepare the ground for revolutionary, military-political manoeuvres (see Gramsci, 1971).

15 One implication of this is that one should not be too hasty in destroying alternative modes of coordination, for they may need to be reinvented in one or another form in response to specific forms of coordination failure. This lesson was relearned in the North Atlantic financial crisis.

Chapter 3

1   A structural contradiction exists when a system is so constituted that its organization or operation tends to produce antagonistic relations or opposed tendencies (for example, capital versus labour, socialization of forces of production versus private appropriation of profit).

2   A strategic dilemma (trilemma, and so forth) exists when agents are faced with choices such that any action undermines key conditions of their existence and/or their capacities to realize some overall interest (for example, treating labour power as a cost of production or source of demand).

3   This could occur in at least three ways: the ecological dominance of the capitalist economy in the structural coupling of different systems; an acknowledged primacy of the economy in (negative and/or positive) strategic coordination; or the secondary coding of autonomous institutional logics through economic values. Such secondary coding leads to questions such as whether it is profitable or unprofitable to apply the distinctions typical of other systems: for example, legal–illegal, true–false, sacred–secular.

4   It therefore involves what my earlier work labelled 'metagovernance', a term I would now reserve for the collibration of all three modes of coordination (cf Dunsire, 1996).

5   Sørensen et al (2009) explicate these principles as follows: (1) network design, which endeavours to determine the scope, character, composition and institutional procedures of networks; (2) network framing, which seeks to define the political

goals, fiscal conditions, legal basis and discursive storyline of networks; (3) network management, which attempts to reduce tensions, resolve conflicts, empower particular actors and lower the transaction costs by providing different kinds of material and immaterial inputs and resources; and (4) network participation, which aims to influence the policy agenda, the range of feasible options, the decision-making premises and the negotiated outputs and outcomes.

Chapter 4

1   This text uses societal projects and societalization projects interchangeably: the former usage emphasizes the social or societal imaginary that informs or guides efforts at societalization while the latter emphasizes the trajectory, processes and practices involved in securing one or another mode and form of societalization.
2   On total institutions, see Goffman's analysis of *Asylums* (1968).
3   See, for example, Jessop (1990b: 327–35; 2002: 24–8; 2010a).
4   This argument holds in the first instance for modern, or functionally differentiated, social formations; it remains to be seen whether it holds for social formations in which segmentation or centre–periphery relations are dominant.
5   My use of STF differs from, but builds in part on, the work of David Harvey (see, for example, Harvey, 1982, 2001, 2003).
6   Marx's actual words were: 'If there is no production in general, then there is also no general production' (1973 [1857]: 84).

Chapter 6

1   The arguments in this section and the next draw heavily on Niemi (2011).
2   A reference to Marx's doctoral dissertation, which cites Aesop's fable about the ass that wore a lion's skin to frighten other animals, but notes that 'the ass was soon revealed under the lion's skin' (Marx, 1975b: 87). See also Isaac (1990).

Chapter 7

1   Miller and Rose declare themselves 'pickers and choosers' rather than Foucault scholars (2008: 8).
2   One source of Foucault's difficulties in linking capital and the state is his tendency to reduce the economy to exchange relations in line with liberal thought: this rendered invisible the contradictions and substantive inequalities in the capital relation. Likewise, when he introduces the logic of capitalism, he does not ground it in a detailed account of the social relations of production as opposed to transferable techniques and/or technologies for the conduct of conduct (Tellman, 2009; cf Marsden, 1999).
3   On the emergent properties of population as an object of government, see also Foucault (1979b [1981]: 24–6, 139–46; 2003: 242–51, 255–6; 2007: 67–79, 109–10, 352–7).
4   Cf Foucault (1977 [1975]: 222–3; 1979b [1981]: 99–100; 2003: 23, 32–4).

Chapter 8

1   This report provoked a response from a Berlin-based tenants' organization, drawing on its own range of national and international policy-makers, advisers and academic experts, which attempted to denaturalize what the World Report attempted to naturalize. See Eick and Berg (2000).

Chapter 9

[1] This argument is largely drawn from work that Jamie Peck and Adam Tickell did with Allan Cochrane (see Cochrane et al, 1996). Thanks to Allan for allowing me to draw so freely on his ideas (see also Peck and Tickell, 1995; Tickell and Peck, 1996; Tickell et al, 1995).

Chapter 10

[1] Material in this chapter benefited from comments by Eva Hartmann and Poul Kjaer.

[2] 'Formal freedom' is counterposed here to the lack of full *substantive* freedom due to the multiple constraints on free choice. The institutionalization of formal freedom is a significant political accomplishment and major element in liberal citizenship, as well as a precondition for functioning (and malfunctioning) market economies.

[3] 'Profit-producing' denotes the place of a particular capital (fraction) in the circuits of capital; it does not entail that every profit-producing capitalist always makes a profit.

[4] This said, the principle of maximizing shareholder value is a valiant effort to find a functional equivalent to competition law.

[5] Cited by Pollitt and Bouckaert (2011: 1), from Filkins (2010).

Chapter 11

[1] On essentially contested concepts, see W.B. Gallie (1956).

[2] I am not trying to suggest that there are only three sets of causes behind the following shifts in principles and practices; many other causal mechanisms are at work, too.

References

Alam, M.S. (2014) 'Two approaches to global competition: A historical review', *Real World Economics Review*, 66: 74–79.

Althusser, L. (1965) *For Marx*, London: New Left Books.

Althusser, L. (1971) 'Ideology and Ideological State Apparatuses', in L. Althusser (ed) *Lenin and Philosophy and Other Essays* (translated by B. Brewster), New York: Monthly Review Press, 127–87.

Althusser, L. (1990) *Philosophy and the Spontaneous Philosophy of the Scientists, and Other Essays*, London: Verso.

Amin, A. and Thrift, N. (1995) 'Globalization, Institutional "Thickness" and the Local Economy', in P. Healey, S. Cameron, S. Davoudi, S. Graham and A. Madani-Pour (eds) *Managing Cities: The New Urban Context*, London: Wiley, 91–108.

Andersen, N.A., Kjaer, P. and Pedersen, O.K. (1996) 'On the critique of negotiated economy', *Scandinavian Political Studies*, 19(2): 167–78.

Arthur, C.J. (2008) 'USA, Britain, Australia and Canada', in M. Musto (ed) *Karl Marx's Grundrisse: Foundations of the Critique of Political Economy 150 Years After*, London: Routledge, 249–56.

Ashby, W.R. (1956) *Introduction to Cybernetics*, London: Chapman & Hall.

Ashcraft, R. (1984) 'Marx and political theory', *Comparative Studies in Society and History*, 26(4): 637–67.

Atkinson, M.M. and Coleman, W.D. (1992) 'Policy networks, policy communities and the problems of governance', *Governance*, 5(2): 154–80.

Baecker, D. (2001) 'Managing corporations in networks', *Thesis Eleven*, 66: 80–98.

Baecker, D. (2006) 'Network Society', in N.O. Lehmann, L. Qvortup and B.K. Walter (eds) *The Concept of the Network Society: Post-Ontological Reflections*, Copenhagen: Samfundslitteratur, 95–112.

Banting, K. and Kymlicka, W. (2017) 'Introduction: The Political Sources of Solidarity in Diverse Societies', in K. Banting and W. Kymlicka (eds) *The Strains of Commitment: The Political Sources of Solidarity in Diverse Societies*, Oxford: Oxford University Press, 1–57.

Baraldi, C., Corsi, G. and Esposito, E. (1998) *GLU: Glossar zu Niklas Luhmann's Theorie sozialer Systeme*, Frankfurt: Suhrkamp.

Barbera, F. and Jones, I.R. (2020) *The Foundational Economy and Citizenship: Comparative Perspectives on Civil Repair*, Bristol: Policy Press.

Barbieri, M. (2008) 'Life is semiosis: The biosemiotic view of nature', *Cosmos and History: The Journal of Natural and Social Philosophy*, 4(1-2): 29–51.

Bateson, G. (1972) *Steps to an Ecology of Mind*, Chicago, IL: University of Chicago Press.

Beel, D., Jones, M.R. and Jones, I.R. (2016) 'Regulation, governance and agglomeration: Making links in city-region research', *Regional Studies, Regional Science*, 3(1): 509–30.

Beel, D., Jones, M.R. and Jones, I.R. (2017) 'City-Region Building and Geohistorical Matters', in J. Riding and M. Jones (eds) *Reanimating Regions: Culture, Politics, and Performance. Regions and Cities*, London: Routledge, 194–204.

Beel, D., Jones, M.R. and Jones, I.R. (2018a) 'Elite city-deals for economic growth? Problematizing the complexities of devolution, city-region building, and the (re)positioning of civil society', *Space and Polity*, 22(3): 307–27.

Beel, D., Jones, M.R. and Jones, I.R. (2018b) 'Regionalization and Civil Society in a Time of Austerity: The Cases of Manchester and Sheffield', in: C. Berry and A. Giovannini (eds) *Developing England's North: The Political Economy of the Northern Powerhouse*, Basingstoke: Palgrave Macmillan, 241–60.

Beel, D., Jones, M.R. and Plows, A. (2019) 'Urban growth strategies in rural regions: Building the North Wales Growth Deal', *Regional Studies*, available at https://doi.org/10.1080/00343404.2019.1669783

Beer, S. (1990) 'Recursion zero: Metamanagement', *Systems Practice*, 3(3): 315–26.

Bell, S. and Hindmoor, A. (2009) *Rethinking Governance: The Theory of the State in Modern Society*, Cambridge: Cambridge University Press.

Benko, G. and Lipietz, A. (1994) 'De la régulation des espaces aux espaces de régulation', in R. Boyer and Y. Saillard (eds) *Théorie de la régulation: L'état des savoirs*, Paris: La Découverte, 293–303.

Bevir, M. (2010) *Democratic Governance*, Princeton, NJ: Princeton University Press.

Beynon, H. (2016) 'Foreword: Overview of WISERD', in M. Jones, S. Orford and V. Macfarlane (eds) *People, Places and Policy: Knowing Contemporary Wales through New Localities*, London: Routledge, xv–xvi.

Beynon, H., Davies, R. and Davies, S. (2012) 'Sources of variation in trade union membership across the UK: The case of Wales', *Industrial Relations Journal*, 43(3): 200–21.

Black, W.K. (2005) *The Best Way to Rob a Bank is to Own One*, Austin, TX: University of Texas Press.

Black, W.K. (2011) 'Neo-classical economic theories, methodology, and praxis optimize criminogenic environments and produce recurrent, intensifying crises', *Creighton Law Review*, 44: 597–645.

Blackaby, D., Drinkwater, S., Murphy, P., O'Leary, N. and Staneva, A. (2018) 'The Welsh economy and the labour market', *Welsh Economic Review*, 26(1): 1–16.

Blakeley, H. and Moles, K. (2019) 'Everyday practices of memory: Authenticity, value and the gift', *The Sociological Review*, 7(3): 621–34.

Blum, W. (2001) *Rogue State: A Guide to the World's Only Superpower*, London: Zed.

Bohman, J. and Rehg, W. (2017) 'Jürgen Habermas', in E.N. Zalta (ed) *The Stanford Encyclopedia of Philosophy* (Fall 2017 edition), available at https://plato.stanford.edu/archives/fall2017/entries/habermas/

Börzel, T.A. and Risse, T. (2010) 'Governance without a state: Can it work?', *Regulation & Governance*, 4(2): 113–34.

Bouckaert, G., Peters, B.G. and Verhoest, K. (2010) *The Coordination of Public Sector Organizations: Shifting Patterns of Public Management*, Basingstoke: Palgrave Macmillan.

Bourdieu, P. (1984) *Distinction: A Social Critique of the Judgement of Taste* (translated by R. Nice), Cambridge, MA: Harvard University Press.

Bourdieu, P. (1990) *The Logic of Practice* (translated by R. Nice), Cambridge: Polity.

Bovaird, T. (1994) 'Managing urban economic development: Learning to change or the marketing of failure?', *Urban Studies*, 31(4/5): 573–604.

Boyer, R. (1996) 'State and Market', in R. Boyer and D. Drache (eds) *States against Markets: The Limits of Globalization*, London: Routledge, 84–114.

Brunkhorst, H. (2005) *Solidarity: From Civic Friendship to a Global Legal Community* (translated by J. Flynn), Cambridge, MA: The MIT Press.

Bryan, D. and Rafferty, M. (2006) *Capitalism with Derivatives: A Political Economy of Financial Derivatives, Capital and Class*, Basingstoke: Palgrave Macmillan.

Bryson, A. and Davies, R. (2019) 'Family, place and the intergenerational transmission of union membership', *British Journal of Industrial Relations*, 57(3): 624–50.

Burchell, G., Gordon, C. and Miller, P. (eds) (1991) *The Foucault Effect: Studies in Governmentality*, Hemel Hempstead: Harvester Wheatsheaf.

Buttigieg, J.A. (1995) 'Gramsci and civil society', *boundary 2*, 22(3): 1–32.

Buttigieg, J.A. (2005) 'The contemporary discourse on civil society: A Gramscian critique', *boundary 2*, 32(1): 33–52.

Campbell, J.L. and Pedersen, O.K. (2007) 'Institutional competitiveness in the global economy', *Regulation and Governance*, 1(3): 230–46.

Campbell, J.L., Hollingsworth, J.R. and Lindberg, L.N. (eds) (1991) *Governance of the American Economy*, Cambridge: Cambridge University Press.

Capello, R. (1996) 'Industrial enterprises and economic space: The network paradigm', *European Planning Studies*, 4(4): 485–98.

Cardoso, J.L. and Mendonça, P. (2012) *Corporatism and Beyond: An Assessment of Recent Literature*, Lisbon: Institute of Social Sciences, University of Lisbon, available at https://repositorio.ul.pt/handle/10451/6770

Castells, M. (1989) *The Informational City: Economic Restructuring and Urban Development*, Oxford: Blackwell.

Cerny, P.G. (1997) 'Paradoxes of the competition state: The dynamics of globalization', *Government and Opposition*, 32: 251–74.

Chandoke, N. (2009) 'Putting civil society in its place', *Radical Politics Today*, 7, available at https://research.ncl.ac.uk/spaceofdemocracy/word%20docs%20linked%20to/Uploaded%202009/chandhoke/chandhoke.pdf

Chaney, P. (2016a) 'Comparative analysis of state and civil society: Discourse on human rights implementation and the position of Roma in the former Yugoslav space', *Ethnopolitics*, 16(5): 431–49.

Chaney, P. (2016b) 'Gendered political space: Civil society, contingency theory, and the substantive representation of women', *Journal of Civil Society*, 12(2): 198–223.

Chaney, P. and Sophocleous, P. (2018) 'Trust, Territoriality and Third Sector Engagement in Policy-Making and Welfare Provision: Exploring the Trust Pathologies of Welfare Pluralism', in A. Cole (ed) *Trust–Transparency Paradoxes: Proceedings of an International Conference*, WISERD Working Paper, Cardiff: WISERD (Wales Institute of Social & Economic Research, Data & Methods), 29–37.

Chesnais, F. (1987) 'Science, technology and competitiveness', *STI Review*, 1: 85–129.

Chomsky, N. (2006) *Failed States: The Abuse of Power and the Assault on Democracy*, London: Hamish Hamilton.

Chouliaraki, L. (2013) *The Ironic Spectator: Solidarity in the Age of Post-Humanitarianism*, Cambridge: Polity.

Clark, K., Drinkwater, S. and Robinson, C. (2017) 'Self-employment amongst migrant groups: New evidence from England and Wales', *Small Business Economics*, 48: 1047–69.

Cochrane, A., Peck, J. and Tickell, A. (1996) 'Manchester plays games: Exploring the local politics of globalization', *Urban Studies*, 33(10): 1319–36.

Cole, A. (ed) (2018) *Trust–transparency Paradoxes: Proceedings of an International Conference*, WISERD Working Paper, Cardiff: WISERD (Wales Institute of Social & Economic Research, Data & Methods).

Conteh, C. (2013a) 'Policy Governance in Multi-level Systems', in D. Cepiku, D. Jesuit and I. Roberge (eds) *Making Multi-Level Public Management Work*, London: Routledge, 85–100.

Conteh, C. (2013b) *Policy Governance in Multi-Level Systems*, Montréal: McGill University Press.

Coulson, A. (1997) '"Transaction cost economics" and its implications for local governance', *Local Government Studies*, 23(1): 107–13.

Cruikshank, B. (1999) *Will to Empower: Democratic Citizens and Other Subjects*, Ithaca, NY: Cornell University Press.

Dalby, S. (1993) 'Just the tonic for Eastlands', *The Financial Times*, 23 June.

Dartford Borough Council (1999) 'Land at North Dartford Planning Brief', available at www.dartford.gov.uk/data/assets/pdf_file/0008/63584/LandatNorthDartfordPlanningBrief.pdf

Davies, J.S. (2011) *Challenging Governance Theory: From Networks to Hegemony*, Bristol: Policy Press.

DCLG (Department for Communities and Local Government) (2006) *Thames Gateway: Interim Plan: Development Prospectus*, Wetherby: Communities and Local Government Publications.

Deacon, B. (2007) *Global Social Policy: International Organizations and the Future of Welfare*, London: SAGE Publications Ltd.

Deacon, B. with Hulse, M. and Stubbs, P. (1997) *Global Social Policy: International Organizations and the Future of Welfare*, London: SAGE Publications Ltd.

Deacon, R. (2002) 'Why the King has kept his head: Foucault on power as sovereignty', *Politeia*, 21(3): 6-17.

Dean, M. (1994) *Critical and Effective Histories: Foucault's Methods and Historical Sociology*, London: Routledge.

Dean, M. and Villadsen, K. (2016) *State Phobia and Civil Society: The Political Legacy of Michel Foucault*, Stanford, CA: Stanford University Press.

de Angelis, M. (2017) *Omnia sunt Communia: On the Commons and the Transformation to Postcapitalism*, London: Zed Books.

Debray, R. (1971) 'Time and Politics', in R. Debray (ed) *Prison Writings*, London: Allen Lane, 87–160.

de Certeau, M. (1985) *The Practice of Everyday Life*, Berkeley, CA: University of California Press.

della Porta, D. and Diani, M. (2010) *Social Movements: An Introduction* (2nd edn), Cambridge: Polity.

Dellheim, J. (2014) *Finanzialisierung, Solidarische Ökonomie, Sozialökologischer Umbau/Sozialökologische Transformation, Imperiale Lebensweise, Kapitaloligarchien*, Berlin: Rosa Luxemburg Stiftung.

Delorme, R. (1995) 'Self-organization and complexity', Paper presented to Conference on Self-Organization in Economics, Paris: CEPREMAP, 9–10 March.

Delorme, R. (2010) *Deep Complexity and the Social Sciences*, Cheltenham: Edward Elgar.

Deutsch, K.W. (1963) *The Nerves of Government: Models of Political Communication and Control*, New York: Free Press.

Dierkes, M., Antal, A.B., Child, J. and Nonaka, I. (eds) (2001) *Handbook of Organizational Learning and Knowledge*, Oxford: Oxford University Press.

DoE (Department of the Environment) (1993) *Annual Report 1993: The Government's Expenditure Plans 1993–94 to 1995–96*, Cm 2207. London: HMSO.

Doheney, S. and Milbourne, P. (2017) 'Community, rurality, and older people: Critically comparing older people's experiences across different rural communities', *Journal of Rural Studies*, 50: 129–38.

Donahue, J.D. and Nye, J.S. (2002) *Governance Amid Bigger, Better Markets*, Washington, DC: Brookings Institute.

Dowdle, M.W. (2013) 'The Regulatory Geography of Market Competition in Asia (and Beyond)', in M.W. Dowdle, J. Gillespie and I. Maher (eds) *Asian Capitalism and the Regulation of Competition*, Cambridge: Cambridge University Press, 11–35.

Dunleavy, P., Tinkler, J., Gilson, C. and Towers, E. (2006) *Digital Era Governance*, Oxford: Oxford University Press.

Dunsire, A. (1993) *Manipulating Social Tensions: Collibration as an Alternative Mode of Government Intervention*, Köln: Max-Planck-Institut für Gesellschaftsforschung, available at www.mpi-fg-koeln.mpg.de/pu/dp93-97_en.asp#1993

Dunsire, A. (1996) 'Tipping the balance: Autopoiesis and governance', *Administration & Society*, 28(3): 299–334.

Edelenbos, J. and Klijn, E.H. (2007) 'Trust in complex decision-making networks: A theoretical and empirical exploration', *Administration & Society*, 39(1): 35–50.

Edelman, M. (1977) *Political Language: Words that Work, Policies that Fail*, London: Academic Press.

Eder, K. (1999) 'Societies learn and yet the world is hard to change', *European Journal of Social Theory*, 2(2): 195–215.

Eick, V. and Berg, R. (eds) (2000) *Und die Welt wird zur Scheibe... Reader zum Weltbericht (Für die Zukunft des Städte – URBAN 21)*, Berlin: Berliner MieterGemeinschaft.

Elchedus, M. (1990) 'The Temporalities of Exchange: The Case of Self-Organization for Societal Guidance', in B. Marin (ed) *Generalized Political Exchange: Antagonistic Cooperation and Integrated Policy Circuits*, Boulder, CO: Westview, 192–216.

Elias, N. (2000) *The Civilizing Process* (2nd edn), Chichester: Wiley-Blackwell.

Esser, K., Hillebrand, W., Messner, D. and Meyer-Stammer, J. (1996) *Systemic Competitiveness: New Governance Patterns for Industrial Development*, London: Routledge.

Etherington, D. and Jones, M.R. (2016) 'The city-region chimera: The political economy of metagovernance failure in Britain', *Cambridge Journal of Regions, Economy and Society*, 9(3), 371–89.

Fairclough, N. (1989) *Language and Power*, London: Longmans.

Fairclough, N. (2003) *Analysing Discourse: Textual Analysis for Social Research*, London: Routledge.

Feilzer, M.Y. and Jones, I.R. (2015) 'Barriers to social participation in later life: Fear of crime and fear of young people', Paper presented at MICRA Seminar Series, University of Manchester, 7 October.

Ferguson, A. (1995 [1767]) *An Essay on the History of Civil Society*, Cambridge: Cambridge University Press.

Filkins, D. (2010) 'Afghan offensive is new war model', *New York Times*, 12 February.

Fischer, F. (2009) *Democracy and Expertise: Reorienting Policy Inquiry*, Oxford: Oxford University Press.

Foucault, M. (1977 [1975]) *Discipline and Punish: The Birth of a Prison* (translated by A. Sheridan), London: Allen Lane.

Foucault, M. (1979a) '"Governmentality", translated by C. Gordon', *Ideology & Consciousness*, 6, 5–21.

Foucault, M. (1979b [1981]) *History of Sexuality: Volume 1: Introduction* (translated by R. Hurley), London: Allen Lane.

Foucault, M. (1979c) *Power, Truth, Strategy* (edited by M. Morris and P. Patton), Sydney, NSW: Feral Publications.

Foucault, M. (1980) *Power/Knowledge: Selected Interviews and Other Writings 1972–1977* (translated by C. Gordon, L. Marshall, J. Mepham and K. Soper), New York: Pantheon.

Foucault, M (1982) 'The Subject and Power' (translated by L. Sawyer), in H. Dreyfus and P. Rainbow (eds) *Michel Foucault: Beyond Structuralism and Hermeneutics* (2nd edn), Brighton: Harvester, 208–26.

Foucault, M. (1989 [1983]) 'An Ethics of Pleasure' (translated by S. Riggins), in S. Lotringer (ed) *Foucault Live: Interviews 1966–84*, New York: Semiotext(e), 257–77.

Foucault, M. (1991) 'Governmentality', in G. Burchell, C. Gordon and P. Miller (eds) *The Foucault Effect: Studies in Governmentality*, London: Routledge, 87–104.

Foucault, M. (1997 [1984]) 'The Ethics of the Concern of the Self as a Practice of Freedom', in P. Rabinow (ed) *Ethics: The Essential Works of Michel Foucault, 1954–1984*, New York: New Press, 281–301.

Foucault, M. (2000) 'Truth and Power', in J.D. Faubion (ed) *Power: The Essential Works of Michel Foucault, 1954–1984*, New York: New Press, 111–33.

Foucault, M. (2003) *'Society must be Defended': Lectures at the Collège de France 1975–1976* (translated by D. Macey), New York: Picador.

Foucault, M. (2007) *Security, Territory, Population: Lectures at the Collège de France, 1977–1978* (translated by G. Burchell), Basingstoke: Palgrave.

Foucault, M. (2008) *The Birth of Biopolitics: Lectures at the Collège de France, 1978–1979* (translated by G. Burchell), Basingstoke: Palgrave.

Fox, S., Hampton, J.M., Muddiman, E. and Taylor, C. (2019) 'Intergenerational transmission and support for EU membership in the United Kingdom: The case of Brexit', *European Sociological Review*, 35(3), 380–93.

Friedman, M. (1962) *Capitalism and Freedom*, Chicago, IL: University of Chicago Press.

Fukuyama, F. (1995) *Trust: The Social Virtues and the Creation of Prosperity*, New York: Free Press.

Gallie, W.B. (1956) 'Essentially contested concepts', *Proceedings of the Aristotelian Society*, New Series, 56: 167–98.

Geoghegan, M. and Powell, F. (2009) 'The Contested Meaning of Civil Society', in D. Boron and P. Kirby (eds) *Power, Protest and Democracy*, Dublin: A. & A. Farmar, 95–110.

Gerber, D. (2010) *Global Competition: Law, Markets and Globalization*, Oxford: Oxford University Press.

Ghai, Y. (1993) 'Constitutions and Governance in Africa: A Prolegomenon', in S. Adelman and A. Paliwala (eds) *Law and Crisis in the Third World*, London: Hans Zell Publishers, 51–75.

Giddens, A. (1984 [1976]) *The Constitution of Society: Outline of the Theory of Structuration*, Cambridge: Polity.

Glagow, M. and Willke, H. (eds) (1987) *Dezentrale Gesellschaftssteuerung: Probleme der Integration polyzentristischer Gesellschaft*, Pfaffenweiler: Centaurus-Verlagsgesellschaft.

Glynos, J. and Howarth, D. (2007) *Logics of Critical Explanation in Social and Political Theory*, London: Routledge.

Goffman, E. (1968) *Asylums: Essays on the Social Situation of Mental Patients and Other Inmates*, New York: Anchor Books.

Gordon, C. (2001) 'Introduction', in J.D. Faubon (ed) *Power: The Essential Writings*, New York, NY: New Press, xi–xlii.

Gough, J. (1991) 'Structure, system, and contradiction in the capitalist space economy', *Environment and Planning D: Society and Space*, 9(4): 433–49.

Gough, J. (2004) 'Changing scale as changing class relations: Variety and contradiction in the politics of scale', *Political Geography*, 23(2): 185–211.

Gough, J. and Eizenschitz, A. (1996) 'The modernization of Britain and local economic policy: Promise and contradictions', *Environment and Planning D: Society and Space*, 14(2): 203–19.

Grabher, G. (ed) (1993) *The Embedded Firm: On the Socioeconomics of Industrial Networks*, London: Routledge.

Grabher, G. (1994) *Lob der Verschwendung, Redundanz in der Regionalentwicklung: Ein sozioökonomisches Plädoyer*, Berlin: Sigma.

Graham, K. (1986) *The Battle of Democracy*, Brighton: Wheatsheaf Books.

Graham, C. and Smith, F. (eds) (2004) *Competition, Regulation and the New Economy*, Oxford: Hart Publishing.

Gramsci, A. (1971) *Selections from Prison Notebooks* (translated by Q. Hoare and G.N. Smith), London: Lawrence & Wishart.

Gramsci, A. (1975) *Quaderni del Carcere, edizione critica dell'Istituto Gramsci*, 4 volumes, Turino: Einaudi.

Gramsci, A. (1995) *Further Selections from the Prison Notebooks* (translated by D. Boothman), London: Lawrence & Wishart.

Granovetter, M. (1985) 'Economic action and social structure: The problem of embeddedness', *American Journal of Sociology*, 91(3): 481–510.

Greenspan, A. (2008) Evidence given on 23 October 2008, Washington, DC: House Committee on Oversight and Government Reform.

Guma, T., Woods, M., Yarker, S. and Anderson, J. (2019) '"It's that kind of place here": Solidarity, place-making and civil society response to the 2015 refugee crisis in Wales, UK', *Social Inclusion*, 7(2): 96–105.

Haas, P.M. and Haas, E.B. (1995) 'Learning to learn: Improving international governance', *Global Governance*, 1(4): 255–85.

Haber, H.F. (1994) *Beyond Post-Modern Politics: Lyotard, Rorty and Foucault*, London: Routledge.

Habermas, J. (1984) *The Theory of Communicative Action, Vol I: Reason and the Rationalization of Society* (translated by T. McCarthy), Boston, MD: Beacon [in German, 1981, vol 1].

Habermas, J. (1987) *The Theory of Communicative Action, Vol II: Lifeworld and System* (translated by T. McCarthy), Boston, MD: Beacon [in German, 1981, Vol 2].

Habermas, J. (1989) *The Structural Transformation of the Public Sphere: An Inquiry into a Category of Bourgeois Society* (translated by T. Burger with F. Lawrence), Cambridge: Polity.

Hajer, M. (2009) *Authoritative Governance: Policy-Making in the Age of Mediatization*, Oxford: Oxford University Press.

Hajer, M. and Wagenaar, H. (2003) 'Introduction', in M. Hajer and H. Wagenaar (eds) *Deliberative Policy Analysis: Understanding Governance in the Network Society*, Cambridge: Cambridge University Press, 1–30.

Hall, P. and Pfeiffer, U. (2000) *Urban Future 21: A Global Agenda for Twenty-First-Century Cities*, London: Federal Ministry of Transport, Building and Housing/E. & F.N. Spon.

Harvey, D. (1982) *The Limits to Capital*, Oxford: Blackwell.

Harvey, D. (2001) 'Globalization and the "spatial fix"', *Geographische Revue*, 2: 23–30.

Harvey, D. (2003) *The New Imperialism*, Oxford: Oxford University Press.

Hastings, A. (1996) 'Unravelling the process of "partnership" in urban regeneration policy', *Urban Studies*, 33(2): 253–68.

Hausner, J., Jessop, B. and Nielsen, K. (1995) 'Institutional Change in Post-Socialism', in J. Hausner, B. Jessop and K. Nielsen (eds) *Strategic Choice and Path-Dependency in Post-Socialism*, Aldershot: Edward Elgar, 3–45.

Hayek, F.A. (1947) 'Opening Address to a Conference at Mont Pélerin', in F.A. Hayek (ed) *Studies in Philosophy, Politics, and Economics*, Chicago, IL: University of Chicago Press, 148–59 [1980, new edition].

Hayek, F.A. (1948) *Individualism and Economic Order*, Chicago, IL: University of Chicago Press.

Hayek, F.A. (1972) 'The Theory of Complex Phenomena', in F.A. Hayek (ed) *Studies in Philosophy, Politics and Economics*, London: Routledge & Kegan Paul, 55–70.

Healey, P., de Magalhaes, C., Madanipour, A. and Pendlebury, J. (2003) 'Place, Identity and Local Politics: Analysing Partnership Initiatives', in M. Hajer and H. Wagenaar (eds) *Deliberative Policy Analysis: Understanding Governance in the Network Society*, Cambridge: Cambridge University Press, 60–87.

Heidenheimer, A.J. (1986) 'Politics, policy and policey as concepts in English and Continental languages', *Review of Politics*, 48(1): 1–26.

Héritier, A. and Rhodes, M. (eds) (2011) *New Modes of Governance in Europe: Governing in the Shadow of Hierarchy*, Basingstoke: Palgrave Macmillan.

Hill, C.R. (1992) *Olympic Politics*, Manchester: Manchester University Press.

Hirst, P.Q. and Zeitlin, J. (1991) 'Flexible specialization vs post-Fordism: Theory, evidence and policy implications', *Economy and Society*, 20(1): 1–56.

Hjarvard, S. (2008) 'The mediatization of society: A theory of the media as agents of social and cultural change', *Nordicom Review*, 29(2): 105–34.

Hodgson, G. (1988) *Economics and Institutions*, Cambridge: Polity.

Hollingsworth, J.R., Schmitter, P.C. and Streeck, W. (1994) *Governing Capitalist Economies: Performance and Control of Economic Sectors*, Oxford: Oxford University Press.

Hood, C. (1998) *The Art of the State: Culture, Rhetoric and Public Management*, Oxford: Oxford University Press.

Howard, D. (2002) *The Specter of Democracy: What Marx and Marxists Haven't Understood and Why*, New York: Columbia University Press.

Hunt, A. and Wickham, G. (1994) *Foucault and Law: Towards a Sociology of Governance*, London: Pluto Press.

Hutcheon, L. (1994) *Irony's Edge: The Theory and Politics of Irony*, London: Routledge.

Hyden, G. (1992) 'Governance and the Study of Politics', in G. Hyden and M. Bratton (eds) *Governance and Politics in Africa*, Boulder, CO: Westview, 1–26.

Isaac, J. (1990) 'The lion's skin of politics: Marx on republicanism', *Polity*, 22(3), 461–88.

Jensen, M. (2011) *Civil Society in Liberal Democracy*, London: Routledge.

Jessop, B. (1982) *The Capitalist State: Marxist Theories and Methods*, Oxford: Martin Robertson.

Jessop, B. (1990a) 'Regulation theories in retrospect and prospect', *Economy and Society*, 19(2): 153–216.

Jessop, B. (1990b) *State Theory: Putting Capitalist States in Their Place*, Cambridge: Polity.

Jessop, B. (1993) 'Towards a Schumpeterian Workfare State? Preliminary remarks on post-Fordist political economy', *Studies in Political Economy*, 40: 7–39.

Jessop, B. (1995) 'The regulation approach and governance theory: Alternative perspectives on economic and political change?', *Economy and Society*, 24(3): 307–33.

Jessop, B. (1996) 'A Neo-Gramscian Approach to the Regulation of Urban Regimes: Accumulation Strategies, Hegemonic Projects, and Governance', in M. Lauria (ed) *Reconstructing Urban Regime Theory*, New York: Sage, 51–73.

Jessop, B. (1997) 'The Governance of Complexity and the Complexity of Governance: Preliminary Remarks on Some Problems and Limits of Economic Guidance', in A. Amin and J. Hausner (eds) *Beyond Markets and Hierarchy: Third Way Approaches to Transformation*, Aldershot: Edward Elgar, 111–47.

Jessop, B. (1998) 'The rise of governance and the risks of failure: The case of economic development', *International Social Science Journal*, 155: 29–46.

Jessop, B. (1999) 'Governance Failure', in G. Stoker (ed) *The New Politics of Local Governance in Britain*, Basingstoke: Macmillan, 11–32.

Jessop, B. (2002a) 'Liberalism, neoliberalism and urban governance: A state-theoretical perspective', *Antipode*, 34(3): 458–78.

Jessop, B. (2002b) *The Future of the Capitalist State*, Cambridge: Polity.

Jessop, B. (2003) 'Governance and Meta-Governance. On Reflexivity, Requisite Variety, and Requisite Irony', in H. Bang (ed) *Governance as Social and Political Communication*, Manchester: Manchester University Press, 101–16.

Jessop, B. (2004) 'Cultural political economy and critical semiotic analysis', *Critical Discourse Studies*, 1(2): 159–74.

Jessop, B. (2006) 'Spatial Fixes, Temporal Fixes, and Spatio-Temporal Fixes', in N. Castree and D. Gregory (eds) *David Harvey: A Critical Reader*, Oxford: Blackwell, 142–66.

Jessop, B. (2007a) 'Knowledge as a Fictitious Commodity', in A. Buğra and K. Agartan (eds) *Reading Karl Polanyi for the 21st Century*, Basingstoke: Palgrave Macmillan, 115–34.

Jessop, B. (2007b) 'New Labour or the normalization of neoliberalism', *British Politics*, 2(3), 282–88.

Jessop, B. (2007c) *State Power: A Strategic-Relational Approach*, Cambridge: Polity.

Jessop, B. (2009) 'Cultural political economy and critical policy studies', *Critical Policy Studies*, 3(3-4): 336–56.

Jessop, B. (2010a) 'From Hegemony to Crisis? The Continuing Ecological Dominance of Neoliberalism', in K. Birch and V. Mykhnenko (eds) *The Rise and Fall of Neoliberalism*, London: Zed, 171–87.

Jessop, B. (2010b) 'Another Foucault Effect? Foucault on Governmentality and Statecraft', in U. Bröckling, S. Krasmann and T. Lemke (eds) *Governmentality: Current Issues and Future Challenges*, New York: Routledge, 56–73.

Jessop, B. (2014) 'Repoliticizing depoliticization: Theoretical preliminaries on some responses to the American and Eurozone debt crises', *Policy & Politics*, 42(2): 207–23.

Jessop, B. (2015) *The State: Past, Present, Future*, Cambridge: Polity.

Jessop, B. (2016) 'The Heartlands of Neoliberalism and the Rise of the Austerity State', in S. Springer, K. Birch and J. MacLeavy (eds) *The Handbook of Neoliberalism*, London: Routledge, 410–21.

Jessop, B. (2017) 'Civil society as a mode of governance: Between network and solidarity', Lecture given at Bangor University, 29 March.

Jessop, B. and Sum, N.-L. (2001) 'Pre-disciplinary and post-disciplinary perspectives in political economy', *New Political Economy*, 6(1): 89–101.

Jessop, B., Peck, J. and Tickell, A. (1999) 'Retooling the Machine: Economic Crisis, State Restructuring and Urban Politics', in A.E.G. Jonas and D. Wilson (eds) *The Urban Growth Machine: Critical Perspectives Twenty Years Later*, New York: State University of New York Press, 141–59.

Johns, N., Green, A., Swann, R. and Sloan, L. (2019) 'Street pastors in the night-time economy: Harmless do-gooders or a manifestation of a New Right agenda?', *Safer Communities*, 18(1): 1–15.

Johnson, C.J. (2000) *Blowback: The Costs and Consequences of American Empire*, Boston, MA: Little, Brown.

Johnson, C.J. (2004) *The Sorrows of Empire: Militarism, Secrecy and the End of the Republic*, New York: Metropolitan Books.

Johnson, C.J. (2006) *Nemesis: Last Days of the American Republic*, New York: Metropolitan Books.

Jones, C., Hesterly, W.S. and Borgatti, S. (1997) 'A general theory of network governance: Exchange conditions and social mechanisms', *Academy of Management Review*, 22(4): 911–45.

Jones, M. (2019) 'The march of governance and the actualities of failure: The case of economic development twenty years on', *International Journal of Social Science*, 68(227–228): 25–41.

Jones, M., Orford, S., Heley, J. and Macfarlane, V. (2016) 'New Localities in Action and Reaction', in M. Jones, S. Orford and V. Macfarlane (eds) *People, Places and Policy: Knowing Contemporary Wales through New Localities*, London: Routledge, 143–73.

Joseph, J. (2016) 'Governing through failure and denial: The new resilience agenda', *Millennium*, 44(3): 370–90.

Joseph, J. (2018) *Varieties of Resilience: Studies in Governmentality*, Cambridge: Cambridge University Press.

Kaasch, A. (2015) 'Conclusions – Complexity in Global Social Governance', in A. Kaasch and K. Martens (eds) *Actors and Agency in Global Social Governance*, Oxford: Oxford University Press, 233–50.

Kaasch, A. and Stubbs, P. (2014) 'Global and Regional Social Policy Transformations: Contextualizing the Contribution of Bob Deacon', in A. Kaasch and P. Stubbs (eds) *Transformations in Global and Regional Social Policies*, Basingstoke: Palgrave Macmillan, 3–17.

Kaminski, B. (1991) *The Collapse of State Socialism: The Case of Poland*, Princeton, NJ: Princeton University Press.

Keane, J. (1988) *Democracy and Civil Society*, London: Verso.

Kelen, A. (2001) *The Gratis Economy: Privately Provided Public Goods*, Budapest: Central European Press.

Kelly, M.G.E. (2009) *The Political Philosophy of Michel Foucault*, London: Routledge.

Kempa, M. and Singh, A.-M. (2008) 'Private security, political economy and the policing of race', *Theoretical Criminology*, 12(3), 333–54.

Keohane, R. (1984) *After Hegemony: Cooperation and Discord in World Political Economy*, Princeton, NJ: Princeton University Press.

Kerr, D. (1999) 'Beheading the King and enthroning the market: A critique of Foucauldian governmentality', *Science & Society*, 63(2): 173–202.

Kickert, W.J.M., Klijn, E.H. and Koppenjan, J.F.M. (eds) (1997) *Managing Complex Networks: Strategies for the Public Sector*, London: SAGE Publications Ltd.

Kitschelt, H. (1991) 'Industrial governance structures, innovation strategies, and the case of Japan: Sectoral or cross-national comparative analysis?', *International Organization*, 45(4): 453–93.

Kooiman, J. (1993a) 'Governance and Governability: Using Complexity, Dynamics and Diversity', in J. Kooiman (ed) *Modern Governance: New Government–Society Interactions*, London: SAGE Publications Ltd, 35–48.

Kooiman, J. (1993b) *Modern Governance: New Government Society Interactions*, London: SAGE Publications Ltd.

Kooiman, J. (2000) 'Societal Governance: Levels, Models, and Orders of Social–Political Interaction', in J. Pierre (ed) *Debating Governance: Authority, Steering, and Democracy*, Oxford: Oxford University Press, 138–64.

Kooiman, J. (2002) 'Activation in Governance', in H. Bang (ed) *Governance, Governmentality and Democracy*, Manchester: Manchester University Press, 79–100.

Kooiman, J. (2003) *Governing as Governance*, London: SAGE Publications Ltd.

Kooiman, J. and Jentoft, S. (2009) 'Meta-governance: Values, norms and principles, and the making of hard choices', *Public Administration*, 87(4): 818–36.

Kouvelakis, S. (2005) 'The Marxian critique of citizenship: For a rereading of *On the Jewish Question*', *The South Atlantic Quarterly*, 104(4): 707–21.

Kouvelakis, S. (2008) *Philosophy and Revolution: From Kant to Marx*, London: Verso.

Larmour, P. (1997) 'Models of governance and public administration', *International Political Science Review*, 63(4): 383–94.

Larsson, B. (2013) 'Sovereign power beyond the state: A critical reappraisal of governance by networks', *Critical Policy Studies*, 7(2): 99–114.

Lazzarato, M. (2005) 'Biopolitique et bioéconomique', *Multitudes*, 22, autumn [cited from 'Biopolitics and bioeconomics: A politics of multiplicity', translated by A. Bove and E. Empson, *Generation Online*, available at www.generation-online.org/p/fplazzarato2.htm].

Lefebvre H. (1991 [1978]) *The Production of Space*, Oxford: Blackwell.

Leftwich, A. (1994) 'Governance, the state, and the politics of development', *Development and Change*, 25(4): 363–86.

Lemke, T. (2019) *A Critique of Political Reason: Foucault's Analysis of Modern Governmentality*, London: Verso.

Lindberg, L.N., Campbell, J.C. and Hollingsworth, R. (1991) 'Economic Governance and the Analysis of Structural Change in the American Economy', in J.L. Campbell, L.N. Lindberg and R. Hollingsworth (eds) *Governance of the US Economy*, Cambridge: Cambridge University Press, 3–34.

Lockwood, D. (1999) 'Civic integration and class formation', *British Journal of Sociology*, 47(3): 531–50.

Logan, J. and Molotch, H. (eds) (1987) *Urban Fortunes: The Political Economy of Place*, Berkeley, CA: University of California Press.

Lohmann, G. (1991) *Indifferenz und Gesellschaft: Eine kritische Auseinandersetzung mit Marx*, Frankfurt: Suhrkamp.

Luhmann, N. (1979) *Trust and Power: Two Essays*, Chichester: John Wiley.

Luhmann, N. (1982a) 'Interaction, Organization, and Society', in N. Luhmann (ed) *The Differentiation of Society*, New York: Columbia University Press, 69–89.

Luhmann N. (1982b) 'The world society is a social system', *International Journal of General Systems*, 8(3): 131–8.

Luhmann, N. (1983) 'Das sind Preise', *Soziale Welt*, 34(3): 153–70.

Luhmann, N. (1988) *Die Wirtschaft der Gesellschaft*, Frankfurt: Suhrkamp.

Luhmann, N. (1992) *Social Systems* (translated by J. Bednarz with D. Baecker), Stanford, CA: Stanford University Press.

Luhmann, N. (1996) 'Politics and economics', *Thesis Eleven*, 53: 1–9.

Luhmann, N. (1997) 'Globalization or world society? How to conceive of modern society', *International Review of Sociology*, 7(1): 67–80.

Luhmann, N. (2005) *Law as a Social System* (translated by K.A. Ziegert), Oxford: Oxford University Press.

Luke, T. (1994) 'Placing power/siting space: The politics of global and local in the New World Order', *Environment and Planning D: Society and Space*, 12: 613–28.

Lundvall, B.-A. (ed) (1992) *National Systems of Innovation: Towards a Theory of Innovation and Interactive Learning*, London: Pinter.

Machiavelli, N. (1988) *The Prince* (edited by Q. Skinner and R. Price), Cambridge: Cambridge University Press.

Macneil, I.R. (1974) 'The many futures of contracts', *Southern California Law Review*, 471 (May): 691–816.

Macpherson, C.B. (1962) *The Political Theory of Possessive Individualism: Hobbes to Locke*, Oxford: Oxford University Press.

Malpas, J. and Wickham, G. (1995) 'Governance and failure: On the limits of sociology', *Australian and New Zealand Journal of Sociology*, 31(3): 37–50.

Mandelbrot, B. (1982) *The Fractal Geometry of Nature*, New York: W.H. Freeman.

Mann, R. (2016) 'East West and the Bit in the Middle: Localities in North Wales', in M.R. Jones, S. Orford and V. Macfarlane (eds) *People, Places and Policy: Knowing Contemporary Wales through New Localities*, London: Routledge, 95–117

Manoïlescu, M. (1929) *Théorie du protectionnisme et de l'échange international*, Paris: Marcel Giard.

Manoïlescu, M. (1934) *Le siècle du corporatisme: Doctrine du corporatisme intégral et pur*, Paris: Felix Alcan.

Marin, B. (1990) 'Introduction. Generalized Political Exchange. Governance and Generalized Exchange', in B. Marin (ed) *Generalized Political Exchange. Antagonistic Cooperation and Integrated Policy Circuits*, Boulder, CO: Westview, 13–65.

Marsden, R. (1999) *The Nature of Capital: Marx after Foucault*, London: Routledge.

Marshall, T.H. (1950) *Citizenship and Social Class: And Other Essays*, Cambridge: Cambridge University Press.

Marx, K. (1973a [1857]) *Grundrisse* (translated by M. Nicolaus), Harmondsworth: Penguin.

Marx, K. (1973b [1857]) 'Introduction to the *Contribution to the Critique of Political Economy*', in K. Marx (ed) *Grundrisse* (translated by M. Nicolaus), Harmondsworth: Penguin, 81–111.

Marx, K. (1975a) 'Contribution to the Critique of Hegel's *Philosophy of Law*', in *Marx and Engels Collected Works, Vol 3*, London: Lawrence & Wishart, 1–129

Marx, K. (1975b) 'Difference between the Democritean and Epicurean Philosophy of Nature', in *Marx and Engels Collected Works, Vol 1*, London: Lawrence & Wishart, 25–107.

Marx, K. (1975c) 'Economic and Philosophic Manuscripts of 1844', in *Marx and Engels Colleced Works, Vol 3*, London: Lawrence & Wishart, 229–346.

Marx, K. (1975d) 'On the Jewish Question', in *Marx and Engels Collected Works, Vol 3*, London: Lawrence & Wishart, 146–74.

Marx, K. (1986a) 'Second Draft of *The Civil War in France*', in *Marx and Engels Collected Works, Vol 22*, London: Lawrence & Wishart, 515–40.

Marx, K. (1986b) '*The Civil War in France*: Address of the General Council of the International Working Men's Association', in *Marx and Engels Collected Works, Vol 22*, London: Lawrence & Wishart, 307–59.

Marx, K. (1987) 'Preface to the *Contribution to the Critique of Political Economy*', *Marx and Engels Collected Works, Vol 29*, London: Lawrence & Wishart, 261–5.

Marx, K. (1989) 'Marginal Notes on the Programme of the German Workers' Party', *Marx and Engels Collected Works, Vol 24*, London: Lawrence & Wishart, 81–99.

Marx, K. (1996 [1883]) *Capital, Volume I*, London: Lawrence & Wishart.

Marx, K. (1998 [1894]) *Capital, Volume III*, London: Lawrence & Wishart.

Marx, K. and Engels, E. (1975) *The German Ideology*, in *Marx and Engels Collected Works, Vol 5*, London: Lawrence & Wishart, 19–539.

Marx, K. and Engels, E. (1976) 'Manifesto of the Communist Party', in *Marx and Engels Collected Works, Vol 6*, London: Lawrence & Wishart, 477–519.

Mason, A. (2000) *Community, Solidarity and Belonging: Levels of Community and Their Normative Significance*, Cambridge: Cambridge University Press.

Massey, D. (1994) *Space, Place and Gender*, Cambridge: Polity.

Mauss, M. (1990) *The Gift: The Form and Reason for Exchange in Archaic Societies* (translated by W.D. Halls), London: Norton [Original work published in 1923].

Mayntz, R. (1993) 'Governing Failures and the Problem of Governability: Some Comments on a Theoretical Paradigm', in J. Kooiman (ed) *Modern Governance: New Government–Society Interactions*, London: SAGE Publications Ltd, 9–20.

Mayntz, R. (2001) 'Zur Selektivität der steuerungstheoretischen Perspektive', in H.P. Burth and A. Gölitz, eds, *Politische Steuerung in Theorie und Praxis*, Baden-Baden: Nomos, 17–27.

Mayntz, R. (2003) 'New Challenges to Governance Theory', in H. Bang (ed) *Governance as Social and Political Communication*, Manchester: Manchester University Press, 27–40.

Mayntz, R. (2004) *Governance Theory als fortentwickelte Steuerungstheorie?*, MPIfG paper 1, Cologne: Max-Planck-Institut für Gesellschaftsforschung, available at www.econstor.eu/handle/10419/44296

McCarthy, G.E. (1990) *Marx and the Ancients: Classical Ethics, Social Justice, and Nineteenth-Century Political Economy*, Savage, MD: Rowman & Littlefield.

McLellan, D. (1973a) *Karl Marx: A Biography*, New York: Palgrave Macmillan.

McLellan, D. (1973b) *Karl Marx: His Life and Thought*, New York: Harper Colophon Books.

McNay, L. (1999) 'Self as enterprise', *Theory, Culture & Society*, 26(6): 55–77.

Messner, D. (1994) 'Fallstricke und Grenzen der Netzwerksteuerung', *Prokla*, 97: 563–95.

Meuleman, L. (2008) *Public Management and the Metagovernance of Hierarchies, Networks and Markets*, Heidelberg: Physica Verlag.

Mill, J.S. (2004 [1848]) *Principles of Political Economy*, Indianapolis, IN: Hackett.

Miller, P. and Rose, N. (2008) *Governing the Present: Administering Economic, Social and Personal Life*, Cambridge: Polity.

Mitchell, T.J. (1991) 'The limits of the state: Beyond statist approaches and their critics', *American Political Science Review*, 85(1): 77–96.

Morin, E (1980) *Le méthode: Volume 2, La vie de la vie*, Paris: Seuil.

Mostov, J. (1989) 'Karl Marx as democratic theorist', *Polity*, 32(2): 195–212.

Moulaert, F. (2000) *Globalization and Integrated Area Development in European Cities*, Oxford: Oxford University Press.

Moulaert, F. and Nussbaumer, J. (2005) 'Defining the social economy and its governance at the neighbourhood level: A methodological reflection', *Urban Studies*, 42(11): 2071–88.

Muddiman, E., Taylor, C., Power, S. and Moles, K. (2019) 'Young people, family relationships and civic participation', *Journal of Civil Society*, 15(1): 82–98.

Muecke, D.C. (1970) *Irony*, London: Methuen.

Musto, M. (2008) 'History, Production and Method in the 1857 "Introduction"', in M. Musto (ed) *Karl Marx's Grundrisse: Foundations of the Critique of Political Economy 150 Years After*, London: Routledge, 6–32.

Nelson, R. (ed) (1993) *National Systems of Innovation*, Oxford: Oxford University Press.

Neocleous, M. (1996) *Administering Civil Society: Towards a Theory of State Power*, Basingstoke: Macmillan.

Nielsen, K. and Pedersen, O.K. (1988) 'The negotiated economy: Ideal and history', *Scandinavian Political Studies*, 11(2): 79–101.

Nielsen, K. and Pedersen, O.K. (1993) 'The Negotiated Economy: General Features and Theoretical Perspectives', in J. Hausner, B. Jessop and K. Nielsen (eds) *Institutional Frameworks of Market Economies*, Aldershot: Avebury, 89–112.

Niemi, W.L. (2011) 'Karl Marx's sociological theory of democracy: Civil society and political rights', *The Social Science Journal*, 48(1): 39–51.

Nimtz, A., Jr (2000) *Marx and Engels: Their Contribution to the Democratic Breakthrough*, Albany, NY: SUNY Press.

Niven, P. (2010) *Balanced Scorecard: Step-by-Step for Government and Non-profit Agencies*, New York: Wiley.

Odysseos, L. (2016) 'Human rights, self-formation and resistance in struggles against disposability', *Global Society*, 30(2): 179–200.

Odysseos, L., Death, C. and Malmvig, H. (2016) 'Interrogating Foucault's counter conduct', *Society*, 30(2): 151–6.

OECD (Organisation for Economic Co-operation and Development) (1986) 'Science, technology, industry', *STI Review*, 1: 84–129.

Offe, C. (1975a) *Berufsbildungreform: Eine Fallstudie über Reformpolitik*, Frankfurt: Suhrkamp.

Offe, C. (1975b) 'The Theory of the Capitalist State and the Problem of Policy Formation', in L.N. Lindberg, R. Alford, C. Crouch and C. Offe (eds) *Stress and Contradiction in Modem Capitalism*, Lexington, KY: D.C. Heath, 125–44.

Offe, C. (1984) *Contradictions of the Welfare State* (translated by J. Keane), London: Hutchinson.

Offe, C. (1987) 'Die Staatstheorie auf der Suche nach ihrem Gegenstand. Beobachtungen zur aktuellen Diskussion', in T. Ellwein, J.J. Hesse, R. Mayntz and F.W. Scharpf (eds) *Jahrbuch zur Staats- und Verwaltungswissenschaft*, Band 1, Baden-Baden: Nomos, 309–20.

Offe, C. (1996) *Modernity and the State: East, West*, Cambridge: Polity.

Offe, C. (2009) 'Governance: An "empty signifier"?', *Constellations*, 16(4): 550–62.

Orwell, G. (1945) *Animal Farm*, London: Secker & Warburg.

Osborne, S. (ed) (2010) *The New Public Governance*, London: Routledge.

Osborne, D. and Gaebler, T. (1992) *Reinventing Government: How the Entrepreneurial Spirit Is Transforming the Public Sector*, Boston, MA: Addison-Wesley.

Ostry, S. and Nelson, R.R. (1995) *Techno-Nationalism and Techno-Globalism*, Washington, DC: Brookings.

Page, N., Langford, Higgs, G. and Orford, S. (2020) 'Implications of spatial and temporal variation in service provision for inequalities in social outcomes 2014-2019' [Data Collection], Colchester: UK Data Service, available at http://reshare.ukdataservice.ac.uk/854037/

Palan, R. (1998) 'The emergence of an offshore economy', *Futures*, 30: 63–73.

Peck, J. (2010) *Constructions of Neoliberal Reason*, New York: Oxford University Press.

Peck, J. and Tickell, A. (1994) 'Too many partners … the future for regeneration partnerships', *Local Economy*, 9(3): 251–65.

Peck, J. and Tickell, A. (1995) 'Business goes local: Dissecting the "business agenda" in Manchester', *International Journal of Urban and Regional Research*, 19(1): 55–78.

Pedersen, O.K. (2011) *Konkurrencestaten*, Copenhagen: Hans Reitzel.

Perez, C. (2002) *Technological Revolutions and Financial Capital*, Cheltenham: Elgar.

Peters, B.G. (2009) 'The two futures of governing: decentering and recentering processes in governing', *NISPAcee Journal of Public Administration and Policy*, 2(1): 7–24.

Pidd, M. (2012) *Measuring the Performance of Public Services: Principles and Practice*, Cambridge: Cambridge University Press.

Piore, M. and Sabel, C.F. (1985) *The Second Industrial Divide*, New York: Basic Books.

Poggi, G. (1979) 'Introduction', in N. Luhmann, *Trust and Power: Two Essays*, Chichester: John Wiley, vii–xix.

Polanyi, K. (1957) 'The Economy as Instituted Process', in K. Polanyi, C.M. Arensberg and H.W. Pearson (eds) *Trade and Market in the Early Empires*, New York: Free Press, 243–70.

Polanyi, K. (2001 [1944]) *The Great Transformation: The Political and Economic Origins of Our Time*, Boston, MA: Beacon Press.

Pollitt, C. and Bouckaert, G. (2011) *Public Management Reform: A Comparative Analysis – New Public Management, Governance, and the Neo-Weberian State* (3rd edn), Oxford: Oxford University Press.

Porter, M. (1990) *The Competitive Advantage of Nations*, Basingstoke: Macmillan.

Poulantzas, N. (1978) *State, Power, Socialism*, London: New Left Books.

Powell, F. (2013) *The Politics of Civil Society: Big Society, Small Government* (2nd edn), Bristol: Policy Press.

Power, S., Allouch, A., Brown, P. and Tholen, G. (2016) 'Giving something back? Sentiments of privilege and social responsibility among elite graduates from Britain and France', *International Sociology*, 31(3): 305–23.

Power, S., Muddiman, E., Moles, K. and Taylor, C. (2018) 'Civil society: Bringing the family back in', *Journal of Civil Society*, 14(3): 193–206.

Provan, K.G. and Kenis, P. (2008) 'Modes of network governance, structure, management, and effectiveness', *Journal of Public Administration Research and Theory*, 18(2): 229–52.

Putnam, R.D. (2000) *Bowling Alone: The Collapse and Revival of American Community*, New York: Simon & Schuster.

Rees, S., Sophocleous, C. and Hirst, N. (2017) *Delivering Transformation in Wales: Social Services and Well-being (Wales) Act, 2014*, Cardiff: WISERD (Wales Institute of Social & Economic Research, Data & Methods).

Rehmann, J. (1999) '"Abolition" of civil society? Remarks on a widespread misunderstanding in the interpretation of "civil society"', *Socialism and Democracy*, 13(2): 1–18.

Reich, R. (1991) *The Work of Nations: A Blueprint for the Future*, New York: Simon & Schuster.

Reinert, E.S. (1995) 'Competitiveness and its predecessors – A 500-year cross-national perspective', *Structural Change and Economic Dynamics*, 6: 23–42.

Reinert, E.S. (2008) *Why Rich Countries became Rich … and why Poor Countries remain Poor*, New York: PublicAffairs.

Rescher, N. (1998) *Complexity: A Philosophical Overview*, New Brunswick, NJ: Transaction Books.

Røiseland, A. (2007) 'Network governance and policy change', available at https://ecpr.eu/Filestore/PaperProposal/2cdfcf88-3794-4206-bcde-270918339139.pdf

Rorty, R. (1989) 'Private Irony and Liberal Hope', in R. Rorty (ed) *Contingency, Irony, and Solidarity*, Cambridge: Cambridge University Press, 73–95.

Rose, N. and Miller, P. (1992) 'Political power beyond the state: Problematics of government', *British Journal of Sociology*, 43(2): 173–205.

Sayer, A. (1992) *Method in Social Science* (2nd edn), London: Routledge.

Sayer, A. (2000) *Realism and Social Science*, London: SAGE Publications Ltd.

Scharpf, F.W. (1993) 'Positive und negative Koordination in Verhandlungssystemen', in A. Héritier (ed) *Policy-Analyse: Kritik und Neuorientierung*, Opladen: Westdeutscher Verlag, 57–83.

Scharpf, F.W. (1994) 'Games real actors could play: Positive and negative coordination in embedded negotiations', *Journal of Theoretical Politics*, 6(1): 27–53.

Senellart, M. (2008) 'Course Context', in M. Foucault, *Security, Territory, Population*, Basingstoke: Palgrave, 369–401.

Schumpeter, J.A. (1962 [1934]) *Theory of Economic Development*, Boston, MA: Harvard University Press.

Schumpeter, J.A. (1975 [1943]) *Capitalism, Socialism, and Democracy* (3rd edn), New York: Harper & Row.

Scott, C. (2006) 'Spontaneous Accountability', in M.W. Dowdle (ed) *Public Accountability*, Cambridge: Cambridge University Press, 174–91.

Seligman, A.B. (1992) *The Idea of Civil Society*, New York: Free Press.

Smith, A. (1976 [1776]) *An Inquiry into the Nature and Causes of the Wealth of Nations, 2 volumes*, Oxford: Clarendon.

Sørensen, E. and Torfing, J. (2009) 'Making governance networks effective and democratic through metagovernance', *Public Administration*, 87(2): 234–58.

Sørensen, E., Torfing, J. and Fotel, T. (2009) 'Democratic anchorage of infrastructural governance networks: The case of the Femern Belt Forum', *Planning Theory*, 8(3): 282–308.

Spivak, G.C. (1987) *In Other Worlds: Essays in Cultural Politics*, London: Routledge.

Springborg, P. (1984) 'Karl Marx on democracy, participation, voting, and equality', *Political Theory*, 12(4): 537–56.

Stewart, M. (1994) 'Between Whitehall and town hall: The realignment of urban policy in England', *Policy & Politics*, 22: 133–45.

Stoker, G. (2019) 'Can the governance paradigm survive the rise of populism?', *Policy & Politics*, 47(1): 3–18.

Storper, M. (1997) *The Regional World: Territorial Development in a Global Economy*, New York: Guilford Press.

Sum, N.-L. (1997) '"Time-Space Embeddedness" and "Geo-Governance" of Cross-Border Regional Modes of Growth: Their Nature and Dynamics in East Asian Cases', in A. Amin and J. Hausner (eds) *Beyond Markets and Hierarchy*, Cheltenham: Edward Elgar, 159–95.

Sum, N.-L. (2018) 'A Cultural Political Economy of Corporate Social Responsibility: The Language of "Stakeholders" and the Politics of New Ethicalism', in R. Wodak and B. Forchtner (eds) *The Routledge Handbook on Language and Politics*, London: Routledge, 557–71.

Sum, N.-L. and Jessop, B. (2013) *Towards Cultural Political Economy: Putting Culture in Its Place*, Cheltenham: Edward Elgar.

Taylor, C. (2001) *Modern Social Imaginaries*, Durham, NC: Duke University Press.

Taylor, C., Fox, A., Evans, C. and Rees, G. (2019) 'The "civic premium" of university graduates: The impact of massification on associational membership', *Studies in Higher Education*, 44: 1–16, available at www.tandfonline.com/doi/full/10.1080/03075079.2019.1637837

Tellman, U. (2009) 'Foucault and the invisible economy', *Foucault Studies*, 6: 5–24.

Teubner, G. (1989) *Recht als Autopoietisches System*, Frankfurt: Suhrkamp.

Texier, J. (2009) 'Società civile', in G. Liguori and P. Voza (eds) *Dizionario Gramsciano, 1926–1937*, Rome: Carocci, 769–72.

Théret, B. (1992) *Régimes économiques de l'ordre politique: Esquisse d'une théorie régulationniste des limites de l'État*, Paris: Presses Universitaires de France.

Thomas, L. and Cousins, W. (1996) 'A New Compact City Form: Concepts in Practice', in M. Jenks, E. Burton and K. Williams (eds) *The Compact City: A Sustainable Urban Form?*, London: E. and F.N. Spon, 286–95.

Thompson, G., Frances, J., Levacic, R. and Mitchell, J. (eds) (1991) *Markets, Hierarchies, and Networks: The Coordination of Social Life*, London: SAGE Publications Ltd.

Thompson, M. (2012) 'Foucault, fields of governability, and the population–family–economy nexus in China', *History and Theory*, 51(1): 42–62.

Tickell, A. and Peck, J. (1996) 'The return of the Manchester Men: Men's words and men's deeds in the remaking of the local state', *Transactions of the Institute of British Geographers*, 1(1): 595–616.

Tickell, A., Peck, J.A. and Dicken, P. (1995) 'The Fragmented Region: Business, the State and Economic Development in North West England', in M. Rhodes (ed) *The Regions and the New Europe: Patterns in Core and Periphery Development*, Manchester: Manchester University Press, 247–71.

Torfing, J., Peters, B.G., Pierre, J. and Sørensen, E. (2012) *Interactive Governance: Advancing the Paradigm*, Oxford: Oxford University Press.

Urry, J. (1999) *Sociology beyond Societies: Mobilities for the Twenty-First Century*, London: Routledge.

Urry, J. (2002) *Global Complexity*, Cambridge: Polity.

Urry, J. (2014) *Offshoring*, Cambridge: Polity.

van Bortel, G. and Mullins, D. (2009) 'Critical perspectives on network governance in urban regeneration, community involvement and integration', *Journal of Housing and the Built Environment*, 24: 203–19.

Villadsen, K. (2016) 'Michel Foucault and the forces of civil society', *Theory, Culture & Society*, 33(3), 3–26.

Wagner, T. (2006) 'Funktionale Differenzierung und ein ökonomischer Primat? Hat die system-theoretische Gesellschaftstheorie ausgedient?', available at www.sozialarbeit.ch/dokumente/oekonomischer_primat. pdf

Wallis, J. and Dollery, B. (1999) *Market Failure, Government Failure, Leadership and Public Policy*, Basingstoke: Macmillan.

Weber, M. (1927 [1923]) *General Economic History*, New York: Greenberg.

Weber, M. (1949) *The Methodology of the Social Sciences*, Glencoe, IL: Free Press.

Weber, M. (1978 [1922]) *Economy and Society, 3 volumes*, Berkeley, CA: University of California Press.

Wickham, G. (1983) 'Power and power analysis: Beyond Foucault?', *Economy and Society*, 12(4): 468–90.

Willke, H. (1987) 'Observation, Diagnosis, Guidance: A Systems Theoretical View on Intervention', in K. Hurrelmann, F.X. Kaufmann and F. Lösel (eds) *Social Intervention: Potential and Constraints*, Berlin: W. de Gruyter, 21–35.

Willke, H. (1990) 'Political Intervention: Operational Preconditions for Generalized Political Exchange', in B. Marin (ed) *Governance and Generalized Exchange: Self-Organizing Policy Networks in Action*, Frankfurt: Campus, 235–54.

Willke, H. (1992) *Ironie des Staates: Grundlinien einer Staatstheorie polyzentrischer Gesellschaft*, Frankfurt: Suhrkamp.

WISERD (Wales Institute of Social & Economic Research, Data & Methods) (2014) 'Wales takes a lead in Researching Civil Society', available at https://WISERD.ac.uk/wales-takes-lead-researching-civil-society

WISERD (Wales Institute of Social & Economic Research, Data & Methods) (2015) 'Introducing the new WISERD Civil Society Research Centre', *WISERD News*, Issue 10, 10 January.

WISERD (2019) 'WISERD to receive major funding from ESRC for continuation of civil society research', News, 3 September, available at https://WISERD.ac.uk/news/WISERD-receive-major-funding-esrc-continuation-civil-society-research

WISERD Civil Society (2020) *Changing Perspectives on Civic Stratification and Civil Repair*, Cardiff: WISERD, available at https://wiserd.ac.uk/sites/default/files/documents/Wiserd%20Civil%20Society%20Booklet%20ENG%20DIGI_0.pdf

WISERD ESRC Centre on Civil Society (2014) *Civil Society: Researching Civil Society for Civil Society*, Cardiff: WISERD, available at https://WISERD.ac.uk/WISERD-civil-society-research-centre

Wolff, R. (2000) 'Marxism and democracy', *Rethinking Marxism*, 12(1): 112–22.

World Bank (1991) *World Development Report: The Challenge of Development*, New York: Oxford University Press.

World Bank (2015) 'Stakeholder analysis', available at www1.worldbank.org/publicsector/anticorrupt/PoliticalEconomy/stakeholderanalysis.htm

World Report (2000) *Weltbericht für die Zukunft der Städte Urban 21* [*World Report on the Urban Future 21*], available at www.bbsr.bund.de/BBSR/DE/Veroeffentlichungen/ministerien/BMVBS/Sonderveroeffentlichungen/2005undaelter/DL_WeltberichtURBAN21.pdf?__blob=publicationFile&v=6?

Zeitlin, J. and Pochet, P. (2005) *The Open Method of Coordination in Action: The European Employment Social Inclusion Strategies*, Oxford: Peter Lang.

Index

structuration xviii, 35, 39, 41, 43f, 90f
Stubbs, Paul 159
subhegemony 63, 88f, 160, 223
subjectivation 146, 149, 219
subjective wellbeing 118f
subjectivity 126, 146, 149f, 157, 171
subjects 13f, 16, 42, 54, 85, 148
  class 93, 143f
  culturally embedded 145, 147
  economic subjects 141, 144f, 147, 202
  entrepreneurial subjects 16, 54, 74, 144
  legal 141, 145, 147, 201f, 219
  of governance 13f, 16, 54f, 59, 63, 74, 82f, 149, 164, 187, 202
  of metagovernance 5, 86
  of struggle 141
  political subject 233
Sum, Ngai-Ling xi, 39, 57, 88, 149
system failure 149, 192, 239

T

technological selectivity 160, 166
temporal horizon 52, 56, 61, 67, 69, 84, 177, 230
temporalization 94
territory, place, scale, network relations 92f, 163f, 183, 236
Thames Gateway 56, 175–8
The Mumbles 112
third way 168, 204, 215, 221f
Tickell, Adam 181, 261
time 23, 45, 47, 52, 58f, 110, 190
time-space compression and distantiation 58, 156, 239
Total Quality Management failure 214
tribalism 226, 235
tripartism 16, 29, 69, 184f, 193f
trade union membership 111, 117f, 123
Trump, Donald 198
trust xvii, 26f, 48f, 63, 66, 71, 110, 112, 179, 188, 212
turnover time 200, 212

U

uneven development 56, 94, 166, 176, 181, 228
United States 16, 28, 52, 137, 173, 179, 181, 198, 207, 209f, 214, 227f
University of Cardiff 103f
University of Greenwich 176f
unmarked sphere 157, 160f, 165
URBAN 21 report 167–73
Urry, John 45, 88, 210
use-value 132, 213

V

Vergesellschaftung 88
  see also socialization
Villadsen, Kaspar 137, 144, 145f, 147, 234

W

wage 132, 200, 213
Wagner, Thomas 192
Wales 100, 103ff, 108f, 112, 235f
Wallis, Joe 10–11
war of manoeuvre 134, 139
war of position 58, 134, 239
Weber, Max 160, 196f, 205, 212
welfare state 16, 17, 29, 114, 169, 181, 226
wellbeing 105, 109, 111, 115f, 117ff, 141–2, 169–70, 235
Wellcome Foundation 176f
Wickham, Gary 29–30, 55, 65, 79, 91, 194
Willke, Helmut 36, 47, 48ff, 56f
WISER 103f
WISERD 5, 22, 100, 103–24, 155, 220, 230, 234f
World Bank xvi, 148–9, 172, 237
world market 23, 125, 161, 166, 171, 187, 189f, 191f, 193, 196, 199, 201, 204–10, 212
world society 4, 46, 90, 158f, 161f, 173, 187f, 191ff
world state 159, 161f, 166